D1715364

THE STATE
ON THE STREETS

THE STATE
ON THE STREETS

Police and Politics in Argentina and Brazil

Mercedes S. Hinton

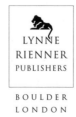

LYNNE
RIENNER
PUBLISHERS

BOULDER
LONDON

Published in the United States of America in 2006 by
Lynne Rienner Publishers, Inc.
1800 30th Street, Boulder, Colorado 80301
www.rienner.com

and in the United Kingdom by
Lynne Rienner Publishers, Inc.
3 Henrietta Street, Covent Garden, London WC2E 8LU

Library of Congress Cataloging-in-Publication Data
Hinton, Mercedes S. 1977–
    The state on the streets : police and politics in Argentina and Brazil /
Mercedes S. Hinton.
    p. cm.
    Includes bibliographical references and index.
    ISBN 1-58826-374-6 (hardcover : alk. paper)
    1. Police—Argentina. 2. Crime—Argentina. 3. Civil society—Argentina.
4. Police—Brazil. 5. Crime—Brazil. 6. Civil society—Brazil. 7. Democratization—
Latin America. I. Title.
HV8178.H56 2006
363.20981—dc22   2005031187

British Cataloguing in Publication Data
A Cataloguing in Publication record for this book
is available from the British Library.

Printed and bound in the United States of America

    The paper used in this publication meets the requirements
∞ of the American National Standard for Permanence of
    Paper for Printed Library Materials Z39.48-1992.

  5 4 3 2 1

Contents

Part 3 Conclusion

Tables and Figures

Acknowledgments

I owe a debt of gratitude to many people and organizations in several countries for their encouragement and support in the research and writing of this book. I am especially grateful to those in Argentina and Brazil who, under difficult circumstances, gave so generously of themselves and their time. For his academic role during my years at Cambridge University, I must start with Geoffrey Hawthorn, whose vigorous intellectual stimulus, tireless enthusiasm, and unerring judgment were crucial in every respect. I am extremely grateful to Guillermo O'Donnell and Laurence Whitehead for their sage scholarly advice, guidance, and encouragement. Years before I met them, it was their writings that initially inspired me, during my undergraduate days, to fully pursue my incipient interest in Latin American democracy and politics. Roberto Saba's support of my project, as well as the friendship he extended while I was in Argentina, leaves me in his debt.

My professional development and publication of this work would not have been possible without the encouragement and mentorship of Robert Reiner at the London School of Economics and Political Science (LSE). Among others at LSE who generously offered intellectual input and advice were Tim Newburn and Declan Roche. To them, George Philip, Francisco Panizza, and all my colleagues in the Government and Law departments of the LSE, where the book was completed, a resounding thank-you. Generous financial suppport for my research was provided by the Faculty of Social and Political Sciences at Cambridge University, Trinity College, the Cambridge Political Economy Trust, the Economic and Social Research Council, and the London School of Economics and Political Science.

For her friendship and the wise advice she has always given me, including the recommendation that I concentrate on the two Latin American countries I knew best, I would like to thank Marzena Szymanska. A lifetime of gratitude to my husband, Geordie Hyland, for his unfailing encouragement and confidence; and to my parents, especially my mother, Mercedes I. Hinton, for her intellectual, emotional, and editorial contributions from start to finish.

—Mercedes S. Hinton

THE STATE
ON THE STREETS

CHAPTER 1

Introduction: Policing in Latin America

"In a democracy, you eat, heal, and educate," declared Raúl Alfonsín, Argentina's first democratically elected postdictatorship president, after taking office in 1983. Yet despite popular hopes and expectations across Latin America that democracy would deliver this and more, the promise of a more prosperous existence has not been realized for the average Latin American. In the past two decades, the stranglehold of poverty and inequality in the region has hardly lessened, while crime and insecurity have soared.

Violence is ubiquitous. The regional homicide rate is the highest in the world, estimated at more than three times the world average (UNDP 2004a: 107). At the street level, muggings, kidnappings, bank robberies, and residential break-ins are daily occurrences. Drug trafficking and gang-related violence, together with death squads and paramilitary organizations, add further layers to the deadly spiral of insecurity. In rural areas, armed clashes between landless peasants and large landowners are on the rise, as are urban confrontations between the police and small armies of the unemployed. For citizens of Latin America, fear of violence is exacerbated by widespread anxiety over predatory police forces and unresponsive governments.

Some of the tensions surrounding crime, policing, and government in the region overall are illustrated by the kidnapping and murder case of Axel Blumberg in Argentina. Blumberg, a twenty-three-year-old middle-class engineering student, was abducted on March 17, 2004, in a leafy suburb of Buenos Aires. A week later, after judicial authorities and the Bonaerense police botched the ransom payment, the rattled gang of kidnappers shot Blumberg five times and left his dead body in a garbage dump. The grieving family chose to go public, making impassioned appeals for justice on behalf of their murdered son and all victims of violent crime. In an unprecedented show of solidarity, 150,000 Argentines of all economic and social classes marched on the capital to demand greater public security and an overhaul of the criminal justice system. Scrambling to investigate, officials uncovered a series of alarming details about the Blumberg case. It was revealed, for example, that four local residents had called the Bonaerense police after seeing the young student being dragged and beaten by his kidnappers in broad daylight. After initial denials, the police finally admitted they had ignored these calls; further investigation revealed that kidnapping rings had been paying the police to look the other way.

As public outcry grew, the government raced to draft an action plan. Three weeks after the massive demonstration, President Nestor Kirchner's minister of justice called a press conference to present a public security megaplan to the media. At the same time, the provincial minister of security responsible for the Bonaerense—the fourth minister to hold the post in two and a half years—was forced to resign. But as there were no takers for a job widely considered to be "the worst in the country," an official who six years prior had resigned due to lack of political support for his proposed police reforms was reappointed as minister. Wasting no time, the new provincial minister of security fired the chief of police (who had assumed office only three months earlier), named a former judge to replace him, announced a massive purge of the Bonaerense, and launched plans to create a new police force for Buenos Aires Province.

As these events unfolded, the government was also forced to confront damaging allegations about the oldest and most elite police force in the country, the Argentine Federal Police (PFA). The PFA, whose jurisdiction encompasses the capital city and federal investigations across the country, was experiencing problems disturbingly similar to those of the provincial force, despite undergoing multiple purges over a period of several years. Several top officials, including the chief of a special squad created only six months earlier to investigate kidnappings, had to be dismissed following allegations of a cover-up of the Blumberg crime.

Even a cursory review of these events raises some troubling questions. Why, for instance, has the Argentine state been unable to establish more effective institutions of police governance since 1983, when electoral democracy was restored? Why does a reactive rather than proactive approach seem to predominate in the face of such recurring problems? What is the likelihood that any security megaplan will succeed in the face of ingrained patterns of misconduct and corruption?

In Latin America, a region with a long history of venal, arbitrary police forces and unresponsive government, these questions are relevant well beyond Argentina's borders. Barely two months after the above-described events, Mexico's capital was rocked by a similar scandal, a case that involved two kidnapped brothers who were executed after their family had paid ransom. On June 28, 2004, a quarter of a million citizens vented their rage in the streets in Mexico City, protesting the lack of personal security and demanding immediate government action.

The Police Role in a Democracy

Elements of the problems described in Latin America are present even in long-established democracies. Indeed, issues such as fear of crime, police corruption, abuse of authority, and institutional racism have been focal points of electoral campaigns in France, the United Kingdom, the United States, and elsewhere. The process of police reform is a notoriously difficult and labored task, in part because of inherent contradictions between the police role and the ideals of democracy. More generally, the coercive capabilities of the police highlight the tensions between the power of the state to compel through force and the representative, consensual, and liberal character of the democratic state. This tension is exacerbated by the fact that in all societies, the police evolved in some measure out of state efforts to extend and consolidate its power and contain the disorderly effects of the "dangerous classes" (Bayley 1975; Marenin 1982; Silver 1967). Even in solid democracies, where the police have moved away from serving as exclusive protectors of the interests of the state to encompass the role of public servant, we find that the police still constitute a socially divisive force, adding to latent structural tensions present in society. This stems in particular from the adversarial character of many police functions, particularly with respect to treatment of suspects and offenders (Bittner 1970; Choongh 1998; Loader 1994). In this adversarial role, the police are often selective in adhering to legalities, directing much of their surveillance and strong-arm tactics toward those groups that are perceived to contribute most to criminality or agitation—the poor and racial minorities.

The features that make the coercive potential of the police difficult to reconcile with democratic norms are all the more apparent in the vastly unequal social context of Latin America. According to the World Bank, Latin America is "unambiguously" the region with the highest levels of income inequality in the world. This has been true as long as statistics have been kept. Even the region's most equal country, Uruguay, is significantly more unequal than the most unequal of Eastern European or industrialized countries (World Bank 2004: ch. 2, 27). In the Latin American context, the concept of "tyranny of the majority" has been historically replaced by the tyranny of the elite and the powerful, a group that, as Guillermo O'Donnell has noted, often perceives the obligations of the law as a "social weakness." In fact, the region has a long tradition of "twisting [the law] in favor of the powerful and for the repression and containment of the vulnerable" (O'Donnell 1999: 312).

That the police themselves are by and large an undemocratic organization is another factor blurring any discussion of the proper police role in a democracy. Even in developed countries, the police are hierarchically organized, have a secretive esprit de corps, resist external interference (preferring to "police themselves"), and are often at odds with legal and procedural codes when gathering criminal evidence and treating suspects (Skolnick 1994). Furthermore, because the police are required to act quickly and decisively in matters involving complex human conflicts and legal and moral questions—often in the face of aggression—their actions are frequently bound to be offensive to one party or another (Bittner 1970: 9).

Even though the police role in any democracy is bound to be contentious, the police in many respects provide the quintessential public service: the protection of life and property (Reiss and Bordua 1967). As this role is accomplished through the threat and use of force, the police (together with the military) embody the coercive potential of the state—a feature viewed by many scholars as the most defining characteristic of the modern state. In the words of Max Weber, the "state is a human community that (successfully) claims the monopoly of the legitimate use of physical force within a given territory" (1958: 78). As Robert Dahl (1989) further asserts, though the state's available means of coercion may be of an economic, social, physical, or psychological nature, it is through firm control over these instruments that the democratic state enforces its laws. And whereas national security is the purview of the military, the police are the state on the streets insofar as law and order are concerned.

A Threshold of Deterrence

Certainly the police have not been as politically decisive or as historically prominent as the military: they rarely perpetrate coups or wrestle power from the state. But through their role as primary legal enforcers and their capacity to serve as deterrents to crime, the police have a fundamental impact on public trust in the legal system and ultimately on the legitimacy of the state itself.

The criminal deterrence literature, akin to the rational choice perspective, emphasizes that people avoid illegal activities out of fear of the perceived consequences.[1] In this view, it is the capacity and perceived likelihood that the police and other institutions of the criminal justice system will detect and punish violations of the law, combined with the overall severity of the punishment, that constitute the main factors underlying obedience to the state's laws. This is not to say that the police are the sole formal institution responsible for deterring crimes or solving them, since even the very best police force cannot be everywhere given finite resources of time, money, and personnel (Bayley 1994: 5–7). Other agencies in the criminal justice system, such as the courts, district attorneys, public prosecutors, and the prison system, are all important in the application of penalties and investigation of crimes. Many policing functions, moreover, are increasingly carried out by private security guards and specialists operating on a commercial basis.

Indeed, in most developed countries, and a growing number of developing countries, private police agents outnumber the public police (Shearing 1992; Bayley and Shearing 1996). Nevertheless, in the public mind, the primary responsibility for fighting crime lies with the state. A uniformed police officer patrolling the streets provides a degree of psychological reassurance to the public that they will be reasonably safe and protected from crime (Kelling 1985). In many countries, this image is favored by the police themselves; they downplay their part in judicial proceedings and prefer to leave to others the analysis of societal and economic factors that contribute to crime (Sherman 1992).

Compliance Through Legitimacy

Yet the police are crucial to crime control and to compliance with the state's laws for reasons much deeper than deterrence alone. Certainly, it would be difficult to imagine widespread compliance with the law were the legal system not backed by at least some minimum threshold of punishment. But if people operated strictly on the basis of calculated benefits and penalties, as the rational choice perspective suggests, then every individual could be thought of as a potential criminal and the state would collapse in the face of impossible monitoring costs. Some measure of normative acceptance and voluntary compliance with the law must therefore complement the state's threat of force in order for the legal system to function adequately.

In some cases, though compliance may first arise for instrumental reasons (such as the threat of force), this in itself may induce a longer-term attitudinal shift as habitual patterns of behavior contribute to the development of voluntary compliance. In many other cases, obedience to the law may result from moral values acquired through family, schools, religion, and prevailing societal mores. Voluntary compliance with the law is also correlated with the degree of legitimacy[2] the government is accorded: where people perceive that the authority or the body enforcing the law is rightful in its capacity to dictate behavior, they are more likely to develop a normative commitment to obeying the law (Tyler 1990).

The police also have an important role in the socialization process. Whether by positive or negative example, the kind of policing young people see on the streets leaves a lasting impression: it can confirm or deny the civic values they learn in the classroom. Even for non–crime related cases,[3] rapid police response to distress calls and their subsequent efforts in assisting victims to seek redress are extremely important to reassuring the public in general and increasing their confidence in the police. Overall, how the police and other agents of the criminal justice system treat people has an important effect on whether they will perceive their government as fair, equitable, and efficacious (Bayley 1995a; Marenin 1996). If people have a reasonable degree of trust in their institutions, they are more likely to believe that compliance, cooperation, and loyalty will best serve their long-term personal interests. Conversely, when the state routinely violates expectations, the social contract is disrupted.

It is respect for the law that underpins property and contract rights and provides the measure of predictability, stability, and confidence necessary for long-term planning and investment—and for sustainable economic and political development. If the police do not respect the law or are corrupt and brutal, public respect for legality and the legitimacy of the state are diminished. Then the state will be limited in its capacity to uphold its laws and policies, protect its citizens, and habitually shape the norms and procedures within its borders.

In the Hobbesian view (1651), people's need for protection from the predatory activities of others is what leads them to consent to the state. Consistent failure by the state to protect the physical security of its population opens the door to such parallel and competing forces as death squads, paramilitary gangs, and private armies, which spring up ostensibly to dispense quick "justice" wherever the state is remiss or unable to act.

The Latin American Context

Democracies paradoxically rest, therefore, on the state's power to coerce. How the state balances the use of force against real or perceived threats, what guarantees it provides against its wrongful or excessive application, and how it punishes those who violate the law are crucial factors in safeguarding civil and political liberties. As Robert Reiner has stated, policing is "both source and symbol of the quality of a political civilization" (2000b: 8). These issues are especially relevant to Latin America, a region that is still struggling to break with its authoritarian past while under the increasing strain of crime and violence.

In Mexico, crime and police corruption are among the most pressing issues on the political agenda. The police were instrumental in enforcing the corrupt state machinery of the Institutional Revolutionary Party (PRI) and in helping to maintain the PRI's virtual monopoly on power between 1929 and 2000. Where vast clientelistic networks did not suffice to achieve political objectives, the government's security forces stifled opponents through the use of wiretaps, beatings, and torture—repressive activities that were particularly intense during the late 1960s and the 1970s. Amid rampant political manipulation of the police and state-sanctioned corruption, organized crime operations such as drug trafficking and human contraband to the United States found a propitious climate in which to grow.

The overlap between the roles of the police and the military in maintaining public order and personal security is a gray area in political life in

Mexico and much of Central and South America. Despite the brutal legacy of military rule, democratic governments still resort to calling on military troops whenever the public security situation deteriorates, and occasionally, they do so also to repress restless police. Even in Mexico, one of the few Latin American countries that has escaped military rule, there have been calls for the militarization of public security. In Venezuela in June 2003, President Hugo Chávez threatened the opposition-controlled Caracas Metropolitan Police with military intervention for agitating against him. Earlier the same year, army troops called in by Bolivian president Gonzalo Sánchez de Losada fired upon a contingent of police officers who were demanding pay hikes in the central square and caused the death of thirty people.

In Peru and Colombia, the destabilizing effects of guerrilla insurgencies and drug trafficking have exacerbated high levels of local and regional insecurity. In Peru, the Maoist Shining Path guerrillas unleashed a war on the state that raged from 1980 to 1993. President Alberto Fujimori enlisted both the army and the police in the bloody but ultimately successful campaign against insurgents, while simultaneously using the police to intimidate and repress political opposition. It is the case of Colombia, however, that provides the most extreme example of insecurity in the region.

Despite Colombia's status as one of Latin America's oldest democracies, it ranked only as a "partially free" country in the 2004 Freedom House Index, an internationally respected democracy barometer. This was in large measure attributable to the fact that the government holds sovereignty over only half of its national territory. The other half, a territory comparable to the size of Switzerland, is held by various opposing factions, including two main leftist guerrilla groups and several right-wing paramilitary organizations. Colombia not only has been torn apart by a civil war now entering its fifth decade but is the source of nearly all of the world's cocaine production; insurgents on all sides rely heavily on profits from the drug trade to finance their campaign against the state and each other. The armed conflict has claimed more than 40,000 lives over the past decade alone and has uprooted some 2.5 million people from their homes (the second highest internal refugee population in the world, after Sudan).[4] In addition to enabling the continuation of the civil war, powerful drug cartels further constrain the rule of law by routinely earmarking parts of their vast profits to corrupt national institutions and public officials—most particularly, the judiciary and the police.

Guatemala, Honduras, El Salvador, and Nicaragua are still grappling with the aftermath of their own bloody civil wars between leftist insurgents and governing elites. More than a decade after peace accords were signed, patterns of land tenure and income are still among the most unequal in the world. These countries are presently experiencing an escalation of crime, in which violent youth gangs known as *maras,* the police, and death squads are all active participants. In spite of large infusions of international funds and technical assistance, especially to Guatemala and El Salvador, to demobilize and retrain former combatants for police work, the police remain abusive and undertrained. Still at the service of traditional elites, the police have an inbred corruption culture that runs so deep that a member of an anticorruption commission in Guatemala has called for a sociologist or psychiatrist to examine it as a type of social pathology.

In the Southern Cone countries of Argentina, Brazil, and Chile, the legacies of the past also continue to cast a long shadow. The police were used as the eyes and ears on the ground during the "national security" military dictatorships of the 1960s, 1970s, and 1980s. During this period, the military sought to root out the perceived threat of communist infiltration through highly repressive tactics that led to the exile, illegal detention, torture, and extrajudicial execution of thousands of opponents. The police not only gathered intelligence on suspected subversives but also allowed many of their facilities, precincts, and training schools to be used as centers for detention and torture. In the postdictatorship period, a considerable number of police personnel were carried over to present-day forces; many repressive methods such as illegal surveillance activities, abusive treatment of the poor, and excessive use of force also survived.

Of the Southern Cone countries, the crime and policing situation in Brazil is by far the most extreme. The levels of social and economic inequality in Brazil are among the highest in the world. With a population of about 185 million it also has Latin America's largest internal market for drug consumption. It was in fact the expansion of the drug trade that, in the mid-1980s, became a catalyst for the deterioration of the public security situation, particularly in urban areas. Illegal entry and transit of drugs from the Andean countries have been facilitated by Brazil's extensive borders, touching upon every other South American country except Chile and Ecuador.

While there is no question that there are many variances in the problems of crime and policing from country to country, there is little doubt that an antagonistic relationship between the police and the population at large is an almost universal problem in Latin America. In a climate of generally weak democratic controls, low police professionalism, and inadequate salaries, the police throughout much of the region have become immersed in lucrative prostitution rings, kidnapping-for-ransom schemes, car theft, and other criminal activity.

Focus and Plan of the Book

Against this backdrop of shared problems, this book focuses specifically on the politics of police reform in Argentina and Brazil in the 1990s. The cases of Argentina and Brazil are illustrative for several reasons. Since they are two of the largest, richest, and most influential nations in Latin America,[5] how they manage crucial political questions of internal security is of interest far beyond their borders. The parallels and disparities between Argentina and Brazil also throw key political issues in the region into vivid relief. Both countries experienced military dictatorships, and these left a similar ideological and tactical legacy within the police force even as the political discourse shifted from subversion to crime. Both countries, moreover, adopted neoliberal reforms in the 1990s to privatize, deregulate, and open their economies. It is on the economic liberalization process and its aftermath, in fact, that much scholarly attention has been focused, leaving the issues of police reform and crime relatively unexplored.

Despite these parallels, there are certain key differences that impinge upon any discussion of policing and reform in these two countries. While in Argentina political violence has long been a feature of national life, violent street crime is a relatively new phenomenon, becoming a national issue only in the 1990s—unlike the case of Brazil, where extreme social disparities have for decades been a contributing factor to high urban crime rates. These differences are reflected in Table 1.1, where it can be observed that in relation to the overall Latin American context, rates of homicide in Argentina are at the lower end of the spectrum while Brazil's are at the middle to high range. It must be noted from the outset, however, that reliable crime statistics are still

Table 1.1 Homicide Rate and Levels in Selected Latin American Countries, c. 2002

	Homicide Rate (per 100,000 inhabitants)	Number of Homicides
Colombia (2002)	217.3	91,244
Venezuela (2002)	42.0	9,617
Bolivia (2000)	32.0	2,558
Ecuador (1999)	25.9	3,217
Brazil (2001)	**23.0**	**39,618**
Paraguay (2001)	15.6	890
Mexico (2000)	14.1	13,829
Argentina (2002)	**9.2**	**3,453**
Uruguay (2002)	8.0	252
Costa Rica (1999)	6.6	245
Chile (2001)	4.5	699
Peru (2001)	5.0	1,298
Panama (1998)	2.0	54

Sources: Interpol (2004). Data pertaining to Argentina drawn from DNPC (2002); Costa Rica and Mexico from United Nations (2004); and Venezuela from Estadística Delictiva/Ministerio de Justicia, División de Estadística, cited in PROVEA (2003).

Note: These statistics do not reflect national differences in legal definitions of crimes or differences in reporting standards.

problematic in both countries—an issue that will be further elaborated in subsequent chapters.

Given that Brazil's population is about 185 million, compared to Argentina's 38.5 million, the scale of social problems in Brazil is much larger. Its population is also much more racially heterogeneous, a factor that undoubtedly contributes to the more extreme polarization of the policing debate and to the tendency to justify police violence with thinly disguised racial code words. Perhaps due to these factors, crime and police abuse scandals in Brazil have received much higher international scrutiny than is the case for events in Argentina. Presently, in both countries and indeed throughout the region, a plethora of new initiatives and attempts at institutional engineering and transplantation are being aimed at police reform. All too often, however, the recommendations of international consultants, as well as locally spawned initiatives, are undertaken without an appropriate assessment of the lessons of the past or without due consideration of the political, cultural, and financial conditions under which the local police operate.

Without an analytical look back, there can be little real understanding of prospects for the future. To address this need, this book assesses the causes that contributed to the deteriorating public security situation in Argentina and Brazil in the 1990s, together with the factors that hindered police capacity to function effectively within the confines of democratic governance. The book provides in-depth analysis of the role and relationship of the police within the state and society, which in the Latin American context is deeply intertwined with a history of democratic interruption, ossified legal frameworks, fragmented civil societies, and ingrained corruption.

Here *public security* refers to the state's capacity to provide its citizenry with an adequate level of protection from crime and violence.[6] Such a concept necessarily has both objective and subjective aspects. Objectively, it reflects an increase in crime that can be analyzed either in aggregate terms or in terms of levels of violence.[7] Subjectively, the concept of public security is tied both to fear of crime and to the perception that the police (and thus the state) are not trusted allies in providing protection or redress from crime. In Latin America, such fears are intensified by political exploitation of the police, by the sensationalistic nature of media reporting on crime, by the spread of crime to previously unaffected areas, or by sudden spurts of specific types of crimes, such as bus hijackings or kidnappings.

The research for this book was carried out in an atmosphere that can best be described as extremely sensitive and secretive. Great care was taken to triangulate all data derived from documentary sources, historical analysis, and 165 interviews carried out in situ in Spanish and Portuguese. Interview subjects included high-ranking police and politicians, community leaders and NGO staff, clergy and prostitutes, lawyers and legislators, businesspeople and shanty dwellers, among other groups. In addition, visits were undertaken to police training institutions, government programs, community forums, and many of the poorest neighborhoods in Argentine and Brazilian cities. Additional details on research and methods are presented in the appendix.

This book argues that notwithstanding differences in the scale of public insecurity, Argentina and Brazil share a common family of problems that have hindered the transformation of the police into an institution capable of providing the kind of public service befitting a democracy.[8] Far from being exclusive to the police, such problems as lack of accountability and corruption are endemic at most levels of the Argentine and Brazilian state (and indeed society). Civil society has not yet demonstrated that it is capable of organizing effectively to ensure the establishment of responsible governance of most core state functions. In both countries, police reform attempts have been framed by a political game whose principal components are uncivic attitudes toward public office, low levels of public accountability, and destructive forms of political competition. The book conceptualizes the political game and its pernicious effects on national life.

Given the complexity and territorial extension of Argentina and Brazil—the eighth and fifth largest countries in the world respectively—this book focuses on policing and the politics of reform as carried out in the cities of Buenos Aires and Rio de Janeiro. Buenos Aires's preeminent role in Argentine life make it a natural choice: it is not only the country's richest city, it is where virtually all important decisions are made.[9] Although the city proper has only about 3 million inhabitants, its greater metropolitan area contains over one-third of Argentina's population of 38.5 million. For its part, Rio de Janeiro is a microcosm of Brazilian social problems—a "symbol of Brazil,"[10] as former president Fernando Henrique Cardoso called it. Neither the mayor of Buenos Aires nor the mayor of Rio directly controls the police forces that operate in their city, a fact that gives rise to frequent jurisdictional battles, political rivalries, and blurred lines of accountability among the municipal, provincial, and federal governments—issues that will be explored in later chapters.

The terms used for Buenos Aires and Rio de Janeiro can be confusing. Buenos Aires is formally known as the Autonomous City of Buenos Aires or Ciudad Autónoma de Buenos Aires. As Argentina's federal capital, it is a separate political and geographic entity from the surrounding Buenos Aires Province, whose capital is La Plata. Rio de Janeiro is both the name of a city and the capital of the state bearing the same name.[11] In this book, unless otherwise specified, the names Buenos Aires and Rio will refer to the cities.

The book contains three parts. Parts 1 and 2 have five chapters respectively, each following a similar organizational rationale. The first chapter in each part analyzes the rise in public insecurity in the postdictatorship period; particular attention is drawn to the police role in the public security crisis.

The second chapter evaluates the culture, organization, and structural framework of the police to highlight the areas most in need of reform. An analysis of the main state initiatives that were undertaken to reform the police is provided in the third chapter, which is followed by an evaluation of the two theories most commonly advanced to rationalize the lack of substantial progress in the reform process. After reflecting on the comparative validity of these arguments, the final chapters of Parts 1 and 2 argue instead that the vagaries of the political game were what undercut reform. In Part 3, the book concludes by assessing the ramifications of the study for the prospects of democratic consolidation in Argentina and Brazil. The book's analysis extends further, suggesting that, far from being isolated cases, many of the same factors that frustrated police reform in Argentina and Brazil are at the heart of the overall failure by most Latin American states to address the primary concerns of the population a quarter-century after the restoration of electoral democracy.

Notes

1. For a review of this literature, see von Hirsch, Bottoms, Burney, and Wikström (1999).

2. By "legitimacy" I mean a belief in the rightfulness of power based on acceptance of the way power is acquired and exercised (i.e., according to established laws), together with a degree of normative acceptance of the rules themselves, as expressed through some measure of consent. For useful reviews of this concept, see Beetham (1991) and Geuss (2001: ch. 1).

3. In developed democracies, 80–90 percent of calls to the police do not involve criminal offenses.

4. Cited in US Committee for Refugees (2003): "Principal Sources of Internally Displaced Persons" (table 6) and the chapter "Americas and the Caribbean: Colombia."

5. In 2003, Brazil was ranked first in Latin America, with a real gross domestic product (GDP) of $868 billion; Mexico second, with $420 billion; and Argentina third, with $272 billion (all figures in US$ at 1996 prices). See Economist Intelligence Unit Data Services (2004).

6. Other terms, such as *public safety, personal security,* and *physical security,* are also commonly used in literature on crime and policing, as is *citizen security,* although the latter term refers more specifically to the inclusion and participation of citizens in public-private partnerships to improve their communities. I have opted for *public security* because this is the term most commonly used in the Latin American context and because my objective is primarily to evaluate the state response to rising insecurity.

7. Crime statistics, however, cannot wholly capture the level of public security, particularly in countries where criminal justice data collection is highly flawed. A variety of factors can affect criminal statistics; in Latin America, in particular, a considerable number of crimes go unreported owing to mistrust of the police and fear of reprisals. If statistics may underrepresent a given problem, statistical increases may, conversely, be attributable not to a rise in "real" crime levels but to

a higher level of reporting or recording. Reporting may be stimulated, for example, by higher numbers of insured victims obliged to file reports in order to claim compensation (auto theft is one case). Police recording of crimes may increase due to improved information technology or pressure to fulfill quotas, in which case even insignificant crimes will be entered. For a full review of these issues, see Maguire (2002).

8. By this I am referring to policing that provides protection, reassurance, emergency assistance, and redress to the public within a framework of law and accountability. For a review of the literature on democratic policing, see Jones, Newburn, and Smith (1996) and Marenin (1998).

9. For more on centralism in Latin America as a whole, see in particular Véliz (1980).

10. Statement by Fernando Henrique Cardoso shortly after his election in October 1994. See "Crime Now Reigns in Brazilian City Renowned as the Source of Romance," *New York Times,* October 25, 1994.

11. Until 1960, Rio de Janeiro was also the capital of Brazil.

PART 1
ARGENTINA

CHAPTER 2

The Rise of Insecurity

Despite a tradition of political instability, violent street crime in Argentina was a relatively unknown phenomenon until the early 1990s. Although Argentina's cities had been among the safest in the Western Hemisphere, by the end of the decade many were experiencing urban problems similar to those of other cities in Latin America. In Buenos Aires, surveys showed that 86 percent of residents expressed fear of crime and that an overwhelming majority did not trust the police (or the state) to help them. This chapter will trace the factors that led to this situation.

The Historical Context of Crime and Instability

Argentines have coexisted with political violence for much of their independent history. Following the declaration of independence from Spain on July 9, 1816, Argentina alternated between brief periods of elected government and decades of extreme instability—including anarchy, civil war, attacks by the indigenous population, genocidal campaigns against the indigenous population, and bilious rivalry between Buenos Aires and the provinces. In 1930 the military staged its first successful military coup. When General José Félix Uriburu ended sixteen years of democratic rule by the Radical Party in September 1930, Argentina entered a long era in which brief periods of democracy were interrupted by a succession of military coups. Military coups were staged in 1943, 1955, 1962, 1966, and 1976: in the eighteen-year period from 1966 to 1984, Argentina experienced civilian rule for only three years, and even in that brief interval (1973–1976) the country was besieged by terrorism and economic and social chaos.

Street crime, however, did not carry over from this history of political turbulence. The capital, Buenos Aires, was known as "the Paris of South America" due to its Europeanized architecture and teeming cultural life.

Women felt safe in the city at virtually any hour, and *porteños* (as residents of Buenos Aires are known) were able to indulge in their fabled nightlife unfettered by personal fear. Strong informal social controls, particularly a tight-knit family structure, relatively low levels of income inequality, and a progressive social safety net first introduced by socialist legislators in the 1920s and expanded later by Juan Domingo Perón,[1] contributed to the sensation of safety. The police relied on tough, mostly illegal methods to keep the visible face of crime off the streets. In the 1950s and 1960s, for example, the police were fairly effective at containing small-scale criminal bands thanks to a network of informants and infiltration methods that had been perfected for purposes of political surveillance since the 1930 military coup. To extract confessions, the police beat up suspects or liberally applied the *picana eléctrica* (electric discharges applied through a rod, usually to the genital area).[2]

The harsh repression unleashed by the military junta that took power in 1976—ostensibly to "reorganize" society and political life—made these methods look quaint by comparison. The military suspended all civil liberties and, with police collaboration, persecuted and tortured anyone suspected of "subversion," which included not only leftist groups but anyone opposed to military rule. Close to 10,000 people were held in captivity, often in police facilities, for more than one year; many were detained for up to seven years. Babies born to imprisoned mothers were given for adoption to members of the security forces. By the time the "dirty war" ended, human rights groups estimated that 30,000 persons had disappeared or been killed, although official records registered only 8,960 (CONADEP 1984).

The armed forces' obsession with perceived communist subversion was matched only by the scope of their economic mismanagement. Between 1976 and 1980 the national debt soared, bankruptcies rose fivefold, and recession caused unemployment and poverty to rise to unprecedented levels. By 1979, Argentina's share of the overall Latin American gross national product (GNP) had fallen to 13.2 percent, from 24 percent in 1950. When the financial system came near collapse in 1981, the currency was devaluated; devaluation was followed by an estimated US$2 billion in capital flight (Rock 1987: 374; Wynia 1992: 136).

In April 1982, in an attempt to reclaim its declining power and distract the restless population from the economic morass, the military decided to gamble on a cause long held dear by the Argentine nation: recovery of the Falkland Islands (Islas Malvinas) from British hands. After months of secret preparations, the junta under the leadership of General Leopoldo Galtieri attempted an invasion of the islands. Roughly three months later, due to the unanticipated strength of the British response, the Argentine military was forced to surrender. The humiliating defeat of the military in conventional war, coupled with mounting dissatisfaction over its handling of the economy, finally forced the ruling junta from power, paving the way for democratic elections in 1983.

Democracy Returns, Prosperity Stalls

Despite the active participation of various police forces in military repression during the dictatorship, police reform did not become a major national political issue until roughly a decade later. During the 1980s, the political agenda was dominated by efforts by President Raúl Alfonsín (1983–1989) to subordinate the military to civilian controls, including prosecution of some of its leaders in regular courts. On the economic front, the priority was to stabilize the heavily indebted economy, left nearly in ruins by the military's failed economic policies and the costly misadventure in the Falklands.

Successive economic plans undertaken by the ruling Radical Party, however, failed to avert a tailspin. By 1984, foreign debt had spiraled to US$48.4 billion (from US$18.8 billion in 1978). With interest payments on the debt absorbing about 60 percent of export earnings and hyperinflation hovering at 1,000 percent annually, Alfonsín was forced to appeal to the International Monetary Fund (IMF) for yet another US$1.5 billion loan and for refinancing of the debt (Wynia 1992: 175–176). When Argentina could not live up to the terms of the IMF agreement, the Peronist opposition, still smarting at its defeat in the 1983 presidential poll, seized every opportunity to further erode public confidence in the government, already besieged by blackouts, soaring unemployment, labor unrest, and food riots. After his Radical Party lost congressional and gubernatorial elections in 1987, President Alfonsín's fate was sealed. Two years later, the Peronist Party was swept back into power; on July 8, 1989, Alfonsín resigned, ceding power to President-Elect Carlos Menem five months ahead of schedule.

President Menem (1989–1999) undertook drastic measures to stabilize the economy, initiating a US$36 billion privatization program that was among the most sweeping in the world (Llach and Cerro 1998; Pastor and Wise 1997). Multinational corporations and the local business elite were invited to bid on most state enterprises and assets, including the national airline and airport, postal service, public utilities and buildings, and oil, natural gas, and coal deposits. While subsidies to local industry and the agricultural sector were suspended, generous tax breaks were provided to foreign investors. For a while, fiscal deficits were slowly brought under control; in 1991, when parity between the Argentine peso and the dollar was established, monetary speculation and currency fluctuation came to an end.

The successive waves of privatization, however, were carried out with limited legislative debate and largely through executive decree. Secrecy was lucrative: the weak regulatory framework under which the privatization process was carried out provided a billion-dollar windfall to the political and economic elite. Amid deep budget cuts for social programs, the previously substantial middle class declined quickly while poverty and inequality rose incrementally. In the Greater Buenos Aires area, the most populous region of the country, unemployment shot up from 6.3 percent in 1988 to 20.2 percent in 1995, according to the National Institute of Statistics and Census, or INDEC (2003). In the wake of economic deterioration, the percentage of urban poor began to resemble rates in neighboring countries: the percentage of people living under the poverty line rose from 17.8 percent in 1992 to 27.1 in 1999 and 54.3 in 2002.

The Rise in Crime

After years of neglect, public services and the educational system entered a state of deep crisis. In the capital, public school teachers camped out for months in front of the parliament building, waging hunger strikes in protest of abysmal salaries. Crime became commonplace in hitherto safe parts of the city, and beggars, vendors, homeless people, broken sidewalks, and garbage-strewn streets became common sights. Banks were being ransacked by armed bandits, and so were private homes and even the administrative headquarters of the Catholic Church. People became wary of hailing taxis on the street, fearing drivers who robbed their own passengers and dumped them in remote areas. Although, as shown in Figure 2.1, most *porteños* attributed the swelling crime rate to the rise in unemployment and poverty, the unprecedented crisis still shook most people to the core.

Lawlessness was far worse, however, in the *conurbano*, or Greater Buenos Aires. In this sprawling suburban area, many crimes involved hostage taking, and shooting sprees between the provincial police (known as the Bonaerense) and criminals routinely resulted in loss of civilian life. Surveys taken in both Buenos Aires and the *conurbano* show how heavily the deterioration of the public security situation was weighing on people's minds. By 1998, public security was rated the second biggest concern for the average citizen, preceded only by unemployment (UNM 1998: 23). A victimization survey conducted by the Ministry of Justice in 1999 showed that approximately 86 percent of the population felt insecure and considered the likelihood of their being the victim of a crime within the following year to be high.[3] Another poll indicated that four out of five people believed that there were more crimes in 1998 than in the prior three years (UNM 1998: 29).

Due to a lack of reliable criminal justice statistics, it is difficult to assess exactly how much crime actually increased in the 1990s. On average, it was estimated that only 30 percent of crimes were being reported. Of these, the recorded crime rate per 100,000 persons increased by 208 percent

**Figure 2.1 Public Opinion Data
on Main Factors Causing the Crime Increase**

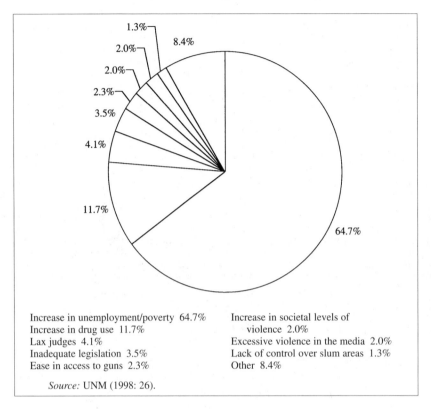

Increase in unemployment/poverty 64.7%	Increase in societal levels of
Increase in drug use 11.7%	violence 2.0%
Lax judges 4.1%	Excessive violence in the media 2.0%
Inadequate legislation 3.5%	Lack of control over slum areas 1.3%
Ease in access to guns 2.3%	Other 8.4%

Source: UNM (1998: 26).

in Buenos Aires between 1990 and 1999, while in the country as a whole it
went up by 69 percent (DNPC 1999). The 1999 homicide rate in Buenos
Aires, for example, while certainly not close to the rates in some Brazilian
cities or even US cities such as Washington, D.C., was higher than in several major European cities (see Table 2.1).

The crime situation in Buenos Aires reveals itself at its most alarming
when measured against its own previous rates: from 1993 to 1999, the
homicide rate jumped from 0.5 to 5.39 homicides per 100,000 inhabitants—
an increase of more than 900 percent. The overall increase in the homicide
rate and levels is reflected in Figure 2.2 (see p. 23). As a United Nations
international crime victimization survey shows, except for homicides,
Buenos Aires residents expressed in 1995 a higher level of victimization
than residents in other Latin American cities—including Bogotá and Rio,
both of which had higher overall crime rates (see Figure 2.3, p. 24).

Table 2.1 Homicide Rate and Levels in Selected International Cities, 1999

Homicide Rate (per 100,000 inhabitants)		Number of Homicides	
Rome, Italy	1.1	Lisbon, Portugal	28
Lisbon, Portugal	1.52	Rome, Italy	29
Toronto, Canada	1.9	Paris, France	43
Paris, France	2.02	Toronto, Canada	48
London, England	2.47	Prague, Czech Republic	64
Berlin, Germany	2.53	Warsaw, Poland	80
Madrid, Spain	3.12	Berlin, Germany	86
Prague, Czech Republic	5.3	Madrid, Spain	90
Warsaw, Poland	4.95	**Buenos Aires, Argentina**	**164**
Buenos Aires, Argentina	**5.39**	Washington D.C., USA	241
New York, USA	9.03	London, England	190
Moscow, Russia	18.85	New York, USA	671
Rio de Janeiro City, Brazil	36.8	Moscow, Russia	1,206
Washington D.C., USA	46.44	Rio de Janeiro City, Brazil	2,058
São Paulo City, Brazil	54.4	São Paulo City, Brazil	5,418

Sources: Buenos Aires figures from DNPC (1999: "Evolución del Homicidio Doloso"); figures for European cities, Moscow, and US cities from Barclay and Tavares (2002); Toronto figures from Toronto Police Service (1999); Rio from Polícia Civil statistics reported by NECVU/UFRJ (2001); São Paulo from Coordenação Geral de Informação, Estatística, e Acompanhamento das Polícias, SENASP, MJ, cited in Kahn (2002).

The Role of the Police in the Crisis

The drastic spike in crime in a previously safe city would have sufficed to provoke a crisis of public insecurity. In both the capital and its metropolitan area, the situation was exacerbated by police forces that had been largely left intact since the days of the dictatorship. Far from fulfilling their roles in a democracy, namely to provide assistance and psychological reassurance, to deter crime, and to give auxiliary support to the rest of the judicial system, the police struggled on each count, actually exacerbating the perception as well as the reality of public insecurity.

Assistance and Reassurance

In general, where the population has a reasonable level of confidence in the police, officers on patrol and their timely response to distress calls afford neighborhood residents an important degree of psychological reassurance. A consistent police presence and the capacity to intervene and follow up appropriately are important affirmations to the public and the criminal element that a state of law and a climate of justice exist (Reiss 1971). As indicated by public surveys, the low level of trust placed by the Argentine population in the police calls into question whether they were fulfilling this

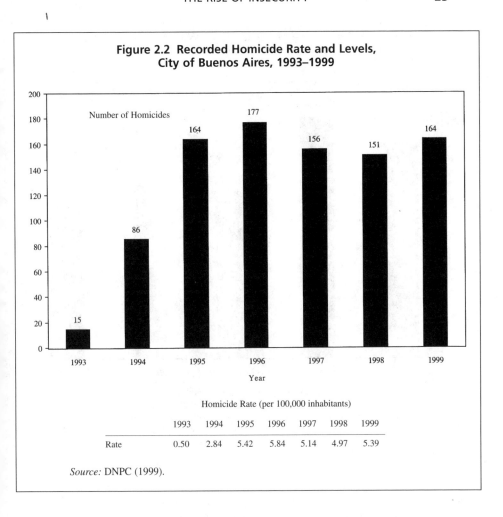

Figure 2.2 Recorded Homicide Rate and Levels,
City of Buenos Aires, 1993–1999

Number of Homicides

Homicide Rate (per 100,000 inhabitants)

	1993	1994	1995	1996	1997	1998	1999
Rate	0.50	2.84	5.42	5.84	5.14	4.97	5.39

Source: DNPC (1999).

role at all. According to Gallup Argentina's annual surveys (1984–2000), throughout the 1990s only 24 percent of the population trusted the police, while another poll taken by Graciela Romer and Associates in 2000 put this figure even lower, at 16 percent (Burzaco 2001: 57). While mistrust of the Argentine police has always been high, in the 1990s it reached an apex due to media coverage of abuses and corruption scandals and by the perception that impunity ruled. Between 1994 and 1997, of 1,056 cases filed against the police for abuse of authority, including verbal or physical abuse, none had resulted in convictions as of 1998 (Ward 1998: 5).

Media coverage of crimes involving harm to hostages had a particularly sharp effect in heightening public panic, because with limited exposure to modern negotiating techniques, the most common police response to

**Figure 2.3 Percentage of Respondents Who Reported Having
Experienced Crime in Selected International Cities**

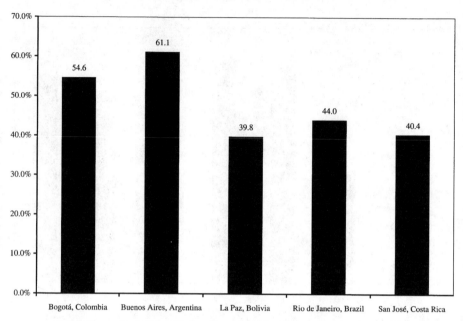

Source: International Crime Victims Survey (1995 statistics), cited in UNDP (2001: 208).
Note: Graph shows victimization for eleven different types of crimes recorded in the survey: robbery, burglary, attempted burglary, car theft, car vandalism, bicycle theft, sexual assault, theft from a car, theft of personal property, assault and threats, and theft of motocycle or moped.

hostage taking by criminals was to display massive force. Between January and October 2000, in Buenos Aires and the *conurbano,* nine bystanders were killed and roughly thirty were wounded in shootouts between the police and criminals.[4] Many of these shootouts and killings were televised by, among others, Crónica TV, part of a conglomerate that also owns Buenos Aires's most sensationalistic newspaper. Prowling the city in fully equipped vans, Crónica TV reporters filmed the wounded and the dead in gory close-up. They also exposed police participation in some of the crimes, lowering even more the levels of confidence in the police. For example, whereas in 1995, 38.6 percent of all property crimes were reported, by 1999 this figure had fallen to 31.3 percent. Reporting rates were even lower for crimes against women and children, white-collar crimes, and political corruption (DNPC 1999). One official survey suggested that the reasons for not reporting crimes could be broken down as shown in Figure 2.4.

Figure 2.4 Reasons for Not Reporting a Crime

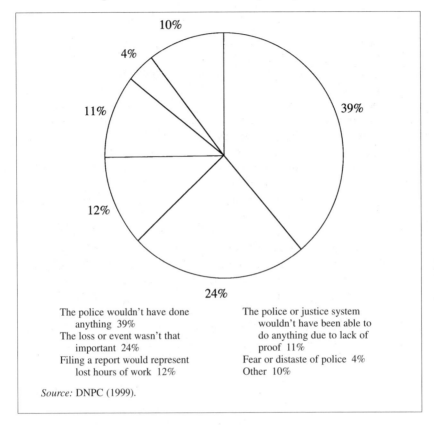

The police wouldn't have done
  anything 39%
The loss or event wasn't that
  important 24%
Filing a report would represent
  lost hours of work 12%

The police or justice system
  wouldn't have been able to
  do anything due to lack of
  proof 11%
Fear or distaste of police 4%
Other 10%

Source: DNPC (1999).

Deterrence Capacity

In the past, the Argentine police had often detained individuals based on "suspicious" physical characteristics, such as having a beard or long hair, looking like a Bolivian, or not carrying the national ID card. They often applied brutal force (*apremios ilegales*) to suspects, holding that these tactics had a deterrent capacity. In the aftermath of the "dirty war," many human rights organizations questioned the validity of arbitrary detention as well as the use of excessive force—issues that will be examined in depth in Chapter 3—and the police were forced to abandon some of their most abusive tactics.

Overall, a rigorous assessment of any police force's deterrence capability is complicated by the difficulty in obtaining hard data on crimes that have been avoided or prevented. Theoretical literature and mathematical models on criminal deterrence rely on how the criminal element perceives the *likelihood* and *severity* of punishment for violations of the law to draw conclusions (Becker 1986; von Hirsch et al. 1999). In Argentina, because of widespread perception that the police are poorly trained, lacking in investigative skills, and prone to bribes, fear of apprehension would not rank high as a deterrent. One official study showed that in 1997 the probability of arrest (the total number of arrests in relation to reported number of crimes committed) in Buenos Aires was only 20.9 percent (Dammert 2000: 38).

Interviews with numerous police officers also suggest that the police themselves believe their deterrent ability to be low. One officer with more than twenty years' experience lamented, "Criminals are not even afraid of us anymore. In the US the police have authority. Here criminals commit robberies 50 meters from where we are standing, and if we get in their way they just shoot us."[5] Not only is police firepower inferior to that of criminals, but many officers lack bulletproof vests and adequate communications equipment, making them even more vulnerable to injury and death. Indeed, in the 1990s, police officers were killed in growing numbers by an emboldened and heavily armed criminal element. In Buenos Aires and the *conurbano,* seventeen police officers were killed in 1990, and the number rose to fifty-three in 1998 (CELS 1999: 2). A comparison with US data shows just how high this figure is. In New York, only three police officers were feloniously killed in 1998. In the entire United States (with a population of about 270 million in 1998, as compared to Argentina's 36 million that year), only sixty-one officers were feloniously killed (FBI 1998).

Investigative Capacity

As discussed in Chapter 1, the third main function of the police in a democracy is to serve as an effective and efficient auxiliary to the judiciary system by making arrests and carrying out criminal investigations within legal boundaries. In the case of the Argentine police, particularly during the 1990s, poor training and methodological and tactical obsolescence tainted their efforts, leading to such a large number of procedural errors and improprieties that judges dismissed many cases outright. In Buenos Aires alone, out of the total 81,320 sanctions for misdemeanors brought forward by the police between March 1998 and June 2000, 85 percent were shelved. Of approximately 12,000 cases that were allowed to continue, only 10 percent were resolved.[6]

Overall, the crime-solving rate in Argentina is consistently low. In 1999, for example, according to official statistics, of all the crimes reported nationwide only 1.25 percent resulted in conviction or sentence. Buenos Aires fared slightly better: its conviction and sentencing ratio was 1.31 percent. To provide an indication of how low this is, in the same year the ratio was 21.5 in England and Wales, where five times as many crimes are reported as in

Argentina.[7] The situation in many of the Argentine provinces was considerably worse. In President Menem's home province of La Rioja, for example, there were only ten convictions in the whole of 1999; that is, only 0.19 percent of all crimes committed resulted in convictions (DNPC 1999).

The investigation of a crime is a very involved and labor-intensive process; the piecing together of a case is usually painstakingly slow, and breaks often result from tips from the public or from a relative of the victim. Without some degree of public cooperation, the difficulty in resolving most cases greatly rises. In Buenos Aires, the unwillingness of the public to assist the police, even anonymously, combined with mediocre training, limited expertise in forensic sciences, and the scarcity of appropriate technology, contributed to the low success rate of most investigations.

The probability of being imprisoned for a crime is also small. According to 1999 official figures, only 0.6 percent of all crimes believed to have been committed in Argentina resulted in imprisonment (DNPC 1999). Even with such dismal conviction rates, the antiquated prison system was overwhelmed, so in 1994 a "probation" system based on the US model was set up to deal with nonfelonious offenses. Instead of being imprisoned, a convicted individual could be sentenced to take a remedial course or perform a certain number of hours of community service. But the two courts with jurisdiction over this system were so saturated that in the year 2000 over 10,000 cases were pending.[8] In addition, sentences dictated under the probation system were equivalent to an unconditional release order, since there was virtually no follow-up system in place to ensure compliance.

According to data from the Ministry of Justice, in 1996, 53 percent of all penal indictments took between six months and two years before resolution, while 23 percent took more than three years (RNR 1996). In most cases, if the culprit was not apprehended on the spot or there were no suspects, the case was shelved. Perhaps owing to frustration with the low levels of resolution of crimes by the formal criminal justice system, one study found that 53 percent of the population believed that taking the law into one's own hands is justified in extreme situations (UNM 1997: 12).

In the 1990s, lack of confidence in the police plummeted even further after allegations that the police might have participated in, or known about, several high-profile crimes. The most notorious was the July 1994 car bombing of the Jewish Argentine Mutual Association (AMIA), which left 85 dead and close to 300 wounded. To this day, neither this case nor a deadly bombing of the Israeli Embassy in Buenos Aires two years earlier has been solved. According to Argentine investigative journalist Raúl Kollman, "To properly investigate this case would have meant to mess with the business of the police and the security services . . . so the investigation has been a complete failure."[9] The journalist added that the likelihood was high that cover-up orders had come from the highest levels of the Menem government. These allegations were revived in July 2002, when a secret deposition leaked to the *New York Times* accused former president Menem of taking a US$10 million bribe from Iranian officials to cover up the bombing.[10]

Conclusion

Certainly the police cannot bear sole responsibility for the increase in crime and insecurity in the 1990s, for its roots reach back into the intense economic and social dislocation produced by the military dictatorship. The military's catastrophic mismanagement was temporarily repaired during the 1990s, but the remedy itself—President Menem's sweeping program of neoliberal reform—contributed to a dramatic escalation of poverty, inequality, and crime amid vast political corruption. While the police were not responsible for the economic and social factors that contributed to crime, their performance contributed to both the sensation and the reality of public insecurity rather than providing a reasonable level of protection, reassurance, and redress to the population. Why did the state allow such deficiencies? The following chapters turn to this issue.

Notes

1. See Rock (1987: 187–189, 262–264) for more on these social reforms.

2. According to historian Ricardo Rodriguez Molas (1985), the use of the *picana eléctrica* as an instrument of torture was first introduced by the police in 1930—the year that marked the first successful military coup and continued use of the police to repress worker movements and political protest.

3. These figures are echoed by other statistics. One survey found that 71.6 percent feared being a victim of some kind of crime. Of this, 45.7 percent were afraid of physical assault, while 41.7 percent were afraid of being robbed. See UNM (1998: 29).

4. "La Ley de la Selva," *Revista Veintitres,* October 5, 2000.

5. Author interview with one of the directors of the University of the Argentine Federal Police, August 29, 2000.

6. "La Ciudad: El 85 por Ciento de las Actas Policiales Realizadas Hasta Ahora Fueron Mal Confeccionadas," *Clarín,* June 10, 2000.

7. Calculated from United Nations (2004): tables 2 and 11.

8. "Probation: Una Prueba con Poco Control," *Clarín,* September 25, 2000.

9. "Interview with Raúl Kollman," by J. Rosenberg, www.atentado-amia.com.ar, July 18, 1994.

10. "Iran Blew Up Jewish Center in Argentina, Defector Says," *New York Times,* July 22, 2002.

CHAPTER 3

Policing in the Seat of Power

If we are to understand the relationship of the police with the Argentine state and society in the 1990s, an examination of the historical and cultural continuum that shaped police institutions from their foundation in the nineteenth century onward is essential. Although it is generally agreed that police-military collaboration in repressive activities during the 1970s was a shameful episode whose consequences still resonate on the police, the institution has in fact been manipulated politically, by both military and civilian regimes, throughout its history. As a result, a system of mutual dependency evolved between the police and the political establishment—an unholy alliance that undermined most efforts to strengthen police governance and improve controls. Nowhere is this more evident that in the capital city of Buenos Aires, the country's economic and political seat of power.

A Brief History of the Argentine Police

Policing in most of the Argentine territory is a provincial matter. Each of the twenty-three Argentine provinces has its own police force, controlled by the provincial governor and the governor's minister of security. The most powerful police presence in the country, however, is the Argentine Federal Police (PFA), a force that beyond its primary theater of operations in the country's capital, the Autonomous City of Buenos Aires, has jurisdiction over investigation of federal crimes in the interior. The importance of maintaining the PFA close to the power structure is evidenced by the fact that it is the president of the republic who directly appoints the head of the PFA, the chief of police. The reasons for this will become more readily apparent through a brief historical overview.

Argentine history is indelibly marked by high levels of political violence and conflict. In the nineteenth century, independence from Spain brought neither unity nor stability to the Provincias Unidas del Río de la Plata, as Argentina was then known. Even after a formal declaration of independence was signed on July 9, 1816, provincial governments continued to wage war against remaining royal armies, against each other, and against dominance by the port city of Buenos Aires. Fratricidal conflict, mixed with campaigns to exterminate the indigenous population and periods of anarchy and external war,[1] lasted for almost seven decades. Within such an unstable context, real or imagined "destabilization" attempts by political opponents and social movements were and have remained one of the paramount concerns of political leaders, both civilian and military, who have long used the police for surveillance purposes to preempt perceived threats. These efforts acquired far higher political priority than the development of solid and stable institutions and particularly affected the development of policing—a historical trajectory that is not always duly considered in contemporary debates over reform.

The first police in Argentine history were created in Buenos Aires in 1580, simultaneously with the second founding of the city by the Spaniard Juan de Garay. During the bloody upheavals of the nineteenth century, the police of Buenos Aires became absorbed in the conflicts between the governor of Buenos Aires Province, Juan Manuel de Rosas (1835–1852), and other provincial chieftains. A wealthy landowner who assumed power with the title "Restorer of the Laws" and ruled through intimidation, Rosas, along with his federalist allies (*federales*), favored a centralized system of government dominated by Buenos Aires Province. They were opposed by the unitarists (*unitarios*), who allied themselves with Brazil and Uruguay to resist the *federales'* attempted domination of the port of Buenos Aires and its lucrative European trade. With the exception of a two-year period of relative calm (1840–1841), war between federalists and unitarists raged between 1837 and 1852, the year Rosas was defeated and sent into exile to England.

In 1840, the internal conflict was temporarily superseded by a war waged against a Bolivian-Peruvian alliance, by a prolonged blockade against Montevideo, and by a French naval blockade of the port of Buenos Aires. This year marks the first time that the police of Buenos Aires were officially militarized into two artillery battalions, reflecting their function as guardians of the laws dictated by Rosas (Rock 1986: 84–85; Rodríguez and Zappietro 1999: 84–85).

When the city of Buenos Aires was federalized in 1880, jurisdiction over the police (which became known as the Police of the Capital) was transferred to the president of the republic through the minister of the interior. It was during the period that followed that Colonel Ramón Falcón laid the main foundations for modern policing in Argentina. Appointed chief of the Police of the Capital in 1906, Falcón charged the uniformed Security Division with maintaining public order in the federal capital, while the two branches of the Investigative Division acted, respectively, as a political police and a criminal or detective police (Kalmanowiecki 2000: 41).

The Police of the Capital gradually acquired numerous other functions and competencies, which were extended to the interior of the country. This expansion evolved during the presidency of José Figueroa Alcorta (1906–1910), when an anarchist movement, brought to Argentina during the wave of Italian and Spanish immigration in the late 1880s, quickly gathered force in many provinces. Although the number of anarchists was small, they were remarkably successful in organizing trade unions, defending workers' rights, and staging strikes, which won them considerable influence in the political and economic life of Buenos Aires. With the spread of the anarchist movement to other provinces, the government authorized the police to deport or imprison suspected anarchists and their sympathizers. Following the attempted assassination of President Figueroa Alcorta in 1908 by a self-declared anarchist, the intelligence-gathering capabilities of the police throughout the country were further expanded.

Creation of the Argentine Federal Police

A few months after being appointed in a military coup that overthrew the government on June 4, 1943, President Pedro Ramírez issued a decree creating a new police force, the Argentine Federal Police. The PFA's jurisdiction would extend to all the national territory with regard to federal crimes; its chief would be appointed by the president of the republic. The PFA gradually absorbed the functions of the Police of the Capital, which was abolished two years later. From 1943 to 1983, a forty-year period, all chiefs[2] of the PFA were military officers, with the exception of four brief appointments that, combined, lasted the equivalent of twenty-six months.

As noted in Chapter 2, the military coup that deposed President Hipólito Yrigoyen in 1930 was the first of six democratic interruptions (not including various failed coup attempts), setting the stage for a police apparatus that mirrored the military's own structure. Militarization of the police is not a problem per se; many democracies, notably Italy and France, have military-style police forces. Militarization can in fact promote greater internal discipline and efficiency in the police, provided there is an effective chain of command fully conversant with, and committed to, the obligations of policing in a democratic society. In Argentina, however, brutal repression and subversion of democratic principles have marked the association between the military and the police.

The 1976 military takeover, in particular, left an indelible negative ideological and tactical legacy among the police, owing to the intensity and scale of the military's repression of suspected communist subversion, reviewed in Chapter 2. Like the military, the police emerged from the dictatorship severely discredited and widely detested due to their active involvement in the dirty war. As a high-ranking official interviewed in the Secretariat of Security put it, "During the dictatorship the police were used by the military as cheap labor for their worst activities."[3] Once democracy was restored, however, while the military were banned from involvement in matters of internal security, the same police who had grown accustomed to operating in a climate of repression, illegality, and impunity were left largely intact to preserve public order and security.

Organization and Training

> [The PFA] is not managed as a big enterprise should be; rather it is managed as an army in battle would be. You can't discuss or contradict orders, or change course, or dispute an order.
> —*A retired division chief of the PFA*[4]

Centralization and hierarchy are two salient characteristics of military organizations. In the case of the PFA, its close association with the armed forces has made unconditional respect and unquestioned obedience to superior officers two of its institutional pillars. Any deviation from strict administrative regulations is subject to punishment: policemen can be imprisoned for arriving late to work or wearing unpolished shoes. Since personal loyalty and obedience to superior officers are sine qua non qualifications for promotion, it is extremely rare for a policeman to denounce corruption or negligence in a precinct (of which there are fifty-three in Buenos Aires). Until 1999, policemen were considered by the state to be on duty twenty-four hours a day and were required to carry arms at all times.[5]

The chain of command has eighteen echelons from top to bottom, with two distinct and separate career tracks: one for officers and one for the sub-officer cadres (akin to enlisted officers in the military). Unlike police in the United States and Britain, whose members can rise from privates to the top echelons, chances for advancement in the PFA are limited: a subofficer can rise only to the position of deputy precinct chief (*subcomisario*), even after obtaining a master's degree or being distinguished for bravery. Social interaction between the two strata is strongly discouraged. The officer class is an elite group constituting roughly 16 percent of the force. On average, their training lasts three years, as opposed to the three months subofficers receive. Officers in training live-in at the Escuela Ramón Falcón; they are allowed to leave the premises only on weekends. Separation of the sexes is strictly enforced; the respective living quarters are located at a considerable distance from one another, and female teachers normally teach female students in separate classes.[6] Posters, pictures, and radios are prohibited in rooms between 8:00 A.M. and 6:00 P.M. Officers in training are required to salute their superiors whenever in their presence; their highly regimented routine creates a tight and closed esprit de corps and generates a high level of indoctrination.

For the subofficer cadres, a high school diploma has been required only since 1996, and the institution of this requirement has not had a significant effect in redressing the low levels of schooling of those who joined the force prior to this date.[7] Initial training at the Escuela de Cadetes lasts roughly three months. Training in the area of investigations is likewise limited. Because until the recent past the police customarily used intimidation and beatings to obtain information, a weak and malformed investigative tradition developed. In the 1990s, with personnel costs accounting for roughly 86 percent of total police expenditures and about 10 percent allocated for fixed costs (such as utilities, vehicles, gasoline, weaponry, and ammunition), resources left over to increase police capacity in forensic sciences and other investigative disciplines were grossly inadequate.[8] The capacity of the PFA to keep pace with advanced technology is very restricted. As a director of one of the police training institutions pointed out, "Once you get off the technology train, it is very difficult to get back on."[9]

As noted above, the subofficer cadres have insufficient training in regular police work, and this is all the more so as concerns investigative work. Because subofficers are usually the first to arrive on a crime scene, by the time Department of Investigation personnel arrive the crime scene has all too often been already compromised. Instances of crime scenes that have been improperly preserved or cordoned off, and of evidence tampering, are well documented (e.g., CELS and HRW 1998). To make matters worse, in Buenos Aires, police officers who perform best on exams and fitness tests are sent to "elite" police precincts, the ones closest to the political and financial hub, where violent crime rates are low. The worst performing officers are sent to the peripheral areas of the city, where crime is more acute.

Use of Force

> In Argentina, either you punish criminals by using illegal force, or there will be impunity for the crimes they commit.
> —*A middle-level official in the Ministry of Justice*[10]

As discussed in Chapter 1, it is a challenge for any society to resolve the tensions between the dictates of democracy and the coercive powers of the police. Indeed, "the potential for police violence and the rhetoric that would justify it are endemic" (Chevigny 1995: 26). This is even more so the case in developing countries, where social instability, violent crime, and inequality are problems of a much larger magnitude than in advanced countries. Nevertheless, in a democracy it is expected that the police will use force more sparingly than in a dictatorship, where accountability is a rare commodity and impunity tends to be the rule. In Argentina, however, a clear and publicly debated doctrine surrounding the use of force by the Argentine police has not become state policy.

Although a wave of legislation designed to contain human rights abuses by the police was passed in the 1980s in the aftermath of military rule, police truculence remained a problem, albeit on a smaller scale. In April 2000, for instance, a 500-strong march protesting against the IMF ended up with many demonstrators beaten, kicked in the genitals, and pushed back with pressurized water, tear gas, and rubber bullets. Under considerable pressure because the whole episode had been televised, the minister of the interior was forced to publicly deplore the PFA's "brutal and savage repression" and order the suspension of twelve police officers.[11] Also televised, this time internationally, were the events leading up to the December 2001 resignation of President Fernando de la Rúa, when twenty-five protesters were shot by the police, seven fatally. In the aftermath of the riots that ensued, which included widespread looting of supermarkets and shops, the former president, the minister of the interior, the secretary of security, and the chief of police were charged with "homicide, illegal imprisonment, and violation of the duties of a public official."[12]

Accurate official statistics on the use of force, particularly with regard to weapons carried and lost by the police, number and type of bullets fired, death and injury rates, or analysis of the circumstances under which police officers and civilians are killed, are only sporadically maintained. One prominent human rights NGO, the Center for Legal and Social Studies (CELS), has long attempted to fill the vacuum by compiling its own independent research. For 1999, CELS data indicated that the PFA reportedly killed sixty-five persons and wounded thirty-three—a reversal of the normal pattern in a democracy, whereby the police normally wound more than are killed.[13] According to CELS, off-duty PFA personnel killed another fifty-four persons and wounded thirty-one more in Buenos Aires Province (CELS 2000: 142–143). In New York, by contrast, the police fatally shot eleven civilians in the same year—this in a city with a homicide rate about 40 percent higher than that of Buenos Aires and with 7,000 more police officers than the PFA (NYC 2001).

Arbitrary Detention

In addition to the ongoing debate surrounding police use of force, other residual methods of "preventive policing" continued into the democratic era. From 1947 until 1996, the police were given de facto legislative authority to issue regulations dealing with misdemeanors, such as loitering, obscene behavior, gambling, and public urination. These regulations were known as *edictos policiales* (police edicts). Police edicts typified not only several categories of suspicious people but situations that were considered to fall under a precriminal stage as well. The edicts allowed the police to detain individuals based on appearance and to determine punishment for misdemeanors—short-term imprisonment, fines, and the like (Lorences 1997). Between 1992 and 1996, for example, the police detained 593,396 people for misdemeanors, many more than the 200,924 detained for crimes (Chillier 1998b: 6).

The police maintained that the ability to detain people based on suspicious appearance or behavior was a primary tool in crime prevention. Opponents argued that the edicts were unconstitutional in that they granted the PFA lawmaking prerogatives, thus enabling it to act as both judge and jury (Oliveira and Tiscornia 1997: 19). Edicts also made it easy for the police to extract bribes from people seeking to avoid detention or fines, including prostitutes, street vendors, and illegally parked drivers. In an interview, a prostitute said that that on average they paid US$400 a week solely to avoid detention.[14] Those who did not or could not pay were imprisoned for twenty-four hours, detained again after release, or forced to provide free sexual favors.

Though the edicts were struck down in 1996 (replaced by the Code for Urban Public Behavior, to be discussed in Chapter 4), the police persisted in gauging the potential threat posed by individuals based on appearance, socioeconomic status, and political orientation. This approach, a residue from military repression, remains ingrained. In fact, during numerous interviews with officials at one of the police educational institutions, I was repeatedly apprised of the high number of "subversive elements" holding political office or working in journalism or human rights organizations and was freely given their names, past associations, and current positions. One official casually mentioned that the ombudsman's office was staffed by elements from the Facultad de Filosofía y Letras, one of the most historically left-leaning of Argentine colleges (not incidentally, it had the highest number of students and professors abducted during the dirty war in the 1970s). As some legislation restricting police powers was inspired by individuals labeled as left-leaning intellectuals, many in the police institution impugn the legitimacy of these laws, viewing them as another weapon in the same confrontation that took place during the dictatorship. This view is echoed by the results of the public opinion poll presented in Figure 3.1.

Many police officers interviewed complained about the restrictions that kept them from being free to preemptively detain and interrogate potential criminals; they argued that under the current legal codes their only option was to stand in the street and wait for a crime to happen. One public opinion poll showed that 83 percent of police officers believed that procedural codes "neutralize police efforts to fight crime" and that the increase in crime can

Figure 3.1 Police Perceptions of Antagonism (percentage)

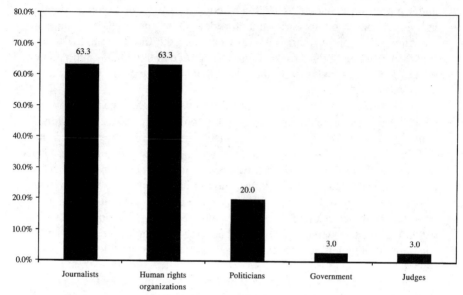

Source: UNM (1998: 106).

be attributed to "soft" procedural and legal codes (UNM 1998). According to one former chief of police, "The new legal codes don't allow us to detain the loiterer or the harasser. If a criminal is scouting out a location for a crime, the cops can't do anything to prevent it. Lots of foreigners are coming here to commit crimes because Argentina is a paradise for criminals. . . . We lack the legal tools to deal with the situation."[15]

A Vocation for Intelligence

Numerous government officials in Buenos Aires have argued that intelligence activities, rather than crime prevention and control, are the primary activity of the PFA. Indeed, engagement of the police in political espionage and intelligence activities, which became widespread in the first quarter of the twentieth century, remained substantial throughout the 1990s. From offices scattered in the provinces, the police generated reports for the minister of the interior and the president on the social situation in each province, including detailed data on student groups and workers' organizations. According to one detective with more than twenty years' experience, the police have "infiltration in the unions, universities, and throughout the whole country. . . . Not even the SIDE [Secretariat of State Intelligence] has as much presence in the interior as the police."[16] One Argentine historian and former adviser to the municipal government on matters of public security said, "The PFA is the best opinion surveyor in the country and has the best intelligence. It dedicates most of its efforts and time to these activities because intelligence is the real source of its power. . . . The PFA's resources go to intelligence, not to the quality of the service provided to the citizen."[17]

A former top city government official stated, "The PFA assumed more intelligence tasks because it could offer information to the executive unmatched by any other agency. . . . The election forecasts of the PFA until the seventies and through the eighties were the best and most accurate in the country."[18]

The PFA also conducted political espionage on the various political parties and opposition candidates in the capital. In one highly publicized instance, the mayor of Buenos Aires found that the wife of one of his chief political strategists was spying for the PFA; numerous other politicians complained of phone tapping and other infiltration maneuvers by the police.

The PFA's Financial and Operational Network

> The paradox of underdevelopment is that the few resources available are all misassigned.
>
> —*A former consultant for the*
> *City Government Program on Citizen Security*[19]

Following the end of military rule in 1983, with human rights and other groups working tirelessly to air the horrors of the dirty war, President Alfonsín rapidly moved to subjugate the military to civilian control. He ordered the prosecution of junta generals Jorge Rafael Videla, Roberto Viola, and Leopoldo Galtieri,[20] among others, and slashed the military budget, the progression of which is shown in Figure 3.2.

During the dictatorship, when matters of "national security" were surrounded by almost total secrecy, the military rewarded police collaboration in carrying out repressive actions with increased budgets. After 1983, Alfonsín curtailed resources to the police, the rationale being that fewer resources would not only reduce their scope of operations but also force them to make more rational use of their funds—an approach that was often advocated by international financing institutions in other government sectors. Successive civilian governments continued this policy, as shown in Figure 3.3.

The PFA, however, learned to accommodate to the new reality of reduced budgets by shifting resources around. It disbursed less money for operational costs (armaments, vehicles, bullets, training, and the like), relied on aging technology, and incurred budget deficits to meet personnel costs (mainly

Figure 3.2 Military Expenditure in Argentina, 1980–1989

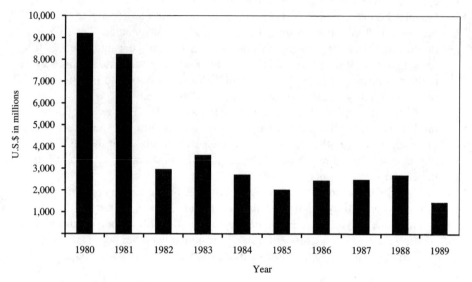

Source: Scheetz (1995).

Figure 3.3 Numbers of Policemen in the Argentine Federal Police

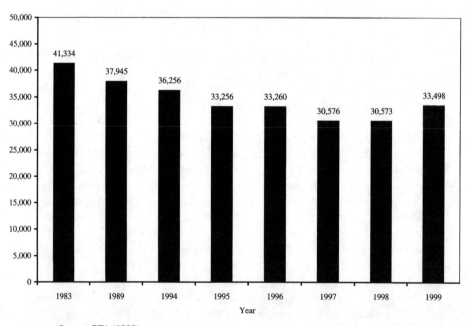

Source: PFA (1999).

salaries and pensions). To compensate for some shortfalls, the PFA organized collection drives in some neighborhoods, with local residents and merchants eagerly making contributions to ensure continued police protection of their homes and businesses. Throughout it all, the PFA remained a huge, centralized, and diversified outfit with many agencies under its control. In the words of a former consultant for the City Government Program on Citizen Security, "The PFA is like a huge government ministry—ministry in the sense of being massive."[21]

The PFA is charged with policing Buenos Aires (in the United States, Washington, D.C., is policed by the mayor's local force), has jurisdiction over federal crimes (handled by the FBI in the United States), provides protection for the president (Secret Service in the United States), and investigates crimes against the national treasury (Internal Revenue Service in the United States). The PFA is also in charge of migratory controls at airports and ports, customs, national passports, and fire fighting in Buenos Aires (and in some locations in the interior). In 1996, the PFA was also given control and jurisdiction over metropolitan public traffic.

But the scope of PFA activities does not end here. In the year 2000, the PFA also owned and managed its own hospital, several radio stations, police bands, a publishing company, magazines, television stations and programs, and summer recreation facilities. The PFA also administers its own university (reviewed in the following chapter).

Salaries and Wages

In the late 1990s, the average patrol officer earned an average monthly salary of US$700. Although compared to salaries in other Latin American countries this figure may seem high,[22] the cost of living in Buenos Aires was so inflated by the artificial parity of the peso with the dollar that an average family of four could not live on it.

Low police salaries are problematic for several reasons, the most obvious one being that they do not attract the best applicants: without adequate remuneration, the probability of getting qualified candidates for risky and dangerous work is low. Second, poor wages automatically place a police officer at the lowest rungs of society, more pliable to corruption and political manipulation. Even if officers remain on the straight and narrow, their economic circumstances will force them to seek a second job or extra shifts, factors that, as noted before, have negative effects on police efficiency.

Monitoring and Control of Expenditures

PFA spending has traditionally been subject to few external controls, which diminishes the incentives for and likelihood of efficient resource allocation by the institution. Although advanced countries also have trouble exercising full control over expenditures, a hallmark of democratic politics is that the decisionmaking process is characterized by greater transparency and access to information than is the case in nondemocracies. In the United States and Europe, the budgets and spending of police forces are subject to examination by external committees and auditors. In Argentina, on the other hand, the two principal control mechanisms, the Auditoría General de la Nación (AGN) and the Sindicatura General de la Nación (SIGEN), are not autonomous, either politically or financially: they depend on the same ministries and officials they are charged with auditing. They operate with limited and undertrained staff, and their investigations are frequently halted, whether for lack of funds or by orders from above. The politicization and lack of transparency of the auditing mechanisms have enabled the PFA to retain substantial autonomy in the use of its resources, at the same time restricting the state's capacity to ascertain the ultimate purpose of these funds or assess how much is obtained through issuing of tickets and fines, passports, and the police's own fund raising.

Internal and External Controls

In light of the deficiencies of the PFA, issues of governmental and internal police controls over police conduct and the efficiency of the mechanisms designed to hold the police accountable to public scrutiny acquire even greater relevance. In a democracy, legal rules are assumed to bind public decisionmaking, public services, and governance, so that in principle all citizens are governed by the same set of institutions and legal rules. In a police context, this implies that "law enforcement is bound by a priori legal codes and does not work outside them" (Sheptycki 1996: 64). Accountability implies transparency, both within the institution itself and in channels of external oversight. Effective accountability is especially important in the case of the police because of their potential to cause physical harm if improperly discharging their duties, and because police brutality or illegality can damage public confidence and diminish respect for the law, as discussed in Chapter 1.

Accountability is almost inevitably complicated, however, by the hierarchical and inward-looking culture of the police, which typically seeks to protect its own (Skolnick and Bayley 1988: 49–51). The police, moreover, are subjected to multiple and competing pressures to provide "results" while concurrently facing demands that they comply with procedural law in situations of imminent danger. Accountability is also influenced by police ability to circumvent procedure in the course of their work and by the wide discretion they typically have in their day-to-day activities, since they often work alone or with only one partner (Goldstein 1977; Skolnick 1994). Further, the police engage in selective law enforcement, as they do not have the resources to enforce all laws at all times and because they are asked to enforce many laws that are unpopular. It is precisely because the police are unlikely on their own to safeguard the tense balance between their powers of coercion and the requirement of legality that the police in a democracy should be accountable to "multiple audiences through multiple mechanisms" (Bayley 1996: 5).

PFA Internal Control

In the 1990s, and indeed to date, lack of accountability remained a particularly troublesome feature of the Argentine police and of the state at large. Instead of concentrating on serious manifestations of deviance, the police's internal controls were effective mostly at punishing violations of personal or administrative discipline, such as impunctuality, failure to salute, improper dress, or slovenliness. As Argentine legal theorist Carlos Nino laments, "In general, there is no accountability in Argentina for the *results* of bureaucratic undertakings, the only accountability incurred is for noncompliance with formalities" (1995: 118). Given this, the police's own control mechanisms have not produced noticeable results in enhancing institutional honesty. Some studies by academics and nongovernmental organizations have posited that the PFA machinery was at its most effective when it was geared toward generating illicit revenue (e.g., CELS and HRW 1998; Chillier 1998a). A legal adviser to the senate said when interviewed that as some precincts provided more lucrative avenues for illicit enrichment than others, an officer who wanted to be transferred there would need to "bid" for the position.[23] Within each precinct, lower-ranking officers were obliged to give percentages of profits to their superiors, who in turn paid their superiors, and so on.[24] In this well-organized system of petty corruption, even the price to turn a blind eye to certain activities was preestablished. One published investigative report asserted that illegal gambling outfits could be expected to pay US$500 per week to the police; unlicensed taxi drivers US$20 per car per week; owners of "saunas" (which double as brothels), US$5,000 per month; and stolen car traffickers US$50,000 per month.[25]

Corruption sometimes swarmed around the police headquarters building itself. In September 2000, two Paraguayan citizens accused of murdering their country's vice president, Luis María Argaña, fled Paraguay and were captured in Argentina. While awaiting extradition, they were jailed in a cell inside the police headquarters building. After careful planning, facilitated by the use of cellular phones brought to them by the wife of a police officer imprisoned in another cell, the Paraguayans bribed the police sentinels guarding them and dashed one morning through a large, palm-fringed open courtyard past the office of the chief of police into waiting cars. After an indignant protest by the Paraguayan government, an embarrassed President de la Rúa pressured the chief of police to investigate. Although the chief launched the largest internal purge of high-ranking police officials in history, he refused to take any personal responsibility, claiming that the escape episode had been engineered by his rivals within the PFA in order to destabilize him.

Under less high-profile circumstances, the usual method of dealing with police corruption would have been to purge only those at the bottom rung. While purges are one way of dealing with abusive or corrupt police officers, it is only when they are accompanied by a cleansing of the structures that enable graft that they have any long-lasting effect. Otherwise, as happened in Argentina during the 1990s, episodes of police corruption and brutality are likely to succeed each other with numbing frequency.

External Oversight: Ministry of the Interior

As discussed previously, since its creation the PFA has been under the jurisdiction of the federal government. In the 1990s, it was the Ministry of the Interior that exercised executive control, within a legal and procedural framework that was set by the legislative and judicial branches. Charged with guaranteeing domestic security, the Ministry of the Interior supervised and coordinated all national security forces, including the Gendarmería Nacional and the Prefectura Naval Argentina.[26] But the ministry's responsibilities far exceeded the scope of public security. Among other functions, the ministry

- Disbursed and monitored federal funds and loans from multilateral organizations to the twenty-three provinces.
- Oversaw all national information and telecommunication systems and emergency assistance to provinces afflicted by natural disasters.
- Participated in national budget deliberations and in judicial reform.
- Coordinated national electoral policy and elections nationwide.
- Elaborated demographic policies.
- Controlled internal and external migration.
- Established norms to fight racism and xenophobia.
- Promoted coordination of national policies among federal, provincial, and municipal governments.[27]

Of all these complex activities, one of the most contentious issues was the adjudication of subsidies to the provinces. As a result, the minister of the interior's direct involvement in oversight of the operational activities and internal affairs of the PFA was far from substantial, and the PFA continued to enjoy a large degree of leeway. In the words of a senior adviser to the minister of the interior, "The police have a certain degree of independence and autonomy. In reality, the government has little control over internal investigations or sanctions. The process by which officers and agents are sanctioned, punished, or investigated is very opaque."[28]

When I asked a former chief of police how much the Ministry of the Interior had affected his management of the PFA, he replied, "I could do more or less what I wanted. Except for the area of resources, the politicians almost never put roadblocks in my way. They gave virtually no political direction and provided no leadership."[29]

Legislative and Judicial Control

Like most of Latin America, Argentina lacks a tradition of strong legislative control on several crucial issues, including public security. When crime peaks or scandals arise, the congress will usually hold hearings or set up special investigative commissions. Many of these commissions, however, do not have sanctioning powers (apart from generating information), and once the particular crisis has faded from the public eye they disband, producing intangible results. Even budget allocations for the police, which are mostly based on spending targets set by the Ministry of the Interior or on prior year allocations, have been routinely approved by the legislature without modification.

But if financial controls over the police were lax, Congress did place formal limits on certain police practices, particularly those that concerned their powers of arrest and detention. Prior to 1991, the PFA was empowered to detain for the "purposes of identification, in circumstances that justified it, for up to twenty-four hours, all persons for whom it was believed necessary to check for a possible police record."[30] These powers, like the aforementioned police edicts, provided significant scope for extortion and frequent human rights violations. In the aftermath of the uproar that followed the case of seventeen-year-old Walter Bulacio—who in April 1991 died from beatings received while in police custody, after he and another thirty youths were detained after leaving a rock concert[31]—Congress acted to curtail PFA powers. In September 1991 it passed a law that introduced the need for probable cause prior to detention for identification purposes and reduced the maximum detention period from twenty-four hours to ten. The law also required that a judge be notified of the detention and granted permission for the detainee to communicate with family or friends.[32] Even though President Carlos Menem initially vetoed the law on grounds that ten hours were not sufficient for the police to perform a thorough identity and criminal record check, enough momentum had built up to push for Congress to override Menem's veto. In that same year, Congress approved a new code of criminal procedures[33] that allowed the police to continue arresting suspects without

warrants in certain restricted situations—for example, in the case of criminals caught in the act or fleeing the scene of a crime, or if overwhelming
evidence of a probable crime was available. In such cases, apprehended suspects could be detained incommunicado without judicial authorization only
for up to six hours. In addition, the police were barred from physically searching individuals or their possessions, including vehicles, unless they obtained
a prior judicial warrant, and interrogations were to be conducted only in the
presence of an investigative magistrate.[34]

Undoubtedly, such measures to control police procedures were a step in
the right direction. Their heavy reliance on the judiciary, however, presented a different set of problems: not only is the judiciary regarded as one
of the most corrupt of all Argentine institutions, it is also perceived to be
thoroughly politicized.[35] In a 1994 public opinion study, only 16 percent of
the general population expressed any confidence in the judiciary, with an
overwhelming 84 percent stating that the judicial system favors the rich and
powerful (Instituto Gallup Argentina 1994). Julio Mafud, a noted sociologist, has said, "The Argentine does not believe in the law or in its representatives. This lack of faith and disbelief is justified by his entire history and
sociology" (1984: 285). There is indeed ample evidence to justify mistrust
of the judiciary, dating back to the nineteenth century, if not earlier.[36] More
recent events demonstrate that little has changed. Between 1990 and 1998,
for example, there were 176 impeachment procedures against judges, 18 percent of which targeted Supreme Court justices (Burzaco 2001: 77). A November 2000 case is emblematic of the atmosphere of illegality that pervades
even highly sensitive cases: the judge charged with investigating a senate corruption scandal was himself placed under investigation for allegedly building
a US$1.25 million home financed by bribes.[37]

Public venting of mutual contempt complicated further the relationship
between the police and the judiciary.[38] The judiciary routinely alleged that
police incompetence forced them to throw out many criminal cases, while
frequent dismissal of criminals on technicalities prompted police accusations that the judiciary was coddling criminals. Although judicial cases
dragged on for years, it was not for lack of funds. Unlike other public institutions, the judicial system did not suffer from acute lack of funds or
judges. According to one study, Argentina spends between 0.8 percent and
0.9 percent of GDP on the judicial system, compared to 0.3 percent in Chile
and the United States. Argentina also has proportionally more judges: roughly
11.5 per 100,000 inhabitants, compared to 8.5 in France, 1.2 in the United
States, and 0.7 in Chile (Burzaco 2001: 71).[39] Nevertheless, as evinced by Figure 3.4, cases take many years to be completed; on average, 66 percent of
accused criminals are incarcerated while awaiting trial, sometimes for years,
as compared to 18.9 and 2 percent in Chile and the United States respectively
(Burzaco 2001: 77).

Figure 3.4 Length of Time Between Indictment for
a Crime and Sentencing in Argentina, 1999

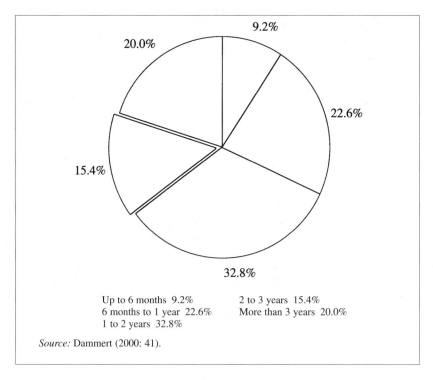

Up to 6 months 9.2%   2 to 3 years 15.4%
6 months to 1 year 22.6%   More than 3 years 20.0%
1 to 2 years 32.8%

Source: Dammert (2000: 41).

The World Bank's Country Assistance Strategy Report echoed domestic concerns when analyzing Argentina's judiciary:

> [A lack of transparency] is exacerbated by a judiciary seen as politicized and demonstrably inefficient. . . . The system suffers from heavy case loads, inequitable distribution of resources, poor infrastructure, little in the way of modern management processes, and overly centralized administration. These weaknesses all contribute to long delays and seeming lack of responsiveness. (2000: 21–22)

Conclusion

It should be acknowledged that the economic and social causes of crime lie beyond the reach of the police. Nevertheless, where police duties are effectively discharged, the police can serve as a deterrent to crime, guarantor of democratic freedoms, and agent of redress and justice. Unfortunately, at the outset of the 1990s, as examined above, police performance in Argentina's most important metropolitan area was negatively affected by historical legacies and by faulty internal and external mechanisms of control. As they were, institutions of police governance lacked the strength and configuration to monitor the financial network of the police or their vast theater of operations and arbitrary practices. There was also a consistent failure to recognize that the police's low social standing (and performance) could improve only through a systematic effort to improve salaries and training. To the detriment of public service, the police remained heavily geared toward corruption and surveillance activities. The state's tacit sanction of these activities, moreover, created yet another layer of suspicion and animosity between the police and the community, already wary of a force that until the recent past had been closely associated with military repression. The reform initiatives that attempted to reverse this situation are the subject of the following chapter.

Notes

1. Notably the War of the Triple Alliance, waged by Argentina, Brazil, and Uruguay against Paraguay (1865–1870).
2. For purposes of clarity, the top police job in the PFA, *jefe* of the Policía Federal Argentina, has been translated as "chief of police"; the *comisarios generales* in charge of the various *superintendencias* will be referred to as "division chiefs"; *comisarios* are denominated "precinct chiefs"; the next rank (*subcomisario*) is "deputy precinct chief."
3. Author interview, August 28, 2000.
4. Author interview, October 18, 2000.
5. The current clause makes the carrying of arms obligatory only while on duty and additional shifts. This law has not significantly altered behavioral practices, however, as most police officers continue to bear arms at all times and get involved in shootings while off duty. A significant number of police and civilian deaths in shootings take place while police officers are off duty. See CELS (2000).
6. Women have been admitted since 1978. In the year 2000, there were roughly 120 women out of 600 cadets. Regardless of education or training, the highest position a woman can attain in the PFA is deputy precinct chief (*subcomisario*).
7. A report published by the Ministry of the Interior in 1996 stated that 39 percent of all security forces had not finished primary school, 31.7 percent had not completed secondary school, and only 3.6 percent had some form of tertiary education. See Burzaco (2001: 46). In US cities such as New York or Boston, in contrast, applicants must have completed a minimum of two years of college to apply to the force.
8. Calculations based on analysis of PFA budgets presented in Secretaría de Hacienda (1993–2000).
9. Author interview, August 29, 2000.
10. Author interview, September 16, 2000.
11. See "Los Graves Incidentes Frenaron la Ley Laboral," *La Nación,* April 20, 2000.

12. The federal judge investigating the case has herself received death threats aimed at stopping her investigation. See "La Investigación de la Jueza Servini Sobre Plaza de Mayo: Hubo un Plan para Matar," *Página 12,* December 26, 2001.

13. To provide an indication of the situation elsewhere: in 1993 the New York Police Department killed twenty-five civilians and wounded sixty-one. See Chevigny (1995: 67).

14. Author interview, October 6, 2000.

15. Author interview, October 20, 2000.

16. Author interview, September 8, 2000.

17. Author interview, September 15, 2000.

18. Author interview, September 8, 2000.

19. Author interview, September 15, 2000.

20. Though members of the security forces were given amnesty by President Menem in 1989. See Acuña and Smulovitz (1995).

21. Author interview, September 15, 2000.

22. And indeed, relative to the situation in the Argentine provinces.

23. Author interview, October 23, 2000.

24. Author interview with a midlevel policeman with more than twenty years' experience, September 8, 2000.

25. "Los Soldados del Diablo," *Notícias,* August 10, 1996.

26. The former is charged with border patrol and numbers roughly 18,000; the latter with patrol of rivers and oceans and numbers close to 15,000.

27. See Ley 24.059 (Ley de Seguridad Interior), Congreso de la Nación Argentina, January 17, 1992, and Decreto 489 (Estructura y Organigrama del Ministerio del Interior), Poder Ejecutivo de la Nación Argentina, June 26, 2000.

28. Author interview, August 24, 2000.

29. Author interview, August 25, 2000.

30. See Article 5, Decreto/Ley 333/58 (Ley Orgánica de la Policía Federal), Poder Ejecutivo Nacional, January 14, 1958.

31. The Walter Bulacio case was subsequently brought before the Inter-American Court of Human Rights by the lawyers of two prominent Argentine human rights groups, CELS and CORREPI. On September 18, 2003, the court ruled that the Argentine state had to continue and complete the investigation of Bulacio's detention and death and bring to justice those found responsible. The ruling established that the statue of limitations was not applicable and that Bulacio's family should be paid US$400,000. The court also called for reform in the laws and practices that had led to Bulacio's detention and death. While the Argentine government paid the reparations to Bulacio's family, the investigation and legal reforms called for by the Inter-American Court remained unconcluded more than two years later.

32. See Ley 23.950 (Averiguación de Antecedentes), Congreso de la Nación Argentina, September 11, 1991.

33. See Ley 25.434 (Código Procesal Penal de la Nación), Congreso de la Nación Argentina, June 19, 2001.

34. Ten years later, in June 2001, police powers were expanded when Congress passed a law granting permission to the police to interrogate a suspect on the scene and conduct an on-the-spot physical and vehicular search without a court order so long as it was carried out openly and under circumstances that justified it. The period to hold suspects incommunicado was again extended to up to ten hours. See Ley 25.434 (Modificación del Código Procesal Penal), Congreso de la Nación Argentina, June 19, 2001.

35. Lack of public confidence in the judiciary is a problem throughout Latin America, owing to heavy backlogs and delays in case adjudication and to a perception of corruption and bias. For more on this see, Frühling (1998) and Ungar (2002).

36. Argentina's national epic, *El Gaucho Martín Fierro,* by José Hernández, first published in 1872, is full of scenes that convey popular contempt for judges. See Hernández (1982).

37. This scandal involved the executive branch and the SIDE, both of which were accused of approving bribes to a dozen senators so they would pass a controversial labor reform law advocated by the IMF. This case, like many others before it, was ultimately swept under the rug, although it led to the resignation of Vice President Chacho Álvarez, an advocate of transparency in government.

38. Mutual contempt does not preclude doing business deals together. In a 1998 case, a high-ranking police officer was accused of owning a chain of male brothels jointly with a federal judge. See "La Renuncia Que Desató una Tormenta," *La Nación,* September 26, 1998.

39. As with the police, roughly 81 percent of budgetary allocations for the judicial system goes to salaries.

CHAPTER 4

Reform the Argentine Way

It is possible that promises are the essential feature of Argentine life.
— *José Ortega y Gasset, 1929*[1]

In the 1990s, when the public security crisis exploded in Argentina, the media feasted on exposés of police misconduct and heinous crimes. Increasingly confronted with a daily reality of grim headlines and angry citizens, the state machinery finally sprang into action, announcing purges, drawing up action plans, pledging additional resources, and creating new institutions. This chapter assesses the main reform initiatives undertaken by President Carlos Menem (1989–1999) and his successor, Fernando de la Rúa (1999–2001). At a time when the police and institutions of oversight were in dire need of a structural overhaul, the administrations of both presidents concentrated on tackling only superficial aspects of core problems.

Shifts in Human and Material Resources

The Menem administration was proactive mostly in avoiding sustainable police reform. At first it denied that there was a crime problem in Buenos Aires; later it claimed that the main threat to the city emanated from foreign terrorists. As mentioned in Chapter 2, there had been in fact two deadly terrorist attacks. The first occurred in 1992, when the Israeli embassy was bombed; the second, which took place two years later, targeted the headquarters of a Jewish-Argentine organization. But though the PFA had made only negligible progress in investigating these crimes and had even attempted to cover them up, various government officials still maintained that the city "remains safe . . . even though there might be a generalized feeling of insecurity."[2]

In November 1997, however, President Menem had to confront a very different reality: a wave of armed assaults, street muggings, and bank robberies had gripped the city. To assuage public fears, he signed a decree reallocating 1,500 officers from the National Coast Guard and the National Border Police to guard public buildings against further terrorist attacks, thus freeing police personnel for street patrol. Finding these measures insufficient in light of the "historically unprecedented wave of delinquency threatening Buenos Aires," twenty-one investigative magistrates sent an open letter to the minister of the interior, the chief of the PFA, and Congress, requesting the immediate hiring of 5,000 additional police. At a press conference, the minister of the interior responded that budgetary restrictions did not allow the government to meet the magistrates' request.[3]

A year later, anxiety over the public security situation was again on the rise. Amid numerous documented reports that the police were taking up to one hour to respond to distress calls, an armed robbery was successfully carried out a few yards from the chief of police's residence. Shortly thereafter, President Menem resolved that he would "reequip the PFA" and pledged US$20 million for this purpose. As the magistrates had unsuccessfully requested a year earlier, this time he promised to hire 5,000 new officers and to purchase 300 new squad cars, three helicopters, communications equipment, and armaments. To meet these costs, the president signed a decree that authorized the removal of US$8 million from the budget of the Office of the Chief of Cabinet and the reallocation of US$12 million from the Ministry of Education's budget.

None of these measures managed to noticeably improve PFA capacity or put a dent on crime. In 1999, President Menem's successor, de la Rúa, found himself with an almost identical public security situation. Instead of belittling its gravity, however, he quickly asserted his commitment to police reform by breaking with tradition: he selected the new chief of police from among the professional ranks of the Scientific Police Division rather than appointing a streetwise operative. The government claimed that the appointment of Rubén Santos would "change by 180 degrees the direction of the PFA,"[4] given his previous untainted record.[5] The new chief created a stir by announcing he would hire handicapped civilians (a first for the city) to man the desks at police precincts so more officers would be freed for street patrol. He forced hardliners into early retirement,[6] replacing thirty-seven of the fifty-three precinct chiefs; he also pledged to add 1,000 officers to the force.

But just how efficient was this saturation strategy in the existing context? Studies carried out in the United States and Britain have concluded that although "saturation policing" does offer psychological reassurance to the population, it has a displacement effect rather than a long-lasting one, as crime simply changes venue. Scholars such as David Bayley have also pointed out that the tangible results of promises to hire additional officers are usually less than they would appear. This is due to the "10-for-1 rule": it actually takes ten officers to increase the visible presence of the police in a given area, because of rotating shifts, desk assignments, training, days off, and so on. "Unless police are everywhere, they will almost never be where they are needed" (Bayley 1994: 6).

In the case of Buenos Aires, there were several factors that detracted from the value of numerical augmentation. First, the deterrent effect of the police was scarcely discernible. The media were saturated with reports of armed robberies (many involving hostage taking) that were committed in restaurants, on sidewalks, and even in banks, right under the noses of police officers. Aware of their disadvantages and fearful for their lives, many officers elected to look the other way; others were allegedly bribed to do so. Given this, new recruits would hardly be positioned to provide psychological reassurance to the population unless their training and skills, as well as their oversight, were substantially increased. Second, the substantial funding required to implement a saturation policy either was not available or was reallocated elsewhere as soon as the crisis died down. Many police officials were bitter about the blatantly demagogic element of politicians' pledges. They complained that politicians talked about a war on crime but did not provide the police with adequate budgets to fight it. As one former PFA division chief noted ruefully, "It is always around election time that politicians make a ceremony out of police acquisitions."[7] This contention is partly borne out by PFA figures, which reflect a sharp decline in police operational budgets between 1990 and 1999; see Figure 4.1.

Barely six months after his election, President de la Rúa broke his promise to allocate more resources for policing by invoking budgetary austerity. Among other measures, he reduced by 8–12 percent the salaries and pensions of officers earning more than US$1,000 monthly. Instead of reallocating the savings to increase the grossly inadequate remuneration of subofficers, the state found another way to deal with the problem of low police salaries: it encouraged the PFA to continue supplementing salaries by moonlighting its own personnel, a practice that had been widespread for years. Under the scheme of *servicios adicionales* (additional services), clubs, soccer teams, and businesses could "rent" police officers directly from the PFA to provide security for special events, with profits benefiting both sides under a payment-sharing formula.

With rising demand for additional services, many police officers typically worked at least an extra six to eight hours several days a week, in addition to a typical work shift of eight hours a day (plus unpaid overtime hours). Even though this arrangement helped make ends meet for many policemen, there is little doubt that it distorted the integrity and quality of public service. In purely logistical terms, the toll was heavy. Adding a private shift of six to eight hours to eight hours of public duty, plus an average of two hours' daily travel time (many policemen live in Buenos Aires Province rather than the city, due to lower living costs), left only six hours for sleep and

Figure 4.1 Operational Budget of the Argentine Federal Police, Selected Years, 1990–1999

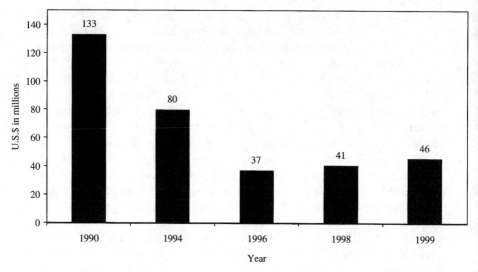

Source: PFA (1999).

family-related activities. As a result, many policemen suffered not only from the stress inherent to their dangerous line of work but also from exhaustion and low levels of concentration—factors that considerably increased their own risk as well as the population's. The system also provided a fresh opportunity for corruption, given that the PFA often overrepresented the number of officers subcontracted for private shifts at mass events in order to overcharge their clients and pocket the difference. As an indication of the large sums involved, soccer clubs alone spent roughly US$10 million annually in security to prevent violent outbursts during games.[8] Although the system of additional services came under attack, the standard official response was that it was preferable to other means the police might devise to supplement their low salaries.

Training

The need to improve training and education levels of the police was one of the few areas that brought almost no disagreement. In 1996, Chief of Police Adrián Pelacchi made a high school diploma a requirement for entry-level positions and additional study a requirement for promotion. The chief also instituted the requirement that new members of the officer class obtain a university degree, or equivalent (Pelacchi 2000: 881–890).

To stimulate the police to pursue higher education, President Menem's administration gave accredited university status in 1992 to the PFA's own institution of higher learning, the Instituto Universitario de la Policía Federal.[9] Located in the middle-class neighborhood of Flores, the continually expanding Instituto Universitario offers various low-cost advanced diplomas, as well as bachelor, master, and law degrees lasting from one to five years. A range of subjects as diverse as public security, criminology, law, nursing, international relations, social work, telecommunications, tourism, and foreign languages are taught by both civilians and police personnel. The university is administered directly by the PFA, with retired high-ranking police officers serving as academic deans.

The police university provides a good illustration of the state approach to police training. Other than providing some policy guidelines and arranging for NGOs to give human rights seminars, the Menem and de la Rúa administrations essentially left the task of training and educating the police to the police themselves. In the Argentine context, this approach signals at least two significant problems. As pointed out by one government official, "The police do not think that there is much wrong with their way of doing things."[10] Since the tight-knit nature of police culture tends to isolate its members from many societal trends, attending a civilian rather than police-run university would have provided police personnel exposure to a wider array of social and political thought. Although many civilians attend the police university, a good number of them are connected to police work or have relatives in the force.[11] In addition, most initiatives were focused on raising the educational levels of the officer class, a group that already receives significant privileges. On the other end of the spectrum are the subofficers, who are in need of serious educational support. Given that the subofficers represent 84 percent of the PFA, this constituted a significant omission.

Transparency and Information Technology

As occurred in many Latin American countries, in the 1990s the use of information technology was greatly expanded in Argentina. At the state level, it was viewed as a dynamic tool that would help modernize technocratic policymaking and increase transparency. In the area of public security, crime maps were developed, and a universal police emergency response telephone number was established—a particularly helpful initiative since 63 percent of residents surveyed in Buenos Aires did not know the phone number of their local precinct.[12]

Provision of standardized statistics and electronic data sharing is another area that was sorely behind the times. Whereas Britain's government, for example, has been collecting national criminal data since 1876, Argentina's police forces have been required to send crime statistics to the federal government only since 1971. Even then, violations of the law requiring submission of crime statistics were so commonplace that in July 2000 a law had to be passed specifying various fines for noncompliance.[13] According to the National Office for Criminal Justice Policy, the lack of such a law had "created serious obstacles to systematic . . . data collection and [governmental] analysis of these statistics" (DNPC 2000: 7). It was hoped that opening up provincial crime statistics to public scrutiny would stimulate competition and transparency.[14] The submissions, however, made it apparent that most of the provincial criminal justice systems would need to undergo fundamental changes before any serious competition could take place. In La Rioja and Santiago del Estero, for example, two of the poorest provinces in the nation, there had only been ten and twenty-two criminal convictions, respectively, in the whole of 1999 (DNPC 1999). As for PFA statistics, they were so incomplete and lacking in detail[15] that energies were poured instead into the generation of an annual victimization survey—an exercise that the United Nations Interregional Crime and Justice Institute (UNICRI) had initially sponsored in 1995.

Extensive (and expensive) diagnostic studies of crime, carried out by international consultants, were also used in the 1990s to analyze and disseminate the causes and effects of crime and violence. Like many other initiatives, however, the diagnostic studies of crime were undertaken within a sort of existential vacuum, related neither to the past nor to the future. Recommendations were rarely implemented. By the time the diagnostic study was completed, more often than not the minister or undersecretary in charge had been dismissed from office, and work was interrupted in anticipation of newly commissioned diagnostic studies and plans. One legislative adviser said wryly, "We Argentines spend our lives doing diagnostics."[16] Another adviser on matters of public security added, "The lens that one uses to assess the situation has an ideological face; the diagnostic here forms part of politics."[17]

There are many examples that substantiate these statements. In July 1999, for instance, an undersecretary in the Ministry of Justice released a victimization report that contained both his own undersecretary's diagnostic study and statistics provided by the police. Incensed by media reporting of such data as "363 robberies are reported each day in Buenos Aires" and "a murder occurs every day and a half," various high-ranking government officials set out immediately to deny or discredit the study. The PFA alleged that the report distorted a crime situation that was "under control," while the minister of justice claimed his own undersecretary's report was "premature and very incomplete" and the statistics allowing definitive conclusions would "not be ready for another four years." Reaction from the Ministry of the Interior was equally damning: the report was termed "completely inconsistent" and "contradictory" and accused of containing "gross mistakes."[18]

Lack of continuity and gross manipulation of statistics affected every facet of institutional life, becoming all the more acute each time a new president was elected. When I asked one official in the Ministry of the Interior for data on several programs initiated during the previous Menem administration, he responded, "They took everything when they left." He said he had found the offices completely stripped down of any information, with even the hard drives of all computers erased.[19] Subsequent interviews with officials in other government ministries revealed that this was not an isolated event.

Legislation

We have too many institutions and laws and too little justice.
— *Lucio Mansilla, 1845*

In 1996, Buenos Aires acquired formal legal status as the Autonomous City of Buenos Aires.[20] With this change, *porteños* could directly elect their mayor (now called *jefe de gobierno* or "head of government") instead of having one appointed by the president. This year also marked the beginning of a protracted battle between the federal and municipal governments for control of the PFA, which, as Chapter 3 noted, is overseen by the national government even though its main theater of operations remains the city of Buenos Aires.

As one of its first acts, the municipal legislature passed a sweeping procedural code pertaining to public disturbances and other misdemeanors to replace the *edictos policiales,* also discussed in Chapter 3. The new code, known as the Código de Convivencia Urbana (Code for Urban Public Behavior), legalized vagrancy and prostitution, two of several misdemeanor offenses that had previously been grounds for arrest. With the establishment of this code, it was believed that the PFA would have fewer opportunities for arbitrary detention, harassment, and extortion.[21] The liberal new code generated immediate controversy, and not only because of the moral issues involved. Almost overnight, tranquil residential neighborhoods became magnets for prostitutes and transvestites, who stood on street corners flashing body parts and throwing condoms. Enraged homeowners, concerned about property values and the negative example for their children, responded by beating several transvestites to a pulp.

With residents protesting nightly and prostitutes countermarching under the banner of the officially recognized Association of Argentine Female Sexual Workers (AMMAR), the situation quickly elicited a media frenzy. The police asserted that since prostitution was now legalized, their hands were tied.[22] The nation's president added to the controversy when he called the code a *mamarracho* (a ridiculous aberration) and mocked the city's mayor, Fernando de la Rúa (whose Radical Party controlled both the government and the legislature in the city).[23] The specific clauses dealing with prostitution were subsequently rewritten several times. At one point, the code required the police not only to provide witnesses to any sexual exchange but to videotape "the supply and demand of sexual services . . . in public spaces"[24]—a requirement that would have been notoriously difficult on several levels. A judge serving on a misdemeanor court complained, "The police do not know how to use this medium: they will film a transvestite standing on the corner, but they don't catch on film any gestures which prove solicitation, nor tape any sounds that prove a particular public disturbance. They end up filming themselves when they stop the transvestite."[25]

A prostitute active in AMMAR complained to me in an interview that "though now prostitutes can't be arrested, [the police] can still harass our clients. Because the men are *cagones* [cowards] and don't want anyone to find out or appear in court, they pay up. And if we don't pay the cops they can make things difficult for our clients and we lose business." In 2004, acrimonious debate over yet another revision of the code led to a riot by a group of sexual workers and informal vendors that ended in the virtual destruction of the legislative building.

The Code for Urban Public Behavior was not alone in unleashing a host of new problems whose consequences would take years to address. A case in point is the Two-for-One Law enacted in November 1994. As in other cases already examined, instead of laying the groundwork for a solution to the main problem—in this instance, extensive judicial backlog—the law attempted a shortcut. Designed to limit the length of time suspects could remain in jail awaiting trial, the law determined that for every day past two years that an accused person spent in jail awaiting trial, two days would be commuted off his sentence.[26] Since complex cases take longer to get to trial, the result was that violent offenders were released from jail faster than others who had been accused of petty offenses. The police claimed that the law set up a revolving door for criminals, as most left jail early only to promptly commit new crimes. Rival politicians also blasted the law, warning, "If the Two-for-One Law isn't struck down, more than 8,000 dangerous criminals will be freed in the coming months."[27] The Two-for-One Law was finally repealed in May 2001, but it was hardly forgotten, since it was frequently cited to warn the public about the dangers of electing "politicians soft on crime."

Both the Code for Urban Public Behavior and the Two-for-One Law are emblematic of the majority of laws passed in Argentina, whether at the municipal or federal level, to deal with public security issues in the 1990s. Often these laws focused on secondary issues, failing to address the most serious problems, such as the need to improve police investigative capacity and judicial rates of criminal prosecution and conviction. Although they served to assuage public concern, laws to harden penalties for specific crimes offered limited deterrence in light of abysmally low arrest and sentencing rates. Laws could also be easily repealed or ignored, since many of them were passed without a technical and financial framework to sustain them. Indeed, regardless of how well intentioned the laws of Argentina are, disobedience of them is widespread.[28] Carlos Nino, a respected Argentine political and legal theorist, says,

> There is a recurrent tendency in Argentine society, and in particular among the powerful groups—including the government—towards generalized anomie and towards illegality in particular, that is to say the nonobservance of legal, moral, and social norms. . . . The existence in Argentine society of a pronounced general tendency towards illegality and anomie is very easy to discern. (1995: 24)[29]

New Institutions

Federal Institutions

As noted in the previous chapter, the PFA had long conducted its operations in a largely autonomous fashion, thanks to limited interference from an overburdened minister of the interior and ineffective external controls. In 1996, the Menem administration decided to strengthen the supervisory capacity over the police by establishing a Secretariat of Internal Security within the ministry. But because Menem's first two appointees as secretaries of internal security were former members of the security forces,[30] it is not readily apparent how these appointments could either increase transparency or facilitate civilian control over the police. Menem's successor, President de la Rúa, tried to redress this situation by appointing a civilian to the post in 2000. His choice for the office, however, seemed once again designed to thwart rather than encourage cooperation and accountability, as the new appointee was a known political rival of the minister of the interior. The new security secretary was encouraged to bypass the minister by reporting directly to the president, a situation that heightened conflict between the two officials and disrupted the security agenda.[31]

Another new institution set up under the auspices of the Ministry of the Interior was the Federal Internal Security Council, whose members included the president of Argentina, provincial governors, high-ranking police officials, and a specially appointed administrative task force. Although members were to meet several times a year, the first all-inclusive meeting did not take place until ten years after the law creating the council was passed.[32] In the aftermath of the first meeting, an ambitious fourteen-point plan was presented. It was designed to upgrade police training, improve police relationship with the community, strengthen security in banks, develop common statistical databases, and coordinate the actions of the PFA with all twenty-three provincial police forces and with the rest of the national security forces (Consejo Federal de Seguridad 2000). But as the PFA was notorious for its lack of coordination with the police of the surrounding Buenos Aires Province,[33] it was natural to wonder whether cooperation on a countrywide scale was feasible. When I asked a high-ranking official of the Federal Internal Security Council if the government had a timetable for implementation of this policy and if funds had been allocated to carry out the plan's ambitious objectives, he responded wistfully, "Unfortunately, debt servicing requirements are bleeding us dry. We have to make up for the lack of resources by straining our imagination. . . These plans are really more of a north star or guiding light for future initiatives."[34]

Municipal Institutions

The city government competed actively with the federal government in efforts to make the PFA more accountable. In 1997, the municipal government set up the Office of the Ombudsman to "defend, protect and promote human rights . . . and other citizen rights . . . against acts committed or omitted by public officials and police forces against them" (Defensoría CBA 2000: 8). The ombudsman was appointed in consultation with NGOs for a five-year term. In order to preserve independence, it was decided that the start of an ombudsman's term would not coincide with election years.

Most of the complaints received by the office dealt with instances of police abuse. As the PFA was not subordinate to the city government, however, the ombudsman and her team did not have authority to initiate internal investigations or take disciplinary measures. All the office could do was to make recommendations and propose solutions. A fact that further complicated their ability to obtain police cooperation was that the Office of the Ombudsman was largely staffed by former left-wing activists who had opposed the military and the police in the predemocracy era.

Other institutions created by the city were the Councils for Prevention of Crime and Violence (Consejos de Prevención del Delito y la Violencia), set up under the auspices of a citywide program on decentralization that was designed to bring the municipal government closer to the community. The councils were envisaged as a kind of community policing program, whereby residents could meet with local precinct chiefs to discuss their security concerns and to learn how best to protect themselves.[35] But since the PFA was not anwerable to the mayor, the municipal government lacked the power to actually resolve most issues raised by residents. As was the case with the Office of the Ombudsman, police cooperation was a voluntary matter. This was a problem from the start, given that the police had not been consulted prior to the councils' creation and that their own average salary was half what a council manager earned for what was essentially part-time work.

Compounding these problems, the councils had been set up to cover geographical areas that did not conform to police precinct zones. For any given area covered by one council, there might be up to three different police precinct zones. This meant that every time local residents held a meeting, as many as three different precinct chiefs would have to be invited, a situation that generated confusion, blame trading, and frustration. Later, the Secretariat of Internal Security authorized the police to create their own separate community-policing group, which bore a similar name: Community Centers for the Prevention of Urban Violence (Centros Comunitarios de Prevención de la Violencia Urbana). Participants were hand picked, and most of them were drawn from various neighborhood Associations of Friends of the Police. Not surprisingly, the two groups were soon competing with each other. According to one organizer of the first program, when precinct chiefs stopped attending their meetings, efforts shifted to trying to convince residents to lobby for a transfer of control over the PFA from the federal to the municipal government.[36] Following the election of a new mayor, the Councils for Prevention of Crime and Violence disbanded altogether.

In 2000, the municipal government also created a Secretariat of Justice and Security, although the city lacked jurisdiction over both the judiciary and the police. When I asked a top official in the secretariat about it, he replied,

> The Secretariat was created in anticipation of the day when the city would control the PFA [an issue under debate since 1996]. It is mostly a job requiring reflection and administration. In a sense it is nice because I don't have any of the operational worries or drama that I might otherwise have. . . . For the time being we are working on a diagnostic of what a local police force might look like.[37]

Plans

In conjunction with the large number of institutions that were created, a plethora of plans were launched by the federal and municipal governments to increase control over the PFA and to encourage civil participation in the fight against crime. For the period March–October 2000 alone, for example, I came across the following plans dealing with the public security issue—and this list is not exhaustive:

- Plan for Prevention of Football Violence (based on an experience in London).

- Plan to Prevent Disobedience to Traffic Laws.
- Federal Internal Security Plan.
- National Plan for Rural Security.
- Plan for Reintegration of Jailed Youth.
- Plan for Gun Prevention (based on a Canadian experience).
- Plan for Neighborhood Watch (based on an experience in Gloucestershire).
- Plan to Provide Technical Assistance on Community Policing to the Provinces.
- National Plan of Community Prevention (based on experiences in Boston and San Diego).
- Plan to Coordinate the Police Forces of the Mercosur Countries.
- Plan to Coordinate the Penitentiary Systems of the Mercosur Countries.
- Plan to Prevent Hijackings of Trucks and Cars.
- Plan to Prevent Cattle Theft.
- Plan to Prevent Drug Trafficking.

When I mentioned these plans to police officials, I was often met with blank looks. Although a few had heard of some of the plans, most had not, since the police had not been asked for input. Lack of prior consultation and collaboration was not an isolated problem; on the contrary, it affected all levels of government service. At one point in 2000 there were two different programs of citizen security scattered between the municipal government and the federal government (the former based on French and Spanish models, the latter with funding from the Inter-American Development Bank).[38] Neither initiative provided for coordination with the Secretariat of Social Development, although both plans contained many elements that converged with projects already under way. In another case, the Ministry of Justice launched several plans for prevention of violence and gun control without coordinating with the Ministry of the Interior. The Program of Comprehensive Reform of the Judicial System (funded by the World Bank) addressed the courts and the prison system but not the police, despite the fundamental importance of the latter to the overall deterrence capacity of the criminal justice system.[39]

Not infrequently, supervising officials produced press releases or quick opinion surveys attesting to a plan's success even when it had never effectively gotten off the ground or had been operational for only a few weeks. For example, it was announced to the press that President de la Rúa's National Plan of Crime Prevention had lowered crime rates just one month after it came into existence.[40]

The National Plan of Crime Prevention, heralded as an important interministerial collaboration between the Ministry of Justice and the Ministry of the Interior, had been launched with considerable fanfare by President de la Rúa himself. Its main objectives were to "reduce street crimes," to reduce the "population's fear of violent crimes," and to "construct new relationships of trust and reciprocity between the security forces and civil society." The plan also laid out numerous development initiatives to be implemented concurrently with the security objectives (MinJus and MinInt 2000).

Despite its name, in reality the National Plan of Crime Prevention was to be implemented in a total of only six neighborhoods, four of which were in Buenos Aires. The plan was launched without appropriate funding. When I interviewed one of its authors, it was explained that they were hoping to get funds soon from the World Bank and the Inter-American Development Bank,[41] as well as from another project that had been halted upon the completion of President Menem's term. When I asked a senior financial officer at the Ministry of the Interior about the possibility of federal funding for the project, he said that had he been consulted beforehand, he would have told the plan writers that there were no such federal resources available.[42] Asked why these details had not been worked out ahead of time, he answered that it really did not matter anyway, as it was common knowledge that every new official wanted to be a protagonist in a high-profile initiative such as this one.

The National Plan of Crime Prevention was itself based on another plan, a modest neighborhood-watch initiative in the locality of Saavedra, called the Citizen Alert Plan. Saavedra, which lies at the foot of the boundary dividing the city from Buenos Aires Province, had been experiencing a rising crime problem. After an officer from the local precinct was killed on duty when he recognized a bank robber as a fellow policeman, residents wrote numerous letters of complaint to various federal and municipal officials, asking for enhanced police presence in their neighborhood. When no reply came, some residents decided to take matters into their own hands. Inspired by Internet chats mentioning some of Britain's neighborhood-watch programs, they decided to create a local variant and called it the Citizen Alert Plan of Saavedra.

The idea was that neighbors would encourage each other to be more vigilant in their own community, reporting to the police any suspicious signs or people. Certain nocturnal activities, such as walking the dog or parking the car, would be undertaken together so as to provide safety in numbers. Because many of the residents on a given block had not met previously, periodic get-togethers were organized. A web page was created, and tips were provided to assist interested parties in setting up block watches.[43]

This modest neighborhood initiative came to wider attention only when an official delegation from England and Scotland Yard, who had been in contact with Saavedra residents over the Internet, visited Argentina and asked government officials to arrange a meeting with the pioneering neighbors. The Ministry of Justice, perhaps recognizing a good opportunity, promptly sent consultants to ascertain Saavedra's needs. Soon some social programs were started in the adjoining poor locality of Barrio Mitre (where much of the criminal element was believed to be based), and a small task force of public prosecutors was set up to facilitate investigation of local crimes. The Ministry of Justice presented the plan to the local media as a successful "integrated social development package"; the government took the plan to international forums as well, and it was subsequently showcased in Inter-American Development Bank (IADB) and United Nations documents as a model initiative.[44]

When I visited Saavedra, I asked one of the community organizers to provide me with some specific details of the plan's accomplishments. The response was that it was impossible to quantify how many people had downloaded details of the plan from the Internet or how many blocks had been organized (with a tone that implied that the sheer numbers involved made this impossible). Only minutes later, in a private meeting, a high-ranking police officer in the Saavedra precinct quantified the number as 20 square blocks out of 500. In a separate conversation with another organizer, it was mentioned that only two square blocks had actually been organized.[45]

Conclusion

Police reform in Argentina's seat of power has been surrounded by an aura of profound purpose. But as this chapter has argued, purges and proclamations, new laws, institutions, and dozens of programs have accomplished only superficial change. In this parallel universe where ephemeral victories replace the arduous business of finding sustainable solutions, the core problems of the police were sidestepped, lest they provide an unwelcome reflection of the unresolved problems of state and society at large.

While several of the adopted mechanisms, whether propelled forward by legislation or by NGO activism, did achieve considerable progress in curtailing the police's arbitrary and violent methods, there were many other areas where the rights and guarantees required for democratic police governance continued to be highly deficient. Police finances, for example, were left largely unmonitored. The PFA continued to devote considerable energy to "profitable" activities (both politically and materially) to the detriment of its essential public role. Although police performance was substandard, the state continued to leave crucial issues of education and training largely in the hands of the police themselves. While various information technology tools were introduced, they did not succeed in reversing the zealous safeguarding of information by the police, let alone habitual manipulation by political authorities. In the absence of strong internal and external oversight mechanisms, and with limited input from a corrupt judiciary hardly positioned to press for change, institutional accountability remained elusive.

These shortfalls were further compounded by the fact that many of the initiatives described in this chapter lacked an adequate framework of institutional and financial support and were quickly reversed or superseded in the whirlwind of personnel changes. The cycle of new plans, laws, and institutions was repeated ad nauseam, with negligible effect on hapless police entangled in their own cycle of failure. If the preceding sections illustrate what was happening in the wealthiest and most advanced city in the country, imagine what the situation was like in the more impoverished interior.

While the police bore the brunt of public condemnation, the preceding sections have shown that deficient state controls and public policies enabled the perpetuation of questionable practices and activities. But since neither Argentine institutions nor Argentine society was composed entirely of inept or ill-intentioned individuals, why were reform efforts so consistently peripheral and unsuccessful? The following two chapters will address this question.

Notes

1. See Ortega y Gasset (1929: 638).
2. "Por Falta de Plata Hay Mil Policías Menos," *La Nación,* August 11, 1996.
3. See "Robos: Preocupación Presidencial," *La Nación,* November 6, 1997, and "Corach: No Hay Fondos para Poner Más Policías," *La Nación,* November 27, 1997.
4. "Perfil Más Técnico para la Policía," *La Nación,* January 7, 2000.
5. Author interview with a senior adviser to the minister of the interior, August 24, 2000.
6. Santos would later claim that these were among the rivals who engineered the infamous Paraguayan assassins' escape from police headquarters—an episode reviewed in the previous chapter.
7. Author interview, August 29, 2000.
8. See "Procesarían el Lunes a Altos Jefes Policiales: Es por la Custodia de los Partidos," *La Nación,* April 14, 2001.
9. Although originally set up as an academy in 1974, it became an accredited university in 1992.
10. Author interview with a high-ranking official in the Secretariat of Security, August 28, 2000.
11. Roughly 60 percent of the approximately 3,500 students are civilians.
12. "La Mitad de los Porteños No Sabe Adónde Recurrir ante un Delito," *Clarín,* September 27, 1998.
13. Ley 25.266 (Estadísticas Criminológicas, Modificación de la Ley 22.117), Congreso de la Nación Argentina, June 22, 2000.
14. Author interview with a high-ranking official in the National Office for Criminal Justice Policy, August 15, 2000.
15. For instance, PFA statistics often fail to differentiate between crimes witnessed by the police and those reported by victims. Basic details, such as the exact location and time of a crime, gender of victims and suspects, and material value of stolen property, are often missing. In addition PFA statistics often fail to distinguish

clearly whether a threat or an actual crime was committed, or whether a crime was "accidental" or "intentional" (e.g., whether a crime related to a traffic accident or a mugging).

16. Author interview, October 23, 2000.

17. Author interview with an adviser to the secretary of justice and security within the government of the City of Buenos Aires, September 21, 2000.

18. See "En el País Se Denuncia un Robo Cada 45 Segundos," *Clarín,* July 25, 1999; "Reacción Oficial por los Datos de un Informe," *Clarín,* July 26, 1999; and "Policías en la Capital," *Clarín,* July 27, 1999.

19. Author interview, August 24, 2000.

20. For more on the process by which Buenos Aires gained its new status, see Herzer (1996). Although the Autonomous City of Buenos Aires is responsible for municipal functions such as garbage collection and maintenance of plazas, it also controls certain functions that normally pertain only to provinces, such as adopting its own procedural codes and managing public health and education services. In federal budget statistics, the Autonomous City of Buenos Aires appears alongside the twenty-three provinces. The federal government, however, retains control over the police and criminal courts. Though already mentioned in an earlier chapter, for purposes of clarity it is important to reiterate that the Autonomous City of Buenos Aires is a separate geopolitical entity from Buenos Aires Province.

21. On average, the PFA detained 150,000 people per year under the old legal codes or police edicts, which allowed the police to bring suspicious people into precincts while they checked for a prior criminal record. It is estimated that only 18 percent of the persons detained had been previously arrested. See Abramovich (1998).

22. The chief of the Metropolitan Division of the PFA stated, for example, "The new urban legal code doesn't work because of what it does to our operational procedures on the streets: until the crime takes place, the police can't act" (quoted in "No Tenemos Medios Ideales,' *Página 12,* August 29, 1998).

23. "Menem: No Queda Otra Salida que la 'Mano Dura' Frente a la Inseguridad," *Clarín,* September 13, 1998.

24. Ley 162, art. 10 (Modificación al Código Contravencional y de Procedimiento Contravencional), March 4, 1999.

25. "El Sexo en el Estrado," *Página 12,* October 15, 2000.

26. Ley 24.390 (Plazos de Prisión Preventiva, "Ley 2 por 1"), Congreso de la Nación Argentina, November 2, 1994.

27. "Otro Caso Que Refleja una Larga y Vieja Disputa," *La Nación,* January 16, 2001.

28. This theme is further elaborated upon in subsequent chapters.

29. See Mafud (1984) for more on this theme.

30. The first was a former air force officer. The second, a former chief of police, was replaced by a civilian by President Menem after the press exposed his links to a squad connected to the disappearance of a labor leader during the dictatorship.

31. The rivalry between Minister of the Interior Federico Storani and Secretary Enrique Mathov was daily fodder for the press.

32. Ley 24.059 (Ley de Seguridad Interior), Congreso de la Nación Argentina, January 17, 1992.

33. I also asked a PFA precinct chief about coordination difficulties with the Bonaerense. He stated that the problem "is similar to the situation American police officers have when criminals flee into Mexico. US police officers cannot cross the border into Mexico, no? We have the same problem when a criminal crosses the General Paz [a major highway] into the province." Author interview, September 6, 2000.

34. Author interview with a high-ranking official dealing with the Federal Security Council, September 13, 2000.

35. Programa de Seguridad Ciudadana (1999a, 1999b).

36. Author interview, September 15, 2000.

37. Author interview, September 21, 2000.

38. They were the Programa de Seguridad Ciudadana under the government of the City of Buenos Aires and the Programa de Seguridad Ciudadana y Protección Civil in the Ministry of the Interior.

39. Author interview with a high-ranking official in the Program of Comprehensive Reform of the Judicial System, September 7, 2000. Also Programa Integral de Reforma Judicial (2000).

40. "Una Encuesta Muestra Que Bajó el Indice de Victimización," *Página 12,* August 20, 2000.

41. Author interview, September 13, 2000.

42. Author interview with one of the chief economists in charge of the budget of the Ministry of the Interior, September 8, 2000.

43. Vecinos Solidarios (1999).

44. See for example, "The Case of Barrio Saavedra: A Pioneering Example of Community-Based Crime Prevention in Argentina," presented by the Argentine delegation at the Tenth United Nations Congress on the Prevention of Crime and the Treatment of Offenders, Vienna, Austria, April 10–17, 2000.

45. Author interviews, September 6, 2000.

CHAPTER 5

Overriding Threats and Priorities?

What can explain the failure by three consecutive governments in the 1990s to approach police reform with the required commitment and continuity? To answer this question, Argentine policy elites invariably invoked one of two theories, and occasionally both in concert. The first was that strong opposition from the police derailed plans for reform; the second, that constant economic turmoil caused a deprioritization of the issue. This chapter examines the weight of these arguments, which were put forward with much conviction. Although both arguments contain valid elements, I conclude that neither police resistance nor economic crisis, alone or combined, could have produced the patterns described in Chapter 4.

Closing Ranks

> The police are not the arm of society; in fact, they own the arm of the politician. . . . They place themselves at the disposal of the political powers that be, but then impose their own conditions.[1]

It is not only in Argentina that policymakers portray the main obstacle to police reform as institutional resistance; the same argument is frequently invoked in most of Latin America and indeed in the industrialized democracies of Europe and the United States. Because bureaucratic resistance to reform is universal, it further complicates a reform process that is already difficult, labored, and lengthy. Bureaucracies typically act as a kind of special interest group within the government, since they often have a vested interest in the status quo. They mobilize quickly to retain their spheres of influence by lobbying for policies that promote their interests, increase their funding, or expand the range of their activities (Krueger 1990: 14–18). Public choice theorists argue that reforms in the public interest often fail to take root precisely because such "rent-seeking" activities are usually successful. This is attributable mainly to the fact that public service providers are likely to control much of the information essential to their own reform and are typically more organized, focused, and politically powerful than the users. Users, moreover, have the added disadvantage of being segmented by varying class and sectoral interests (Bates 1981; Grindle and Thomas 1991; Olson 1965).

If reform of the average public service is difficult, police reform is all the thornier, as the police are not only a sizable bureaucracy but also an armed, secretive, and politically strategic one. Even in developed countries, the police have a secretive esprit de corps and are selective in the laws they enforce and resistant to external interference (Goldstein 1977; Skolnick 1994). Changing an occupational police culture is considered extremely difficult, and all the more so when attempts are forced from outside the institution (Bayley 1995b; Chan 1997; Goldsmith 1990).

In Argentina, the PFA's vast holdings, some of which are believed to derive from involvement in gambling, prostitution, and car theft rings, have enabled the institution to exert considerable influence over politics.[2] Some politicians have often turned a blind eye to these illegal activities because they benefit handsomely from *pactos mafiosos*—unholy alliances with rogue police elements—or because they consider tolerance for some level of police corruption as a reasonable trade-off for keeping control of the streets. Politicians have long relied on the PFA to contain political demonstrations in the city and to provide crucial intelligence on unrest in the provinces. In the two years President de la Rúa was in office (1999–2001), for example, there were nine general strikes to protest social conditions; major provincial trucking routes were cut off a total of 2,149 times by angry protesters, requiring police intervention to displace picketers from the roads (UNM 2003). A former chief of police put it as follows,

> If we were experiencing a situation of social peace, it would be one thing to try to dismantle and overhaul the existing structures. But trying to do that when the population is experiencing such tremendous insecurity could be a potential disaster. It is like dismounting from your horse in the middle of a river when you are only halfway across. You can be swept away by the current.[3]

The belief that the police can manipulate crime to destabilize the political situation remains widespread. As one adviser to a former minister of the interior said, "Politicians are reluctant to take on the police for fear that the police will delay investigations, 'boycott' their role of crime control by allowing crimes to occur, or worse, actively stimulate the criminal underworld to commit more crimes and create public panic."[4]

Boycotting Crime Control

In the 1990s in particular, many politicians were hesitant to risk the potential fallout of police reform because the hypothesis that the police were willing to stage "crime boycotts" was at least partly borne out by events such as those that occurred after the enactment of the Code for Urban Public Behavior in 1996. As noted in the previous chapter, before the code was passed, high-ranking PFA officials had argued that curtailment of their powers of preemptive arrest would seriously hamper their ability to maintain public order. Once the code was enacted, the police proved their point by standing by while prostitutes and transvestites engaged in nocturnal bacchanals in upper-middle-class neighborhoods in Buenos Aires. As might be expected, indignant residents soon began to rally in demand of the code's abrogation. The code was revised, although the new version was ambiguous enough that the police's low-level extortion activities could continue largely unencumbered.

A Change in Status

The PFA's handling of the Code for Urban Public Behavior was also interpreted as a veiled warning to politicians not to carry out the *traspaso,* a proposed transfer of the PFA from federal to municipal control. This proposal, first introduced in 1996 and still being debated, contemplated the reorganization of the PFA into two entities: one police force for the city of Buenos Aires, to be controlled by the mayor, and a second one, under presidential control, whose interventions would be restricted to federal crimes such as drug trafficking.

The transfer proposal was adamantly opposed by the PFA from the start. The police distrusted the reasons behind the proposal, which tended to crop up whenever the federal government needed to trim government expenditures to meet IMF demands, as well as the vague blueprint for its implementation. Similar to the scant thought given to the role of the state in the aftermath of the sale of its assets, the transfer proposal raised some troubling questions. What would happen after policing functions were transferred to the municipal government? How would the existing pensions and benefits of police officers be handled? Would the security forces be able to coordinate their activities amid the rancor entailed by the split? Funding to combat crime would severely diminish, the police alleged, since city tax revenues would be used rather than federal funds; performance would suffer, and cooperation—such as it was—would give way to paralyzing rivalries.

Not least, the PFA also resisted the transfer out of fear of losing status and prestige: institutions under the aegis of the executive enjoy much higher prestige—and considerably better wages and social benefits—than do those under local or provincial jurisdiction. Several police officers interviewed stated that under no circumstances did they want to see the PFA, the oldest and most professional police force of the country, turned into a local force subordinated to a mere mayor. In stressing the detrimental effects of the transfer and heightening the possibility it could breed more chaos, the police cunningly appealed to the public's inherently conservative view that a known evil is better than a new one. As one former chief of police put it, "The PFA has been around for 170 years. I don't see how the security situation could be improved by replacing us with a new and inexperienced force."[5]

A Nation's Obsession

Another theory strongly advocated by many experts interviewed is that the state assigned low priority to police reform because of the disproportionate weight that economic issues have on Argentine political life. In many nations the success of political agendas are often linked to the state of the economy, and this is all the more so in developing countries, where the array of social problems is much larger and deeper than in more advanced countries. Emerging economies are typically more vulnerable to external factors, such as currency and commodity price fluctuations, speculation, and protectionism. Thus governments in developing countries are prone to place economic policies aimed at achieving investment and growth at the forefront of their public agenda—frequently at the expense of other needs—in the belief that entrenched poverty will worsen if economic growth falters.

Many Argentine interviewees across sectors argued that this is the main reason why police reform has not been meaningfully addressed. They maintained that Argentina's economic crises, coupled with pressures by the IMF to restructure the economy and engage in fiscal austerity in order to remain eligible for further loans, totally overshadowed other policy issues.

Descent from Opulence

In Argentina, which in a few decades went from economic might to near bankruptcy, concern over economic issues is nothing new: generations of frustrated citizens have been waiting for Argentina to return to past glories. In 1910, in per capita terms, Argentina was the world's ninth wealthiest nation, with standards of nutrition, consumption, health, access to higher education, labor, and social legislation that were ahead of most European countries (Waisman 1987). When the collapse of commodity prices devastated the export-oriented economies of Latin America following the Great Depression, Argentina's economy entered a period of stagnation from which it never fully recovered. By the mid-1990s, almost a third of the population was unemployed or working in the parallel economy. In 2000, factors such as chronic balance of payments crises, economic contraction, political instability, corruption, and a rising ratio of foreign debt to gross domestic product (GDP) made Argentina the second worst risk investment among emerging markets in the world, after Nigeria. In January 2002, economic problems culminated in the largest sovereign debt default in history. By 2002, official data indicated that the numbers of the poor had swelled to more than 57.5 percent of the population; in some of the poor northern provinces this percentage reached 71.5 percent (INDEC 2002). In a country celebrated for its agricultural wealth and its exports of grain and beef, hunger and death from malnutrition came to pose increasingly visible and pressing social problems.

The seeming intractability of Argentina's economic problems, both under authoritarian rule and under electoral democracy, has preoccupied not only the country's own political elites but noted economists and social scientists everywhere, for whom the Argentine question remains a "riddle" (e.g., Diaz-Alejandro 1970; Waisman 1987; Weil 1944). As will be examined next, international financing institutions (IFIs) put macroeconomic issues at the forefront of their push for reform in Argentina—and left issues such as public security and police reform absent from their immediate agenda throughout the 1990s.

Outside Agendas

The increasingly influential role that IFIs came to have on domestic public policy became more apparent after the return to democracy in 1983, although many factors at play during the dictatorship actually led to this eventual outcome. Some of these factors include the military regime's own economic mismanagement, rising indebtedness, worldwide recession after the oil-price shocks of the 1970s followed by tightening of monetary policies, and the exhaustion of a development model centered on import substitution industrialization (ISI) (Fishlow 1986; Frieden 1991; Weyland 2002). Like many other Latin American countries, Argentina could not meet its external financial obligations and resorted to asking for new loans. Because the IMF and the World Bank tied the granting of new loans, as well as renegotiation of debt servicing requirements, to structural reform, the *dirigiste* state-centered model of development[6] was abandoned in favor of market-oriented neoliberal policies. Primarily, the structural reform packages (of which police reform was not part) included a mix of macroeconomic and management measures. Known as the Washington Consensus, these demands were (1) fiscal discipline to eliminate budget deficits; (2) redirection of public expenditure away from defense and toward social and physical infrastructure and elimination of state subsidies for food, fuel, and other services; (3) strengthening tax collection and accounting systems; (4) liberalization of interest rates; (5) liberalization of the exchange rate; (6) liberalization of trade, with an emphasis on outward orientation; (7) openness to foreign direct investment; (8) privatization of state enterprises; (9) deregulation of the private sector; and (10) reforms to ensure greater legal protection of private property (Williamson 1993).[7]

In Argentina, the influence of IFIs on economic policy was cemented when Finance Minister Domingo Cavallo pegged the peso to the dollar in 1991 in an effort to curb runaway inflation, which had shot up to 5,000 percent the year before. Though this and other measures helped to stabilize the economy, the combination of an overvalued currency and trade liberalization soon strangled the export sector, depressing local industry and cementing high rates of unemployment. Large international and domestic conglomerates gradually took over the industrial base, which President Perón had considerably expanded in the late 1940s and early 1950s. Argentina found itself increasingly vulnerable to external economic shocks and highly dependent on foreign investment and loans to meet its obligations—a kind of vicious circle that made the country's public policies extremely malleable to pressure from abroad. Between 1983 and March 2000, for example, Argentina was induced to carry out a total of eight IMF stabilization and structural adjustment programs (Kearney 2001).

In this environment, decisions on budgetary allocations to public services, including the police, were made less on the basis of policy objectives than on the basis of IMF-imposed targets. The federal outlays contained in the annual budget approved by Congress in December were routinely adjusted throughout the year because of government overestimation of economic growth, shrinking tax revenues, domestic emergencies (e.g., floods), or increased country risk ratings, which caused interest rates on debt servicing requirements to climb. With each adjustment, funding for public programs and services was shifted or curtailed, causing projects to be abandoned halfway and state salaries and pensions to go unpaid for months at a time. Any public service could find itself with 10 percent less total revenue than initially allocated, or paralyzed by the suspension or delay of disbursements. These factors made forward planning, resource management, and most reform efforts exercises in divination and improvisation.

A Closer Look

This chapter has examined two of the explanations most frequently advanced by Argentine policy elites to explain the derailment of police reform. The first argument, that the police themselves subverted reform, is certainly persuasive, as the hierarchy certainly had the means and the tools to resist meddling they deemed contrary to their interests. The police's vast intelligence network granted them an important measure of power over the political establishment, which they used to accumulate prerogatives, expand their involvement in both legal and shadowy activities, and raise the specter of a boycott of crime control as a bargaining card.

Nevertheless, from the 1990s onward, taking on the institution would have elicited strong popular support: with polls consistently showing dismally low levels of trust in the police, and crime and insecurity ranking at or near the top of public concerns, latitude for government leadership in this regard was greater than ever before. In addition, there were progressive elements within the police that could have become allies in making a break with the past, if governmental efforts to overturn the police's structural and operational deficits had been comprehensive and resolute.

Many policy elites in Argentina also advanced the rationale that the absolute priority of the economic agenda contributed to the lack of attention to police reform. As surveyed in this chapter, the country's economic woes appeared to be so chronic and bewildering as to lend an unassailable logic to this argument. Is it, however, rational for a state to concentrate all its financial and human capital in addressing only one issue, especially when growing crime exponentially increases the stakes of instability? In strictly financial terms, the paucity of available resources was never so extreme as to have allowed no room for reform. For example, between 1993 and 2000, even as the PFA's share of federal budget allocations decreased by 17 percent, the judiciary's allocations were increased by 27 percent.[8] As surveyed in Chapter 4, furthermore, Argentine governments did in fact generate a panoply of often costly reform initiatives.

The problem must then lie in other variables. Were the reforms superficial rather than systemic because surface changes are more easily revoked? The role of Argentine civil society in promoting adoption of sustainable public policy is another element that requires examination, particularly because with their comparatively high levels of literacy and political savvy, civil society groups in Buenos Aires appeared advantageously placed to exert effective pressure on the state. The issues are analyzed in Chapter 6.

Notes

1. Author interview with an adviser to an influential Peronist senator, August 16, 2000.
2. Author interview, September 8, 2000.
3. Author interview, August 25, 2000.
4. Author interview, August 16, 2000.
5. Author interview, October 20, 2000.
6. The prevailing paradigm of development throughout much of Latin America between the 1930s and the 1980s was a nationalistic, state-led model of import

substitution industrialization. To encourage the production of import substitutes, governments erected barriers to foreign competition, controlled bank credit, and gave preferential rates for needed inputs and subsidies—all combined with over-valued exchange rates, pricing policies, and export taxes on agricultural products. To manage and coordinate state industries, investment, and regulations, an extensive bureaucratic apparatus was created, together with a network of corporatist political coalitions designed to co-opt and mobilize labor groups and business elites around these policies. For more on Latin America's experience with ISI, see Montesinos and Markoff (2001) and Smith (1998).

7. Though number 10 could, in theory, have included measures dealing with the police, in practice measures were largely restricted to judicial reform, which was not in any case the main thrust of the first wave of reforms in the 1980s and 1990s carried out in Argentina.

8. Federal funds allocated to the PFA declined from 1.64 percent of the total budget in 1993 to 1.40 percent in 2000, as compared to federal allocations to the judiciary, which in the same period increased from 1.29 percent to 1.64 percent. Author calculations based on data in Dirección de Gastos Sociales Consolidados (2000) and in the Secretaría de Hacienda (1993–2000).

CHAPTER 6

The Argentine Political Game

If police resistance and the national obsession with the economy could not account for the derailment of police reform, what other factors were at root? This chapter will argue that the erratic nature of the reform process, far from being an aberration, was one of the typical manifestations of the *political game,* an enduring ethos shaped by historical, cultural, and institutional factors that continues to permeate every aspect of national life. It is when examined through this lens that the politicization of the police and the haphazard formulation and implementation of reform initiatives acquire their own (perverse) logic.

Political Culture and Accountability

> Argentina grows thanks to the fact that its politicians and authorities cannot steal while they are sleeping.
> — *Georges Clemenceau, 1910*

Ideally, democratic politics, as theorized by Robert Dahl (1971), are based on a government's continuing responsiveness to the preferences of a citizenry who are considered political equals. Responsiveness is achieved through institutionalized mechanisms, principally free and fair elections, through which the population can express approval of or dissatisfaction with authorities. Underpinning such mechanisms are guarantees for civil and political liberties, such as freedom of speech, freedom of the press, and freedom of association and assembly, that are essential for political debate and competition. As Guillermo O'Donnell has highlighted (1998), equally important to vertical accountability mechanisms are "horizontal" checks and balances across and within different branches of government. These mechanisms not only ensure that elected officials are responsive to public

75

agendas on the enactment and implementation of legislation and mandates but also enable the government to effectively police itself to prevent malfeasance.

In Argentina, traditional patterns of executive branch hegemony, uncivic attitudes toward public office, low levels of vertical accountability, weak checks and balances, tolerance for corruption, and generalized impunity have generated few incentives for elected officials to act in the interests of the common good. In the absence of strong mechanisms of oversight, state reforms are rarely carried out openly or consistently.

Tolerance for Corruption

Argentina is one of world's most corrupt countries. According to Transparency International's 2004 corruption index, it is ranked 108th out of 146 on a scale of least to most corrupt (see Table 6.1).

In Latin America overall, the use of public office as an opportunity for personal enrichment rather than as a means of rendering public service has deep historical and cultural roots (e.g., Lagos 1997; O'Donnell 1998; Philip

Table 6.1 Corruption Perception Index, 2004

	Country Rank	Country	CPI 2004 Score
Least corrupt	1	Finland	9.7
	2	New Zealand	9.6
	3	Denmark	9.5
	[...]	[...]	[...]
	11	United Kingdom	8.6
	[...]	[...]	[...]
	17	USA	7.5
	[...]	[...]	[...]
	54	Bulgaria	4.1
	[...]	[...]	[...]
	59	**Brazil**	**3.9**
	60	Colombia	3.8
	[...]	[...]	[...]
	108	Albania	2.5
	108	**Argentina**	**2.5**
	108	Libya	2.5
	[...]	[...]	[...]
	144	Nigeria	1.6
	145	Bangladesh	1.5
Most corrupt	145	Haiti	1.5

Source: Transparency International (2004).

Note: The Transparency International Corruption Perceptions Index (CPI) is a composite of corruption-related data from surveys that were carried out by a variety of reputable institutions to assess the degree to which businesspeople and expert analysts perceive corruption to exist among politicians and public officials.

2003). Despite the fact that most Latin American countries based their legal and constitutional systems on the US presidentialist model, no Latin American country has come close to duplicating the political stability and institutional soundness enjoyed by the United States. While there are many complex reasons behind this divergence, one of the most important is cultural (Fukuyama 1999). While the United States inherited from British law and custom a tradition of individualism, self-reliance, and legality, strengthened further by the moralistic, hardworking tradition of sectarian Protestantism, Latin America inherited an imperial and religious tradition from Spain and Portugal that encouraged centralism and dependence on the state and Catholic Church.

As far as the law was concerned, the unwritten principle that guided the colonial administration in Latin America was "to obey but not to comply" (Aguinis 1989: 58; Mafud 1984: 281). From the earliest years of conquest, the Iberian colonialists used their powers for personal aggrandizement, defrauding the royal treasury and ignoring laws set by the crown for the regulation of land, mineral, and labor use (McFarlane 1996: 49). The colonial legacy of familism and clientelism that viewed the national patrimony as subject to distribution among family and friends proved resilient: the political culture it shaped[1] has continued to flourish through the centuries right into the present day.

These features shaped the institutional framework in Latin America[2] and are important factors in explaining why such a vast region shares many recurrent political and economic problems, including the culture of corruption. Indeed, military regimes in Argentina and Brazil, as in other countries, rationalized their coups d'état as a commitment to "reorganize" political and economic life and do away with "selfish" and "corrupt" politicians. The words of General Jorge Videla, who headed the military junta during the Argentine dirty war (1976–1981), in a 1976 speech are illustrative of some of the arguments the military invoked to justify their actions:

> With the country on the point of national disintegration, the intervention of the armed forces was the only possible alternative in the face of the deterioration provoked by misgovernment, corruption, and complacency. . . . The management of the state had never been so disorderly, directed with such inefficiency [because] of general administrative corruption accompanied by general demagoguery. (quoted in Loveman and Davies 1978: 199)

By the 1980s, views on how to combat corruption had become grounded on the neoliberal argument that as state intervention and political manipulation of markets were reduced, opportunities for favoritism and rent seeking would also be reduced (Bhagwati 1982; Klitgaard 1988; Krueger 1990;

Theobald 1990; World Bank 1983). These views became a major component of the Washington Consensus, an agenda whose acceptance, as previously discussed, the IFIs made a condition for the granting of new loan packages. Instead of the predicted decline in graft, however, the exact opposite occurred: throughout Latin America, the sums of money extracted from corruption in recent years have reached tens of millions of dollars, and in some countries hundreds of millions, drastically raising the stakes of past corruption scandals (Weyland 1998: 110).

In Argentina, several murders have been linked to attempts to investigate how state assets were liquidated; one such case is the unsolved January 1997 assassination of photographer José Luis Cabezas. Particularly during the first Menem administration, much of the national patrimony, including oil and gas deposits, was sold at rock-bottom prices under shady regulatory and contractual terms. Even national industries and utilities that were profitable and efficiently run were disposed of, with political insiders keeping for themselves a large part of the profits. Insiders also solicited bribes, which international conglomerates willingly paid: in 1990, for example, a Spanish consortium reportedly disbursed US$80 million in bribes to public officials to gain control of the national airline. In the same year 10,000 kilometers of highways were privatized by executive decree and without open bidding (Manzetti and Blake 1996: 678).

President Menem, his family, and his political associates were at the center of corruption allegations during both his terms.[3] Even after Menem left office, however, he was formally charged with corruption only in connection with the illegal export of arms to Croatia and Ecuador. Despite having been a signatory to a UN-sponsored arms embargo and an arbiter in the 1995 Peruvian-Ecuadorian border war, the former president was charged with having authorized the transaction and of having covered it up. Expecting that he might flee, the judge ordered him jailed. Menem's attorneys, however, invoked a law that prevents the aged or infirm from being imprisoned and obtained his release under house arrest. The not-so-infirm president installed himself in a borrowed palatial home in the suburb Don Torcuato, under the charge of his former Miss Universe wife, who soon announced that they were expecting a child. Six months later Menem was released for insufficient evidence; the hefty profits from the illegal arms sale were not recovered.

The fact that many high officials have been able to circumvent the law to profit from public office has contributed to creating a perception of invulnerability that widens the spiral of noncompliance with the law. It also encourages an atmosphere in which corruption, though not openly condoned, is certainly tolerated, expected in public office, and widely practiced at all levels of society. Societal demands to halt corruption are weakened by the widespread assumption that while people demand discipline from others, few would resist temptation if provided with the same opportunities.

Vertical Accountability

In Argentina, normative attitudes of tolerance toward corruption are linked to the weakness of formal mechanisms and channels of vertical accountability—the citizenry's capacity to make itself heard, whether through elections, advocacy, or other forms of political participation. Although popular protests and demonstrations became commonplace after the 1983 democratic elections, the concept that living under democracy also entails using and analyzing public information to scrutinize government activities remains elusive. In the words of a director of a prominent NGO involved in stimulating popular participation, "The population doesn't systematically monitor the activities of leaders; people don't use the law of access to information, they don't go to public seminars or meetings. . . . Information remains privatized in Argentina in the hands of the government . . . and the population has not systematically tried to make it public."[4]

During Menem's ten years in power there was ample awareness that illegal enrichment was rampant in government circles. Even as local industry was being decimated and unemployment surged, the Argentine population did not use the power of the vote to oust those who were brazenly betraying public trust. Many, in fact, idolized Menem for his charismatic personality. They forced the ouster of Menem's successor instead, the colorless Fernando de la Rúa. Although many Argentines initially hailed President de la Rúa's resignation in December 2001 as the triumph of popular will over an incompetent executive, the following year it became apparent that a familiar cast of characters was back on the scene.[5]

Political parties. In Argentina, the lack of strong mechanisms of vertical accountability is partly a function of a weak political party system—a universal development that seems to have peaked in Latin America. In 2003, for example, the Latinobarometer survey showed that of all regional institutions, political parties inspired the least confidence (UNDP 2004c: 38). In a democracy, political parties should normally channel, aggregate, and represent popular interests and act as pressure points on government agendas. They help to "put order into what would otherwise be a cacophony of dissonant conflicts. Parties help reduce the costs of voting, making it easier for citizens with little time and little political information to participate in politics" (Mainwaring and Scully 1995: 3). Yet in many Latin American countries, the ad hoc quality of parties that appear and vanish quickly from the political scene diminishes their credibility.

Further, for the electoral system to serve as a deterrent to public malfeasance and a stimulus to responsiveness, the vote must be used as a tool to reward or punish politicians. Often, however, parties and campaigns alike are dominated by charismatic personalities who are pursuing their own agenda instead of acting as representational agents. In such weakly institutionalized party systems, voters often have only a limited, if any, idea of what they are voting for (Mainwaring and Scully 1995). If most voters do not know the name of their representative or the party she or he represents,[6] if they vote instead on the basis of patronage or charismatic appeal, neither the record of a public official nor the candidate's programmatic ideas will be a determining factor for votes cast.

While political parties in Argentina tended in the past to be more institutionalized than in other Latin American countries such as Bolivia, Brazil, and Ecuador, in recent years they have become just as fragmented. Not only are they dominated by cults of personality and vicious infighting—themes that will be expanded upon in a later section—but by the mid-1990s their ideologies became so diffuse that voters were hard pressed to correlate candidates with a specific set of policies. Adding to the confusion, once elected to office, politicians all too often made abrupt turnarounds from their previous pronouncements.

Other channels for popular participation. Apart from political parties, other less traditional vehicles of political participation such as the press, labor unions, NGOs, and community associations can, in theory, also help to promote vertical accountability and ensure higher government responsiveness to the citizenry. Although the Argentine press enjoys a deserved reputation for vigorously exposing wrongdoing and corruption in political circles, the vast majority of media exposés enjoy only a limited run in the limelight since new scandals are forever beckoning. Even when proof of malfeasance is offered, moreover, the state usually drags its feet in pursuing prosecutions and convictions of public officials. As a result, continuous media exposure of corruption scandals further feeds public cynicism and disaffection about the honesty of public officials and the effectiveness of the justice system.

On the whole, in the 1990s the population remained weary of and reluctant about political participation. A powerful reason may have been its vivid memories of the fierce military repression of the 1970s and early 1980s, when a person could be kidnapped and "disappeared" for suspected political dissent or for the "wrong" associations. Given that there was almost no relief from acute economic crises, it should not come as a surprise that, for most Argentines, issues of day-to-day survival took precedence over all others. Perhaps more significant, however, were certain ingrained societal traits that have consistently inhibited effective collective action and maintained a high level of social disharmony.

As examined in previous chapters, fear of political destabilization generated widespread distrust. This in turn bred a normative lack of reciprocal obligations—except where bonds of patronage and clientelism make it imperative to consider others. In such a setting, compromise and consensus were often perceived as a loss of face rather than as mutually reinforcing mechanisms for effective cooperation. In a biographical analysis of Perón, Joseph Page has this to say about the excessive individualism of Argentine culture:

> Each Argentine not only holds his own political views, he is thoroughly convinced of the irrevocable truth of his vision. As a result, he rejects the possibility to compromise, and tends towards rhetorical and behavioral extremism. These factors, together with the morbid suspicion that every Argentine feels towards his compatriots, dramatically limits the viability of democratic institutions and carries a predisposition towards authoritarianism. (Page 1983: 25)

And in the words of political scientist Gary Wynia (1992), "Argentina's social classes form a nation whose members share no common understanding of what membership in a national community demands of them" (1992: 29).[7]

In the 1990s, the fact that many organized societal groups showed little inclination toward internal dialogue or forming coalitions with other groups for common projects was reflected in the splintering of virtually all the major labor unions, political parties, and NGOs into dissident groups. Not only did these factions not cooperate, but more often than not they worked at cross-purposes. The Peronist Party, for example, even during Perón's lifetime, was convulsed by internal power struggles between extremist right- and left-wing elements.[8]

Between 1966 and 1973, the national labor federation, the Confederación General de Trabajadores (CGT), was consumed by fierce internal divisions that resulted in a bitter split. One faction (CGT Azopardo), grouping some of the most powerful unions, adopted a moderate position against the military government, while the other (CGT de los Argentinos) was more confrontational. Still, they had one thing in common: almost all union members belonged to the Peronist Party. During Menem's first presidential term (1989–1995), there were new subdivisions and reunifications, culminating in the appearance of a third splinter group called the Congress of Argentine Workers (CTA). In 1994, there was yet another dissident faction, the Movement of Argentine Workers (MTA).[9]

Nongovernmental organizations were not immune to the fever of protagonism. The most renowned of the Argentine human rights groups, the Association of Mothers of Plaza de Mayo, whose courage in facing up to the military dictatorship on behalf of their disappeared children gained the admiration and support of people around the world, was torn apart by a bitter feud. In 1986, a group calling itself the Founding Line of the Mothers of Plaza de Mayo seceded from the main group, wasting no time in mounting strident public attacks questioning the main association's moral authority. In February 2000, the Mothers' Founding Line circulated an open letter castigating a proposal by some European legislators to submit the main group's candidacy for the Nobel Peace Prize and alleging that it was the Founding Line who deserved the prize, since the rival group was dominated by "increasingly dictatorial, unqualified, and libelous policies" and a "growing and unacceptable authoritarian attitude and marked personalism."[10]

Two groups representing victims of police repression and their families, Committee of Relatives of Innocent Victims of Social Violence (COFAVI) and National Coordinator Against Police and Institutional Repression (CORREPI), were also deeply antagonistic, each making claims of moral superiority. While COFAVI exclusively represented "innocent" victims of police repression, CORREPI represented "not only VIP victims, but all victims." Similarly, most NGOs were reluctant to cooperate with the influential Catholic Church even when their social work clearly overlapped, because they maintained that the Catholic Church had been an accomplice of the dictatorship and that it remained excessively conservative. Because the local philanthropic tradition is underdeveloped, many Argentine NGOs depended almost totally on foreign funding from European or US organizations. Their already feeble collaborative spirit was further strained during incessant rounds of competition with other deserving developing-country NGOs. This process nevertheless had to be endured, as few local NGOs had deep roots in local society. In the absence of an effective umbrella organization that could have provided added power, there were serious limits on their ability to pressure the government on issues of common good.[11]

Horizontal Accountability

As noted in Chapter 3, due to shortcomings in the democratic electoral process, governments should ideally play an active role, in the republican sense, of monitoring themselves. In this area state agencies, having greater access to public information than the electorate does, are expected to play an important role, promoting responsibility and self-control in the Madisonian republican tradition. But whereas an effective network of horizontal accountability is normally a bedrock of governance in stable democracies, in most Latin American countries a lack of effective checks and balances across government is a well-observed phenomenon (O'Donnell 1998).

Excessive concentration of power in the executive, which in the 1990s was further exacerbated by economic emergencies and by the near-secrecy in which the neoliberal reform process was carried out, is one of the primary factors underpinning weak checks and balances. O'Donnell (1994) has dubbed countries such as Argentina, Brazil, and Peru "delegative democracies"—countries where the population, although distrustful of politicians, ironically places nearly all hopes and expectations on the figure of the president, delegating to him or her the obligation of solving the nation's problems.[12] In Argentina these patterns were perhaps most readily observable during Carlos Menem's two administrations (1989–1999). To expedite his economic reform agenda, Menem issued a total of 545 decrees—a staggering number in relation to the 35 decrees that had been issued in the 134-year period between 1853 and 1989.[13] At the same time, with an eye toward ensuring that his contempt of the legislature would not be ruled unconstitutional, Menem also enlarged the Supreme Court and packed it with his acolytes. He also removed several members from agencies charged with investigating irregularities in government accounts in order to ensure minimal refutation of his policies (Manzetti and Blake 1996: 672–673).

These patterns were enabled by a cultural tradition embedded in the belief that others are responsible for national salvation. As a high-ranking official of the Argentine catholic hierarchy put it, "Argentina is a *caudillista* country. We are used to being led by strong men: salvation always comes from above."[14] In a context where messianic beliefs are compounded by the absence of an authoritative or normative hold of the law on the country, as previously discussed, the concentration of power in the executive can be more fully understood. With both legislative and judicial branches themselves frequently enveloped in allegations of suspicious activity, compliance with the law is generally a function of instrumental calculations rather than of an inherent belief that obeying the law is the right thing to do. The servility of the legislative branch, in particular, has placed limits on its capacity to serve as a credible balance to the power of the executive. The judicial branch has experienced similar problems, heightened by the perception that judges' interpretation of the law is vulnerable not only to political considerations but also to bribery. Indeed, judges are often placed under investigation for the same crimes they are charged with prosecuting. In a particularly notorious case, in November 2000 the federal judge who was heading the investigation into a bribery scandal involving eleven senators was himself placed under investigation for illicit enrichment.[15] Perhaps unsurprisingly, according to the UN Development Programme, 92 percent of Argentines believe that a poor person will never, or almost never, succeed at securing equal treatment before the law (UNDP 2004b: 253).

In a context where virtually the entire Argentine political class is tainted by corruption and self-interest, it is hard for even well-intentioned politicians to muster the credibility and political will to propel meaningful reform, particularly given little pressure from society and other branches of government to do so. While these factors alone could have been sufficient to forestall police reform, still other problems deserve our consideration.

Competition Without Bounds

We in Argentina live in a permanent campaign.
—*A senior legal adviser for the Argentine senate*[16]

The lack of effective mechanisms of vertical and horizontal account-ability gave virtually free rein to Argentine politicians to follow their individual, particularistic interests—to hold on to office, to extract spoils as quickly as possible, and to vilify the opposition in the process. Unlike in previous decades, when they could depend on a strong party support base, candidates in the 1990s waged long, drawn-out, expensive, and destructive electoral campaigns to gain office; once elected, they spent most of their energy fending off perceived destabilization attempts by the opposition. Appointed officials had a very short life span, since they were conveniently blamed for every crisis whenever the tide turned against their political patrons. Rather than devote scarce political time to systematic study of social or institutional problems with a view to assembling the elements required for reform, most politicians and their teams spent their time contriving schemes to prevent early displacement.

The Politics of Destruction

Because the development process involves creation and destruction of sources of wealth, in most developing countries political competition tends to be unusually fierce and highly conflictive, with bitter clashes among various groups holding opposing interests. The inherently conflictive nature of the development process has been exacerbated in Latin America, a region of vastly unequal multiethnic societies, historically weak institutions, and a tradition of authoritarian leadership. The inability of political institutions to channel and absorb the often conflicting demands of different groups has frequently led to political demagoguery, violence, social disorder, power vacuums, political chaos, and military coups (Huntington 1968; Loveman and Davies 1978).

Argentina has certainly been no exception to this pattern of zero-sum politics; if anything, it has been one of the more extreme cases. Although the political class has learned the lessons of democratic rhetoric—ruling out physical force, intimidation, and coercion as legitimate means of political competition—the viciousness and protracted nature of political contests has hardly diminished; it has been propelled to ever higher intensity by intrusive media. This style of competition reached its zenith during the Menem era. In the early 1990s, he relied on his personal charisma and political acumen to convince his support base that even if his neoliberal economic measures violated nearly all of the traditional Peronist Party principles, they would in the end benefit everyone. When questions were raised on the extent and nature of these reforms or the rampant corruption that accompanied them, Menem bypassed objections by issuing decrees, packing the Supreme Court with his acolytes, and emasculating the legislature.

During his decade in power, Menem fought, ostracized, or derided all emerging rivals within his party, doggedly attempting to remain its dominant figure. One of his potential rivals was his finance minister, Domingo Cavallo, whose prestige soared in the aftermath of an economic program that managed to rein in hyperinflation. When Menem dismissed Cavallo, both men publicly engaged in accusations of corruption and mismanagement: Cavallo subsequently left the Peronists to head his own political party, running unsuccessfully first for the presidency and then for mayor of Buenos Aires.

Similarly, Menem fell out with his former vice president Eduardo Duhalde, also a Peronist. By the time Duhalde ran for president in 1999, Menem was wasting no opportunity to publicly mock his capacity—allegedly out of spite that Duhalde had helped block a constitutional amendment to allow Menem to run for an unprecedented third presidential term. On the day that Duhalde lost to de la Rúa, signs proclaiming "Menem 2004" appeared all over the country.

Bitter internal dissension was not confined to the Peronist Party. Barely six months after de la Rúa was elected president, the ruling coalition came to a crash. His vice president, Chacho Álvarez—who had broken with Menem and the Peronist Party to create his own party, the National Solidarity Front (FREPASO)—resigned from office to protest de la Rúa's alleged involvement in a senate bribery scheme. President de la Rúa also had to endure a barrage of vitriol from the head of his own Radical Party, former president Raúl Alfonsín, who, owing to his role as the first civilian president following the dictatorship, had retained considerable prestige in spite of his own economic mismanagement.

The destructive style of political campaigns extended to public discussion of important issues: instead of presenting a platform of alternative solutions, politicians trivialized debate by ruthlessly mocking their opponents' positions. This was exactly what transpired when public security became a salient feature of political campaigns.

Public Security as Missile

As fear of crime was widespread among all social classes, public security became a major campaign issue in the 1990s primarily because its sensationalistic appeal ensured the media spotlight for any candidate eager to use it as a springboard.[17] In the extremely destructive context described above, this issue also contained many facile elements that appealed to politicians—chief among which was that crime and inefficient policing could be instantly blamed on the mismanagement and indifference of political opponents. As discussed in Chapter 4, blame trading reached the highest levels during a wave of street prostitution in Buenos Aires. President Menem had blamed the Buenos Aires legislature for passing "soft" legislation. The city government, then headed by Fernando de la Rúa, claimed in turn that the only solution for the public security crisis would be to partition the PFA, with most of its functions transferred to municipal control. For its part, the PFA viewed the transfer issue as a ploy by Mayor de la Rúa to bolster his presidential ambitions. As one former chief of police put it, "The PFA was caught in the middle of a political tug of war. The city government launched missiles at us in the press saying we were a total disaster . . . and claiming that public security would improve only if we were transferred under their control."[18]

Once de la Rúa was elected president in 1999, however, he virtually abandoned the idea of transferring the PFA to the municipal government. Politicians in the city nevertheless held on to public security as a major campaign issue: in the 2000 mayoral race, both frontrunners' platforms boosted imported strategies as remedies for the crime epidemic. The Radical Party candidate, Aníbal Ibarra, campaigned on a strategy of community policing, bolstered by his visit to the headquarters of the London Metropolitan Police and his contacts with UK advisers. One of his rivals in the mayoral campaign was Domingo Cavallo, who had been finance minister under Menem and whose neoliberal economic program had been hailed for taming hyperinflation. Cavallo, however, was now under vicious attack for having "created" the crime problem. Cavallo's response was to hire William Bratton, a former top police official in New York City, whose adoption of "zero tolerance policing" was credited with dramatic declines in that city's crime rate. When I asked about transplanting zero tolerance to Buenos Aires, one of the architects of Cavallo's mayoral campaign said,

> The whole campaign from the start was prone to catchy slogans and unrealistic, oversimplified solutions. We knew that we couldn't carry out any of the policies promised in our campaign, but we were forced into this position because we needed to differentiate ourselves from the [Radical Party]. . . . They were responsible for the invasion of prostitutes and transvestites everywhere—the furious reaction [to their attempt to legalize prostitution] was another factor that made us swing far more to the right than we wished.[19]

The Radical Party won both the mayoral elections and the subsequent presidential race. Almost immediately, the government's security policies received blistering criticism from Carlos Ruckauf, the Peronist governor of Buenos Aires Province, who had his own presidential ambitions. Accusing the government of turning the criminal justice system into a "festival for criminals,"[20] the governor instructed a provincial official to broadcast the weekly number of criminals released early from jail as a result of the Two-for-One Law, discussed in Chapter 4. Attempting to placate public uproar, the minister of the interior told Ruckauf he should concentrate instead on fixing his province's own "highly deficient damned police." The minister was referring, of course, to the notorious Bonaerense, a force he accused of meriting only 4 out of 10 possible points in a scale of police competence.[21]

The political tug-of-war culminated in the aftermath of the December 2001 *cacerolazo,* the popular uprising that led to President de la Rúa's resignation. In its wake, ousted officials and many others suggested that the Peronist Party was behind the riots, pointing to the fact that Governor Ruckauf had ordered the Bonaerense to stand by in the face of widespread looting and violence so as to give the government its final coup de grace. Although there were demands that Ruckauf be prosecuted for treason, barely three months later the fifth president-designate, Eduardo Duhalde, appointed Ruckauf as Argentina's foreign minister.

Conclusion

This chapter has attempted to shed light on the factors that underlay the inability of the Argentine state to reform the institutions most crucial to its own legitimacy. With a political game dominated by uncivic cultural attitudes, disrespect for norms, feeble or nonexistent checks and balances, and an unbounded style of political competition, it cannot surprise us entirely that police reform initiatives were improvised, inadequate, and quickly forgotten. Each of these characteristics alone could have adversely affected institutional reform; the combination of all of them led to an absurd universe of inconsequential measures and partial solutions that were cast aside only to be repackaged as soon as another crisis or election loomed.

Since the public security crisis did not show any signs of abating, it might be deduced at best that many of the consultants working around the clock to formulate a dizzying array of initiatives genuinely hoped that some might possibly catch on and work. At worst, it could be assumed that this whirlwind represented various officials' conscious efforts to dupe the population into thinking that the government was proactive on their behalf. The creation of an army of new laws and institutions to promote civilian oversight might be optimistically read as a welcome movement toward increasing accountability over the hermetic PFA. But closer examination shows that much of the hastily approved legislation was either partially applied or disregarded altogether and that community involvement in oversight functions tended to last the length of a specific crisis.

It might also be wondered why candidates for mayor of Buenos Aires ran on platforms featuring public security despite the fact that the mayor lacks legal power over the PFA and the penal system. Perhaps they expected that once in office they would somehow obtain the political backing required to change these circumstances; in any case their subsequent actions frequently belied their promises. While politicians squabbled year after year over whether the transfer of the PFA from federal to municipal control would improve the public security situation, the population remained just as beleaguered by crime as before.

Operating under constant threat of destabilization by opponents, politicians not only lacked the technical expertise to make informed decisions on security issues but also lacked the political time to develop this knowledge. Reluctant to risk the political consequences of institutional reform and aware of veiled threats of crime boycotts by the police, politicians opted instead for measures that could give the *illusion* of decisive action. The fact that public security and police reform became salient campaign issues exacerbated the tendency for hollow treatment of issues, since crime and corruption provide much fodder for the kind of effective sloganeering that ensures media coverage. Thus, instead of engaging in reasoned debate, politicians devoted themselves to unrelenting public condemnation of police performance—which served mostly to alienate the average citizen from the police even further. The relentless and destructive pace of political competition, coupled with the revolving-door nature of government service, also significantly hindered the sustainability of the reform process, because each new appointee brought along a new team of advisers ready to tear down any initiatives launched by their predecessors.

Civil society was part of the same self-perpetuating dynamic. Although collective anger was manifestly high, few organized entities succeeded in systematically channeling popular demands to the government so as to obtain results. Beset by fractiousness and a fever of protagonism, the citizenry largely dissipated its energies through incessant street protests, marches, and accusations.

These salient features of the Argentine political game were aggravated by the disproportionate influence of international financial institutions— which, owing to Argentina's dependence on loans and foreign investment, came to represent a more powerful interest group than the population itself. When IFIs and foreign investors pressured the government to expedite the adoption of a specific economic agenda as a precondition for continued loans or investment, the state rushed to comply. Since more often than not quick compliance meant skipping public debate, passing reforms by decree, forgoing the payment of public employees' salaries and pensions, or giving away hard-won social and labor benefits, pressure from abroad had the net effect of reinforcing existing tendencies toward insular and autocratic decisionmaking. Given that the interest of international institutions was not focused on controversial police reform issues (except in limited areas, such as the provision of information technology to compile crime maps and other statistics), the state did not feel pressure to prioritize these issues.

If, as these chapters have sought to demonstrate, the Argentine state failed to accomplish police reform primarily due to the characteristics of its political game, it follows that all sectors of society must assume responsibility for changing its corrosive nature, even against the formidable odds examined here. Argentina has limped from crisis to crisis for generations. Between the close of December 2001 and early 2002, the world watched in astonishment as the president was forced out of office and the country veered toward anarchy. Dozens of citizens were shot in clashes with the police, bank deposits were impounded, and default on the external debt was declared. In a country that had been a haven for impoverished foreign immigrants, fear of crime and increasing poverty were now forcing many Argentines to seek emigration papers. While these developments came as a shock to many, to paraphrase Gabriel García Márquez, they were in reality "a death foretold." Whether the Argentine state will continue to default on the guarantees that allow its democratic existence is a question whose answer lies in the hands of the Argentine people themselves.

Notes

1. After Almond and Verba, "political culture" is used to mean "the attitudes toward the political system and its various parts, and attitudes toward the role of the self in the system" (1963: 12).

2. Countries such as Chile, Costa Rica, and Uruguay appear to have come closer to overcoming this legacy than their neighbors.

3. For more on these and other corruption scandals linked to privatization, see Manzetti and Blake (1996) and Verbitsky (1991).

4. Author interview, August 25, 2000.

5. President Eduardo Duhalde and his foreign minister, Carlos Ruckauf, were both former governors of Buenos Aires Province as well as vice presidents under Menem. In the Nestor Kirchner administration, there have been many former Menem associates (including the president).

6. In multiparty systems such as those found in Latin America, the task of keeping track of one's political representatives is far more complicated than it would be in a two-party system. Even in the United States, where there are only two major parties, only 25 percent of the electorate know the name of their representatives; in Latin America the percentage is bound to be lower given lower literacy levels and the greater number of parties and candidates competing for office (Geddes and Neto 1992).

7. Also writing on Argentine individualism, cynicism, factionalism, and the absence of a civic culture are Tomás Filliol (1961), Julio Mafud (1984), and Thomas McGann (1966).

8. Patrice McSherry (1997: esp. ch. 3) provides extensive information on the often bloody struggles of the mid-1970s and particularly on the origins and operations of the leftist Montonero organization and the extreme right Argentine Anti-communist Alliance (AAA).

9. For more on the Argentine labor unions in the 1990s, see Murillo (2001: ch. 6).

10. See "Carta Abierta Respecto a la Identidad de Madres de Plaza de Mayo, Línea Fundadora," Madres de Plaza de Mayo, Línea Fundadora, http://madres-linea fundadora.org/noticias/, February 25, 2000.

11. Some human rights NGOs, especially CELS, have made important strides in promoting greater vertical accountability by bringing the horrors of the military dictatorship to light and by trying to prevent people associated with torture and repression from joining the state security forces. Even so, for most NGOs it is not common practice to consistently champion particular causes over time.

12. This is a function of the tradition of *caudillo* or strongman, the embedded cultural influence of the Catholic Church, which prophesies salvation from above, and perhaps the perception that in a country so beset by problems, change can come only in dramatic swoops rather than through incremental reforms. For more on the tradition of *caudillismo,* see Hamill (1992).

13. His successors have continued this trend. In his first eleven months in office, President Kirchner signed sixty-five decrees—even more than Menem signed in the same period in his administration. See Delia Ferreira Rubio and Matteo Gorretti's figures in "Ofensiva Opositora Contra los Decretazos," *La Nación,* May 23, 2004.

14. Author interview, October 27, 2000.

15. It was alleged that the senators were bribed with funds from the SIDE, at the behest of President de la Rúa, to approve a controversial labor reform law advocated by the World Bank. Executive reluctance to pursue a full investigation led Vice President Chacho Álvarez, an advocate of transparency in government, to resign in protest. The case was still dragging on at the time of writing, more than five years later.

16. Author interview, October 23, 2000.

17. The popularity of public security as a campaign issue appears to be a trend elsewhere as well, as evinced by the 2002 presidential elections in France. Police and crimestoppers TV shows have become popular in numerous countries, including Britain, France, and the United States. But because controls over rights to privacy, graphic content, and parental warning requirements for minors barely exist in Latin America, or are ignored altogether, TV and press depictions of violence are all the more explicit and macabre, with color pictures of bloody corpses appearing on magazine covers.

18. Author interview, August 25, 2000.

19. Author interview, August 28, 2000.

20. "Según la Bonaerense, los Jueces Liberan al 90% de los Detenidos," *Clarín,* October 27, 2000.

21. "Entrevista Federico Storani: Federico Storani, Ministro del Interior," *Clarín,* December 24, 2000.

PART 2

BRAZIL

CHAPTER 7

The Spillover of Crime

The escalation of urban crime and violence in Brazil's urban areas coincides with the transitional period from military rule to electoral democracy, although its origins were far longer in the making. Between 1964 and 1985, the military regime's repressive policies were fairly effective in containing political opposition and encasing the poor within "their" boundaries. But by 1985, the enormous socioeconomic disparities that have historically characterized Brazilian society were a fertile breeding ground for the explosion of the drug trade, which soon spilled over from the *favelas* or slums into all socioeconomic classes.

Public perception that the police and the state were either unwilling or incapable of dealing with the drug and crime epidemic set the stage for events that would eventually turn Brazilian cities into virtual battlegrounds. By the 1990s, Rio de Janeiro, previously known as the Marvelous City, became emblematic of the urban chaos that threatened newly won democratic freedoms.

The Historical Context of Crime and Repression

During the dictatorship of Getúlio Vargas (1930–1945), and to a lesser degree during his elected presidency (1951–1954), the application of torture and other heavy-handed methods against political prisoners and common criminals was routinely tolerated, if not encouraged (Cancelli 1993). In 1958, it was reported that Army General Amaury Kruel, chief of the police force of the Federal District of Rio de Janeiro (a position then directly appointed by the president, as Rio was still the country's capital), had ordered special squads to capture and "kill dangerous criminals" to contain a wave of theft, assault, and bank robberies that posed a threat to

93

businesses, provoking bitter complaints from Rio's chamber of commerce (Huggins 1997: 212).

But although this type of property crime was fairly common, and knifings, illegal gambling, and prostitution had long been widespread in poor areas, violent street crime remained a relatively rare phenomenon until the 1980s. As put by Paulo Francis, a well-known Brazilian cultural commentator, in the 1950s, "Of course the *pau-de-arará* [a torture method used by the police[1]] existed, and so did the poor, and the odd character in the hills . . . but in a far smaller and *non-intrusive* scale. The streets of the Zona Sul [the affluent Southern Zone] were 'ours': they belonged to the middle class and above" (Ventura 1994: 19).

A Watershed in Latin American Civil-Military Relations

In the 1960s and 1970s, it was fear of political repression that gripped a generation of intellectuals and much of the middle class. Departing from previous coups (in 1930, 1945, 1954, and 1955), in 1964 the Brazilian armed forces overthrew leftist president João Goulart with a view toward longer-term governance. Driven by a national security doctrine that had evolved from fears that threats from within posed the gravest danger to Latin America, the military took control of political institutions, repressed trade unions, and persecuted opponents and communist sympathizers. In the 1950s, conventional armies had been defeated by revolutionary groups in China, Indochina, and Algeria, but it was the 1959 trouncing of the Cuban army by Fidel Castro's small band of revolutionaries, in particular, that inspired a new set of counterinsurgency and anticommunist strategies for the region. Brazil was singled out for special attention by the US government, owing both to its size and to the ties that developed after Brazil had sent ground troops to fight alongside the Allies in World War II. This collaboration had increased the links between key Brazilian military officers and their US counterparts, particularly between 1948 and 1960, and created a special bond between the two countries unmatched in the Southern Cone (Stepan 1971: 126–128). Although some Brazilian military officers were given special training in the United States, it was the Rio de Janeiro Superior War College, founded in 1949 with US assistance, that became the center of Brazilian counterinsurgency theories. The chief ideologue of the Superior War College, General Golbery, said in 1959, "Latin America now faces threats more real than at any other time, threats that could result in insurrection, uprisings that could attempt (though not openly) to implant . . . a government favorable to the communist ideology and constitute a grave and urgent danger to the unity and security of the Americas and the Western world" (quoted in Stepan 1973: 56).

A Symbiotic Relationship

During the twenty-one years the Brazilian military held power, it formally merged all provincial police forces under its direct control to prevent local power brokers from using these forces to countervail the power of the regime.[2] The police received special training in the application of torture and other coercive methods to control political dissent and suspected subversives. Heavily armed mobile shock squads, such as the notorious Rondas Ostensivas Tobias de Aguiar (ROTA) of São Paulo, were formed to serve as a vanguard of political repression and to keep a vigilant eye over the population at large (Barcellos 1992; Caldeira 2000). Constitutional guarantees such as habeas corpus were suspended, the mandates of congressional representatives and mayors were canceled, trade unions were closed, and the press came under tight censorship (Alves 1985: 95–98). While the middle class bore the brunt of political repression, the regime also monitored the shantytowns (*favelas*) in key urban centers to prevent communist infiltration (Ramsdell 1990: 167). These policies not only weakened Brazil's legal and political institutions but also set in motion several processes that would ultimately lead to a crime explosion.

A Temporary Miracle

Through import substitution, price controls, directed credit, targeted expenditures, heavy investment in infrastructure, and state control of such key industries as transportation, iron, and steel, the military regime sought to use the state as the "motor of development" (Hagopian 1996: 76–77). Unlike their Argentine counterparts, the Brazilian military regime's economic policies succeeded in generating impressive annual growth rates, particularly between 1968 and 1974, when industry expanded in real terms at an annual 12 percent average rate—a process that became known as the Brazilian "economic miracle" (Bonelli and Malan 1987: 16). With emerging heavy industries desperately in need of cheap labor, particularly in car and chemical manufacturing, the military regime deliberately encouraged rural migration to cities,[3] and with partial funding from the Kennedy administration's US Alliance for Progress, it created a National Housing Bank in order to build affordable housing.

Within a few years, however, the rural exodus had outstripped construction and overwhelmed public services in the new housing projects.[4] Forced to squat in squalid *favelas,* migrants found themselves socially and economically isolated. Between 1977 and 1984, the numbers of the poor rose from 40.7 million to 56.9 million (from 39.6 percent to 50.5 percent of the population), while the number of indigents reached 25.1 million, or 23.6

percent of the population. By 1983, Brazil had become one of the most unequal countries in the world, with the richest 10 percent of the population enjoying 47.7 percent of total income while the poorest 40 percent received only 8.1 percent of total income. These ratios would remain almost unchanged at the close of the century (Barros, Henriques, and Mendonça 2000: 40).

If the rise in urban poverty and inequality can be attributed to the military's policies, some have argued that the roots of *organized* crime can similarly be traced to the practice of imprisoning political prisoners together with common criminals. In Rio de Janeiro, prisoners were sent to the Cândido Mendes prison at Ilha Grande, an island three hours from the city. In this isolated outpost leftist militants provided criminals with the intellectual tools and strategies to organize more effectively against the military regime, in the distorted belief that, as victims of social injustice, those convicted of crimes would be the leftists' natural allies in the class struggle.[5]

A by-product of this transculturization process was the formation of the Red Command (Comando Vermelho) and other notorious criminal gangs (Amorim 1993; Coelho 1987; Lima 1991). Originally, the main functions of organized prison gangs were to provide protection against other prisoners and prison guards, to obtain food and other commodities from the outside, and to gain freedom by bribing corrections officers. Later, these gangs took their growing organizational skills beyond prison walls, quickly proliferating in the *favelas* of Rio and other large cities, where they became instrumental in the explosion of the drug trade (Leeds 1996: 52–58).

The Marvelous City Loses Luster

While Brazil's economic growth lasted, the combined force of military and police repression managed to contain violent crime largely within impoverished areas. By the 1980s, however, the economy was in the midst of a sharp decline, owing in large measure to the after-effects of the oil shocks of the 1970s and the subsequent Latin American debt crisis. With millions of workers unemployed, the combination of accelerating poverty and state neglect of the *favelas* proved combustive at a time when the Colombian drug cartels and the expansion of coca cultivation in Peru and Bolivia brought a flood of cocaine and other narcotics into Brazil—a vast country sharing borders with every South American nation except Chile and Ecuador.[6] Rio de Janeiro became a major transit point for the export of cocaine to the United States, Europe, and South Africa and for domestic consumption as well: with a population of about 185 million, Brazil itself was a huge magnet for the drug cartels. By the end of the 1990s, it was estimated that Brazil was the second largest market for cocaine consumption in the world, after the United States (UNODOC 2000: 193).

In Rio de Janeiro, the rise of the drug trade became indelibly associated with the first government of Leonel Brizola (1983–1987). A brother-in-law and political ally of the deposed left-wing president Goulart, Brizola had won the first direct elections for governor in 1982, despite the best efforts of the military and the powerful media conglomerate Rede Globo to block him. To maintain control of the process of political opening (*abertura*), the military had enacted a law requiring that voters select a straight party ticket for all elective offices. While this strategy enabled the military-backed Democratic Social Party (PDS) to retain a majority both in Congress and in the electoral college that would choose the first civilian president in 1985, in Rio the strategy backfired (Gay 1994: 28–29). It was Brizola's Democratic Labor Party (PDT),[7] not the PDS, that swept to victory amid joyous popular celebration.

Once in office, Governor Brizola took immediate steps to dismantle the repressive apparatus left from military rule. One of his first acts of office proved the most controversial: he ordered the police to stop entering the *favelas* without judicial authorization (Cerqueira 2001: 165–166). Because the police had long relied on unannounced raids to search homes, confiscate weapons, and detain suspects, often causing significant damage, the banning order became instantly popular among *favela* residents, while spreading panic everywhere else. Ensconced in the now off-limit *favelas,* drug traffickers proceeded to exploit the intense public discord to consolidate their power and expand their business. Bloody turf wars were fought openly by rival gangs while the police watched in frustration, their hands tied by the governor's banning order. As if the crime wave alone did not suffice, the federal government withdrew funds for public health, transportation, and sanitation in Rio in order to further discredit Brizola's administration and derail his presidential aspirations.

The Role of the Police in the Crisis

To protect themselves from the crime and drug violence that had enveloped the city, Rio's affluent classes turned to private security services for themselves and their businesses, rode in bulletproof vehicles, and hired armed personnel to watch their gated communities. According to one study, between 1983 and 2000, the number of registered private security guards in Brazil increased by 600 percent, from about 50,000 to 350,000.[8] Those who could not afford private protection were gripped by panic and helplessness, fueled by the perception that the police could not or would not protect them.

Assistance and Reassurance Role

As discussed in Part 1, the frequent visible presence of police officers on patrol, coupled with rapid and effective police response to distress calls, can provide psychological reassurance and help to prevent fear of crime.

Unfortunately, this positive dynamic has not taken root in Rio de Janeiro. Like the residents of Buenos Aires, *cariocas,* as Rio residents are known, have almost no trust in the police. In 1995, according to the United Nations International Crime Victim Survey, 79.6 percent of *cariocas* were dissatisfied with the police, with only 15.4 percent expressing satisfaction (UNI-CRI 1998: 109). In outlying areas of Rio, scores of cadavers are regularly found that do not match any missing person reports and are not subsequently claimed by family members, and these deaths are not investigated (Zaluar 1996). A victimization survey conducted by a prominent Brazilian university in conjunction with a human rights NGO showed that only 20 percent of victims reported robberies to the police (CPDOC-FGV/ISER 1997: 38). The results of one poll surveying the reasons for not reporting crimes are shown in Figure 7.1.

In the 1990s, mistrust of the police across socioeconomic lines was fanned by sensationalistic reports in newspapers such as *O Dia* and television

Figure 7.1 Reasons for Not Reporting a Robbery to the Police

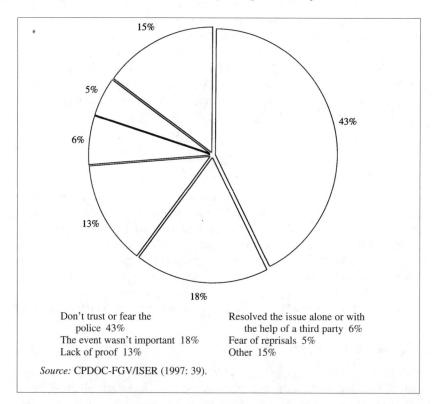

Don't trust or fear the
   police 43%
The event wasn't important 18%
Lack of proof 13%

Resolved the issue alone or with
   the help of a third party 6%
Fear of reprisals 5%
Other 15%

Source: CPDOC-FGV/ISER (1997: 39).

programs such as the *Jornal Nacional* and *Cidade Alerta,* which exposed the complicity of rogue police elements in car theft, kidnapping, and drug trafficking. The working poor had to cope with constant harassment as well: the police not only returned to raiding the *favelas* but routinely solicited bribes to file police reports, to allow illegal vendors to operate, and to allow wrongdoers to avoid arrest for misdemeanors. A former chief of the investigative police in Rio, Hélio Luz, went as far as to state that "nothing is trafficked in this city without the collusion of the police."[9] One editorial written in a prominent newspaper expressed the mood of the period:

> The community doesn't have anyone to turn to when it feels threatened. Organized crime is protected by the police and indeed feeds off the police. The police do not even act within the minimum bounds of decency. The criminals are even more effective than the police, killing and robbing with efficiency. The police no longer know how to be efficient.[10]

In 1994 the army was called in to restore public order, harking back to the days of the military regime. By the close of the 1990s, the public security situation remained grim.

Statistical Overview

As is the case in Argentina, it is difficult to determine exactly how much crime increased in Brazil since the end of the military regime in 1985, as police statistics are frequently unreliable and crime categories are often blurred.[11] In much of Brazil, official police statistics, when they are available, are typically available at the state (provincial) level instead of being disaggregated by city or municipality—one reason being that the boundaries of police precincts do not always correspond to municipal boundaries. The federal government, for its part, does not publish the statistics recorded by the country's police forces and state governments.

A prominent Rio-based university research institute, the Center for Studies of Citizenship, Conflict, and Urban Violence within the Federal University of Rio de Janeiro, has sought to compensate for official shortcomings by compiling its own criminal database. Its data, drawn from recorded civil police statistics, show that the homicide rate in Rio State increased by about 63 percent between 1985 and 1994—from 4,105 to a staggering 7,431 in absolute numbers. (To provide a point of comparison: this is more than ten times the 726 homicides recorded in the whole of England and Wales that year,[12] yet their combined population of about 50 million in 1994 far exceeded the 13.2 million residents of Rio State.) And the alarming increase in homicides in Rio State was exceeded by the homicide rate in the city of Rio, where the homicide rate more than doubled, as shown in Figure 7.2.

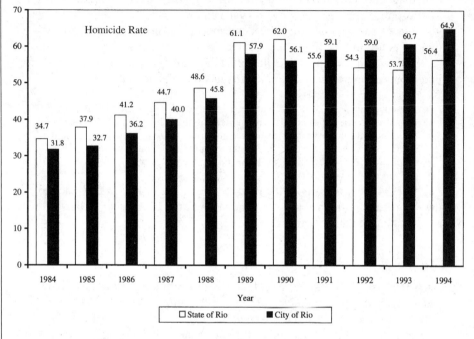

**Figure 7.2 Recorded Homicide Rate and Levels,
State and City of Rio de Janeiro, 1984–1994 (per 100,000 inhabitants)**

Number of Homicides

Region	1984	1985	1986	1987	1988	1989	1990	1991	1992	1993	1994
State of Rio	4,105	4,542	4,996	5,483	6,023	7,654	7,858	7,126	7,008	7,013	7,431
City of Rio	1,663	1,724	1,922	2,135	2,463	3,131	3,055	3,241	3,251	3,367	3,622

Source: Numbers of intentional homicides recorded by the Polícia Civil, cited in NECVU/ UFRJ (1984–2000).

As the new millennium began, hopes for improvement quickly faded. In June 2000, a live TV broadcast of the hijacking of bus 174 near Rio's botanical gardens shook the whole nation. For several hours, millions watched anxiously as the hijacker held terrified passengers at gunpoint and a befuddled police force could not agree on a course of action. As tensions mounted, the police botched a rescue attempt, wounding a young female schoolteacher who was being used as a human shield by the hijacker. The hijacker killed the teacher and shot himself, though not mortally, at which point the police captured him. By the time they reached the nearest hospital, however, the hijacker was dead from strangulation—a denouement that the five officers in the squad car attributed to self-defense.[13] In the aftermath of this episode, thousands of people were frightened off public buses for several months.

Deterrence Capacity

As noted in Part 1, the second crucial role for the police is to provide a minimum threshold of criminal deterrence. In most societies, deterrence is closely linked to criminals' calculation of the likelihood of apprehension and to the application and severity of criminal penalties. In Argentina and Brazil during the military period, the preferred tool for containment of crime was indiscriminate use of force by the security forces, supplemented by harsh penalties that courts dictated for perpetrators of even petty crimes. Once democratic rule was reintroduced, it was expected that police deterrence activities would be conducted within a framework of procedural guarantees and respect for civil liberties. But as will be seen in the following section, the investigative capacity of the police and the judiciary had been too consistently weakened. The criminal justice system overall was in such disarray that even when criminals were finally incarcerated, they escaped from prison on a routine basis: in 1994, the Ministry of Justice reported that successful escapes from Brazilian prisons averaged about nine per day (cited in US Department of State 1996: sec. 1c).

In Rio, in whose prisons convicts often staged violent rebellions and where hand grenades, bombs, assault rifles, and machine guns were easily available, violence levels were said to be approaching those in Colombia.[14] In 1995 alone, 27 on-duty and 162 off-duty police officers were killed (Garotinho et al. 1998: 77).

Police Investigative Capacity

During the twenty-one years that Brazil was ruled by the military, the state's civil institutions were systematically weakened and power was heavily centralized. The judiciary in particular was divested of much of its authority and resources, as was the Polícia Civil (PC), the investigative branch of the police. Some of the PC's investigative duties were transferred to the Polícia Militar (PM), the uniformed branch that during this period was controlled by the army. By weakening the investigative capacity of the PC and instigating rivalry with the PM, the military unwittingly compromised the overall capacity of the state to deal with the crime and drug-trafficking epidemic of the 1980s and 1990s.

The magnitude of both problems became particularly acute in the 1990s. Although the police were constitutionally set up as two separate forces, their functions are theoretically complementary: the PM is charged with keeping order and arresting criminals caught in flagrante delicto, while the plainclothes PC is charged with criminal investigation post facto. In practice, however, the two were bitter rivals, rarely sharing information and operating under a veil of mutual suspicion and secrecy. They are housed separately as well: the uniformed PM in armylike barracks (*batalhões*) and the PC in common precincts or *delegacias*. Until 1999, even their crime statistics were issued independently.

Compounding this lack of cooperation was an astounding lack of adequate training in most areas of criminal investigation. A 1992 study showed, for example, that for even the most serious of crimes—intentional homicide and robbery followed by murder—the evidence gathered by the police was so inadequate that after two years only 8.1 percent and 8.9 percent of cases, respectively, could proceed to trial. By that point many witnesses and police officers had only a dim recollection of events. The remaining cases had to be archived altogether for lack of evidence or suspects (Soares et al. 1996: 230–239). In the United States in that period, by comparison, an arrest was made and the case brought to court in 65 percent of all recorded murder cases (FBI 1995: sec. III).

Conclusion

As shown in this chapter, from the 1960s through the mid-1980s the military regime and the police were ruthlessly efficient in containing political opposition and ensuring that violent crime did not spill out from the slums into the "respectable areas" of Rio de Janeiro. This capacity became increasingly strained, however, as a result of policies that encouraged wide-scale rural-urban migration in order to meet the demands of a rapidly industrializing economy. By the time the global expansion of the drug trade began in the early 1980s, the numbers of urban poor had far outpaced the state capacity (or willingness) to accommodate them, and lack of state presence in the *favelas* made these an ideal ground for the drug trade. The democratization process that was under way during this period brought no relief to the explosion in drug-related crime and violence. On the contrary, drug lords cunningly exploited the fact that after twenty-one years of military rule, civil institutions were severely weakened, the police were widely feared and mistrusted, and there was no agreement on how to address the crisis.

If the police were to be transformed into a reliable ally against crime, more than a few changes would be needed. How the state addressed this problem is examined in the following chapters.

Notes

1. The "parrot's perch" was a bar from which bound victims were suspended upside down while they were subjected to electric shocks.

2. For more on the police role during the dictatorship, see Huggins (1998: esp. ch. 8).

3. The shift in the country's rural-urban balance accelerated dramatically: urban dwellers more than doubled, from an estimated 44,667,700 in 1967 to 97,624,000 in 1985 (in percentage terms, from 52.4 to 72 percent of the population). See United Nations (1976, 1991).

4. The Banco Nacional de Habitação (BNH) was created in 1964. For more on BNH and the removal of *favelas* to Rio housing projects such as Vila Kennedy and Cidade de Deus, see Ramsdell (1990). For the case of Belo Horizonte, see Fernandes (1995: ch. 5).

5. Similarly, Nelson Mandela recounts in his autobiography how South African authorities had put a handful of hardened criminals together with political prisoners, to "act as agent provocateurs." Mandela, however, "saw the gang members not as rivals but as raw material to be converted" (1994: 407–408).

6. For more on the expansion of drug trafficking in South America, see Stares (1996: ch. 2).

7. The Democratic Labor Party (Partido Democrático Trabalhista, PDT) is a center-left populist party. It was founded by Leonel Brizola and was formally approved by the Federal Superior Electoral Tribunal (TSE) on November 10, 1981.

8. See IB Teixeira study cited in "Efetivos de Particulares É Quase o da PM," *Folha de Sao Paulo,* July 8, 2000.

9. See "Hélio Luz: O Tira-Cabeça," *Revista da Folha,* October 8, 1995.

10. "Shows de Violência," *Jornal do Brasil,* September 27, 1994.

11. Murdered robbery victims are considered victims of armed robbery (*latrocínio*), and murdered rape victims are recorded as victims of rape followed by murder (*estupro seguido de morte*). Many cases in which the police kill a suspect are not incorporated into homicide statistics. For more on the various statistical irregularities of the Brazilian criminal justice system, see Zaluar (1996: ch. 3), Cano and Santos (2001), Carneiro (1999: 12–18), and Lemgruber (2002).

12. Crime in England has been considered enough of a problem that on occasion, the British press has dubbed England "the crime capital of Europe." See, for example, "Mugged by the Smiling Face of Gimmick Justice," *London Times,* February 25, 2001.

13. In a strange twist, it emerged that the twenty-two-year-old hijacker had been a survivor of the massacre at the Candelaria Church, an event that will be discussed later in this work. All five policemen who were charged ended up acquitted on the grounds of having acted in self-defense.

14. Due to a forty-year civil war and its infamous drug cartels, Colombia has been widely used as a yardstick for violence and crime in Latin America. Despite the absence of civil war in Brazil, a team of doctors from Rio's largest emergency-room hospital, the Souza Aguiar, who had been sent to Israel for training in dealing with gunshot wounds and trauma, returned prematurely after the Israelis realized that the Rio doctors had more training in coping with gunshot wounds than they did. Indeed, in the municipality of Rio de Janeiro between December 1987 and November 2001, eight times the number of adolescents were killed with firearms as were killed in the bloody Israeli-Palestinian conflict. See "Deserção na Emergência," *O Globo,* June 15, 2001, and Dowdney (2003: 143).

CHAPTER 8

Policing the Marvelous City

In the 1990s, extermination of street children and police participation in death squads and involvement in crime rings were the material of international headlines that scared tourists away from Brazil. In Rio de Janeiro, in particular, these events tended to reoccur at a disturbing rate, raising the question of what kind of policing was being carried out in the *cidade maravilhosa* in the years after the end of military rule. This chapter provides a portrait of the police in Rio de Janeiro within the broader Brazilian context. Overwhelmed by the drug trade, beset by a culture of impunity, and caught between unenforceable extremes, the Rio police were not only vulnerable to the vast power of the drug trade but also malleable to co-optation by the political and economic elites. As a result, fear of crime and insecurity continued to permeate the life of the average citizen.

Structure and History of Policing in Brazil

As is the case in Argentina, the police in Brazil are convened primarily at the state (provincial) level.[1] Unlike Argentina's constitution, however, Brazil's national constitution draws a clear division between the functions of the state police forces. Specifically, the constitution adopted in 1988 specifies that each of the twenty-six Brazilian states and the Federal District of Brasilia have jurisdiction over their own police forces, which are composed of two distinct, if complementary, outfits: the Military Police (PM) and the Civil Police (PC). The PM is not a military entity per se, although it has at various times been subordinated to the armed forces; its main function is the preservation of public order. The PM patrols the streets and guards public spaces, arresting suspects caught in flagrante delicto or pursuant to a warrant. The PC is a plainclothes judicial or investigative entity charged with criminal investigation. As mentioned in the previous chapter, each force is

105

housed separately: the PM in military-style barracks and the PC in precincts or *delegacias*. Heading each force is a chief[2] who nominally reports to the secretary of public security, but it is always the state governor who exerts ultimate control.

The police structures that were adopted in Brazil were modeled on institutions that were initially created in Rio. The first full-time police force in the territory was the Royal Guard Police Force of Rio de Janeiro (Guarda Real da Policia), created in May 1809 by the Portuguese royal family, the Braganças, who had fled Portugal in 1808 during the Napoleonic wars. After the installation of the royal court in Rio, Brazil was declared a kingdom united with, and equal to, the Kingdom of Portugal—a singular event in colonial history.

Since 1549, virtually all economic activity in the territory had been dependent on slavery; by the early 1800s, with nearly half the population of Rio enslaved, fear of slave revolts ran high. To contain the threat and maintain public order, in 1808 the Portuguese established a General Police Intendency of the Court and State of Brazil, and the aforementioned Royal Guard Police Force a year later. These two institutions gave origin to the dual system of policing in Brazil.

The General Police Intendency, on which the PC would later be modeled, was charged not only with overall administration of public works but also with determining which actions and behavior constituted criminal offenses. The intendent alone mandated the laws that governed the arrest, prosecution, and sentencing of criminals (Bretas 1997: 41).[3] For this purpose, the police intendent held the rank of *desembargador* (high court judge). As a government minister wielding the delegated authority of the monarch, he had responsibility for criminal judges, as well as the Royal Guard Police Force.

The Royal Guard soon became feared for its ruthlessness. It brutally punished slaves for the slightest insubordination and laid siege to hideouts of runaways, called *quilombos,* in order to starve them. According to historian Thomas Holloway, the Royal Guard established patterns of policing that would still prevail well after the dissolution of the empire in 1889. Members were drawn from the free lower classes, and the guard's organization followed the military model, so that the use of force could be controlled through hierarchy and discipline. From the earliest days, the police in Rio were conceived as a

> standing army fighting a social war. . . . Unlike warfare against an external enemy on the battlefield, however, the objective was not to exterminate or eliminate the adversary. The goal was repression and subjugation and the maintenance of an acceptable level of order and calm, enabling the city to function in the interests of the class that had made the rules and created the police to enforce them. (Holloway 1993: 37)

The Royal Guard was replaced in October 1831 by the Permanent Municipal Guard Corps, which in 1866 became the Military Police of the Court. Despite the name changes, "physical injury continued to be part of an arsenal of techniques used to keep the behavior of the population within bounds and to instill fear" (Holloway 1993: 283); the police's overwhelming preoccupation remained "the preservation of the Court and the threat represented by the large number of slaves" (Bretas 1997: 42). Though neither force was created as an intrinsic part of the army, it was common for army officers to head both; it was not until 1983, in fact, that a career policeman was appointed to command the Rio PM. The militaristic orientation of the police was further reinforced by their participation in various civil conflicts, as well as external wars—most notably the war against Argentina (1851–1852) and the war of the Triple Alliance against Paraguay (1865–1870).

The 1934 constitution specified that the Rio police were to be considered a "reserve of the army"; two years later it was determined that they should be formally structured in accordance with the functional ranks of the army infantry and cavalry (Muniz 2001: 183). In 1969, the military dictatorship formally merged all state police forces into the national army to prevent local power brokers from using them to countervail the power of the regime. Although formal subordination of the police to the military was revoked by the 1988 constitution, the document stipulates that the police can be called into active military service in an emergency situation.[4]

As examined in the previous chapter, during the various military regimes but most particularly after the 1964 coup, the police also received special training in the application of torture and other coercive methods to control political dissenters and subversives. With the return to democracy, the specially trained shock squads lost their original mandate and were reintegrated into regular police forces, but they maintained the same militaristic style (Pinheiro 1991: 169).

Role, Culture, and Organization

A primary problem of policing in Rio, and indeed throughout the whole of Brazil, is that from the earliest days, political authorities have assigned to the police the role of buttress for a highly stratified social order. Similar trends can be discerned in Argentina and in fact have been common in most of Latin America. In Brazil, though, the role of the police was distinctively molded by an imperial tradition that lasted from 1808 until 1889, when the country was transformed into a republic, and by a slaveholding tradition that began in the early sixteenth century and ended only in 1888. Brazil was the last country in the Americas to abolish slavery.

Since then, the buttress role of the police has not been fundamentally altered, though it has become increasingly difficult to sustain. Calls for reform following the democratic transition were complicated by the intensification of urban poverty: between 1991 and 2000, for example, the population in Rio's *favelas* grew nearly seven times faster than in the formal city. According to the Brazilian Institute for Geography and Statistics (IBGE), the combined *favela* population, as counted by the 2000 census, was over a million inhabitants. The actual figure is likely to be significantly higher owing to the politically sensitive nature of these data and the difficulties attached to polling squatter settlements, such as poor infrastructure and local fear of providing information. Whereas in 1991 there were 384 *favelas* in the city, by 2002 the IBGE had placed this figure at 681. In other words, during the 1990s new *favelas* were springing up at a rate of twenty-seven every twelve months, with no sign of abatement.[5] Not even the Southern Zone, the affluent area that contains most of the postcard views of the city, was immune from creeping favelization. Built on hills that tower over bays, lagoons, and the Atlantic Ocean, the decrepit shacks of some of Rio's largest shantytowns are perched in a medinalike maze of dark corridors and mud alleys just a stone's throw from the gleaming Southern Zone, forcing an uneasy comingling of rich and poor. One former chief of the PM mused, "I don't know anywhere else where these contrasts live side by side."[6] While *favelas* provide the bustling city with most of its cheap labor, they have also become a breeding ground for the drug traffic—a trade perceived by many poor adolescents as the only means of achieving the consumption standards they observe all around them.

A Difficult Dichotomy

The average police officer in Rio inhabits the First World by day and goes home to the Third World at night. While on duty, police officers protect middle-class and elite neighborhoods from the predatory activities of people of their own social class; they tend solicitously to the needs of tourists, to whom the municipality provides various comforts and services that the typical officer's own neighborhood lacks. Officers are widely scorned by the same communities they attempt to protect from drug wars. The open presence of armed drug traffickers in the *favelas* is an affront to police officers' training, which conditions PMs to defend the state monopoly of the legitimate use of force.[7] Nevertheless, it was due to the state's reluctance to assert its presence in such areas that the drug gangs took possession of them.

The state is particularly absent from the Northern Zone, a grim industrial district where beaches and boulevards are nowhere to be found. The Northern Zone is home to many working-class communities and to some of Rio's meanest *favelas* as well, built near putrid swamps, landfills, or chemical waste. Here there are few jobs, recreation facilities, or public services; unlike Southern Zone *favelas* such as Rocinha or Pavão-Pavãozinho, here you will see no foreign tourists coming for organized *"favela* tours."[8] Since the rise of the drug trade, a "safe-conduct" must be negotiated in advance with the drug lords whenever public officials wish to enter into "occupied territories." It is the drug lords, and not the neighborhood associations, who enforce "the law of the hills" (*a lei do morro*), deciding what, how, and when things will be done. In a few cases, drug bosses have shown cunning ability to gain adherents, either by parading a flashy lifestyle or through Robin Hood–like actions such as distributing free medicines, buying school supplies, and providing meals; most frequently, however, they control their community through brutality and intimidation.

Indeed, social progress, except in the form of token modernization, would pose a serious threat to traffickers' profits and modus operandi, as the unpaved and twisting alleys of the *favelas* offer ideal hiding places, while lack of opportunity provides them with steady streams of willing young recruits. According to one investigative report published in a prominent newsweekly, by 1987 Rio dealers took an estimated US$10 million per month.[9] By 2004, the drug trade had expanded so dramatically that the same source estimated that this was now the monthly take by dealers in the Rocinha *favela* alone.[10] Another study estimated that drug trafficking generated 9,000 jobs, noting that police estimates placed this figure even higher: 11,340 jobs spread out among 4,800 leaders, 4,400 "soldiers," 1,400 lookouts, and 740 sellers (Resende 1995: 46, 207). Based on his own sources, the mayor of Rio declared in 2002 that there were 10,000 heavily armed traffickers operating in local *favelas*.[11] According to a former chief of the PM, not only does the drug trade feed most crime in the city,[12] but "the life of one in five *cariocas* is under the traffic's direct control."[13]

A Militarized Approach

As is the case for the PFA in Argentina, the militarized attributes of the uniformed police have hindered the PM's capacity to evolve into a force capable of rendering a broader public service role. In Brazil, however, public mistrust of the police has stemmed not so much from their participation in repressive activities during the military regime as from the fact that the police still closely mirror military tactics, where the need to defeat or eliminate an enemy through force, with no value judgment, is paramount. Such "overwhelming" force is normal in war, where the goal is to "gain total supremacy over an enemy" (Brodeur 1999: 80); modern policing, on the other hand, rests on a minimal use of force. Moreover, the application of a militaristic modus operandi to policing detracts from the flexibility needed to formulate suitable responses to complex situations.

Training

The rigidly stratified structure of the PM does not encourage self-improvement efforts: a high school diploma has been required of all recruits only since 1992. Regulations limit mobility between ranks, so an individual who has not gone to officer training school while unmarried and under the age of twenty-five cannot rise to become a lieutenant or above. There will always be six ranks above this person; even a master's degree will not change the situation. A high premium is placed on personal loyalty and internal discipline; promotion often depends on it. Denouncing corruption or abuse of authority can make a police officer liable to sanctions, demotion, imprisonment, or expulsion. Indeed, a PM is prohibited from making statements to the press or talking about the institution without permission from the high command.

Initial training for low-ranking *praças* (who represent roughly 85 percent of the institution) lasts only six months, as compared to three years for the officer class. One investigative report published in a prominent newspaper claimed that due to lack of funds, new recruits could fire only fifty shots in the course of training.[14] Merit recognition in the PM derives primarily from a quantitative orientation: fulfilling arrest quotas, capturing armaments and drugs, and the like. If a judge releases a suspect due to improper police procedure, the only fact entered into PM statistics is the arrest itself. It is numbers that provide recognition for individual police officers and praise for a particular precinct. In the words of a mid-level PM, "The problem with *preventive* policing is that since no crime takes place, it does not show up in the statistics. The government is interested in showing numbers; it is for the same reason that they prefer to invest in new cars rather than in improving the intelligence and investigative capacity of the police."[15]

Heavy-Handed Tactics

There can be little argument that the police in Rio, and indeed throughout Brazil, routinely use excessive force. Some public officials have argued that both the PM and the PC resort to excessive violence because they are backward and inefficient (Soares 1999). But the reasons run far deeper than inefficiency per se. As previously noted, police brutality dates back to the time of slavery, when the primary police role was to suppress all forms of incipient rebellion. This ethos of violence was reinforced by the free rein that the police were given to crush subversion during the period of military rule. Further boosting police immunity was an amnesty law passed in 1979 that barred prosecution of military or police officers for crimes committed during this period (Human Rights Watch 1997: 21). As a result of this amnesty, many police officers schooled in repression remained in the force. As put by Paulo

Sérgio Pinheiro, "In today's war on crime, the PM behave as if they were confronting an 'internal enemy' who must be liquidated" (Pinheiro 1991: 173). This tendency is partly evinced by a study carried out by a sociologist at the Institute for Studies on Religion (ISER), a prominent Rio-based NGO that conducts religious and human rights studies in addition to sociological research. In analyzing the years 1993–1996, he found that the Rio police rarely fired to immobilize: half of those they killed were found with four or more bullets, most often in the head and shoulders. A significant number of cases showed execution-style deaths, with victims shot at close range after being restrained. In many cases, forensic examination revealed that victims had not attempted to resist arrest or were unarmed (Cano 1997: 70–78). In a chilling reversal of policing patterns elsewhere, the same study found that the PM killed on average two and a half as many as they injured (Cano 1997: 30). Despite a 1997 law making torture a crime, reaffirmed by the 1988 constitution, torture is still used as a means of punishing criminal suspects and of extracting confessions, information, or money (UNCHR 2001). A former public security state secretary admitted, "We are trying to move our system away from the procurement of confessions, towards the production of proof, but we are not there yet."[16]

Throughout the 1990s, human rights organizations made public numerous cases of police brutality. In spite of the severity of the charges, their cause did not find a receptive audience, in part because the human rights movement in Brazil has not gained the prominence it reached in Argentina.[17] Brazilian society is more conservative, rural lore is deeply ingrained among the poor, and the notion of an eye for an eye remains culturally strong across the board. The value of universal human rights is far from being widely embraced: a large proportion of the population holds the view that only upright and hardworking citizens should be entitled to human rights. According to one NGO representative, the popular classes draw a clear distinction between abuse of an honest "worker" (*trabalhador*) and abuse of a criminal (*marginal*). While the killing of a *trabalhador* by the police is usually met by public outrage, reaction is exactly the opposite when the victim is a suspected criminal.[18]

In 1995, a human rights group analysis of official police records of civilians killed by the police revealed that on-duty PM officers killed 287 civilians in Rio City, as compared to 27 police casualties in the entire state—a ratio of 13:1 (Cano 1997: 29).[19] According to Paul Chevigny, an expert on police violence, when the ratio of civilians to police officers killed exceeds 10:1, it suggests that deadly force rather than self-defense is being employed (1991: 192). To provide an indication of just how high Brazil's figures are: in the United States, a country that in 1995 had a population of more than 250 million relative to Rio State's some 13 million, 389 civilians were justifiably killed by the police in the line of duty relative to 74 police deaths (a ratio of 5:2). And police brutality is not confined to Rio de Janeiro. According to the São Paulo ombudsman, the PM in São Paulo State killed 1,421 civilians in 1992. While this figure fell to 577 in 1999, the ombudsman reported that 57.5 percent of those killed did not have prior police records; this places in doubt police claims that the majority of the victims had died in shoot-outs with the police (Ouvidoria SP 1999: 48).

Interviews conducted by the Inter-American Commission on Human Rights (IACHR) with the PM in both Rio and São Paulo reveal a staunch belief that killing suspected criminals, not detaining them, is the most effective means of fighting crime (IACHR 1997: ch. 3, sec. 48). To a large extent, this view emanates from the perception that the investigative police are corrupt and inefficient; it also derives from overall police mistrust of the judiciary and the prison system. Accordingly, many PMs opt to serve as both judge and executioner, particularly when there is actual or suspected involvement by such marginalized groups as blacks, the poor, the unemployed, "street girls," or "street boys" (IACHR 1997: ch. 3, sec. 16). When the PM enters a *favela* it is often with the mentality and tactics of an occupying army: the main entry points are "strangled" to prevent the transit of criminals and drugs, massive house searches are conducted, and people are detained on flimsy grounds. In some cases, the flag of a particular police battalion is raised as a symbol that the area has been taken over by the police. During my visit to the Complexo do Alemão, a Northern Zone *favela*, I observed the black flag with white crossbones of the Special Operations Battalion, known as the BOPE (an elite squad used in high-risk situations), flying from a pole erected at the highest point in the *favela*.

Following the democratic *abertura* process, when police violence came under increasing attack by human rights organizations, many disgruntled officers joined death squads to mete out a quick brand of justice under a cloak of anonymity. Although their primary targets were adult members of the criminal underworld, homeless children as young as seven were also summarily executed. The belief that these derelict youngsters were a threat to society, while not universally shared, was widespread, particularly among business owners, who complained that street children scared away customers. According to the Center for Reporting Extermination Squads, an organization established by the Rio State government, of 159 persons arrested between April 1991 and June 1993 for involvement in death squads, 53 were PM officers (IACHR 1997: ch. 3, sec. 36–41). By the early 1990s, Rio State had already identified more than 180 death squads; according to an anonymous survey, 22 percent of PM officers had been approached to join a death squad (Human Rights Watch 1993: 19). In other cases, death squads were formed by armed persons seeking to guarantee the safety of their own neighborhood, or by security guards hired by merchants and shopkeepers to protect their businesses (Panizza and Barahona de Brito 1998: 37). Because security guards routinely lost their jobs if they did not stop robbery attempts, they tended toward extreme violence in their methods.

Opposing a death squad was extremely risky. In Rio alone, thirty-one community leaders who complained about their actions were executed by death squads between 1991 and 1993 (IACHR 1997: ch. 3, sec. 43). Reportedly, local police authorities did not often interfere with their activities, either due to their own involvement or because death squads were considered by many a necessary evil to rid slums of their criminal element. Some residents of working-class areas depended on the police to resolve interpersonal conflicts and to "put the squeeze" on thieves to return stolen property (Cerqueira 1994: 15). The general public showed tolerance to varying degrees, in the belief that death squads, while ruthless, were able at least to administer justice expeditiously. In fact, due to a combination of factors such as intimidation of witnesses and prosecutors, the slow pace of investigations, and the overall inefficiency of the judiciary in reaching sentence, many death squads operated with total impunity.

Resources

Like the PFA in Buenos Aires, the police in Rio frequently complain about the level of resources allocated to the institution.[20] Although personnel expenditures represent 90 percent of the PM budget, salaries for the average officer are very low, and operational budgets are continually affected by serious deficits. In part, this is attributable to the fact that public security resources must be divided between the two separate and competing police entities: the PM and PC have their own vehicles, training institutions, pension schemes, hospitals (the PM itself has two), and social benefits. Public security resources are further stretched by the fact that police doctors, drivers, forensic specialists, photographers, and the like are not hired as civilians but as police personnel. These peripheral personnel, who carry a badge and gun and receive pensions and other social entitlements similar to those of staff carrying out security tasks, constitute a significant drain on public security resources.

Mainly, however, public security resources were sharply cut following the transitional period from military rule, as illustrated by Figure 8.1, even though crime increased dramatically over the same period. Not only were public security resources reduced as part of overall budget cuts, but their percentage of the total state budget also decreased significantly through the 1980s and 1990s.

As discussed in the previous chapter, when Leonel Brizola became governor of Rio State in 1983, during the political *abertura* period, he immediately sought to distance himself from the worst abuses of the military

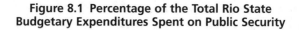

Figure 8.1 Percentage of the Total Rio State
Budgetary Expenditures Spent on Public Security

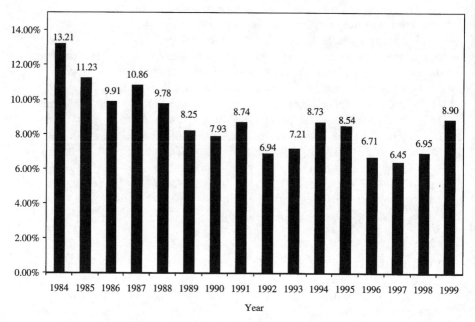

Source: Tribunal de Contas do Estado de Rio de Janeiro (1986–1999); 1984 and 1985 figures based on Tribunal de Contas statistics cited in Teixeira (1994).

government. One of his strategies was to slash the percentage of budget expenditures for public security. Although the governor was sending a clear message that intimidation and force were no longer permissible policing methods, no comprehensive alternative was put forward to contain crime. By the mid-1990s, with drug-related crime spilling over from the *favelas* into the city at large, allocations for public security began to climb back, as shown in Figure 8.2, although allocated funds did not come close to meeting the need to bring police technology, training, and salaries up to competitive standards.

Pay Scales

Even though efforts have been under way to improve low police salaries in some Latin American countries, the problem remains serious throughout the region. In Brazil, salaries are so inadequate that the PM has often resorted to strikes, leaving the population bereft of even minimal protection. In July 1997, for example, the PM carried out strikes in seventeen out of twenty-six

Figure 8.2 Rio State Public Security Budget Expenditures

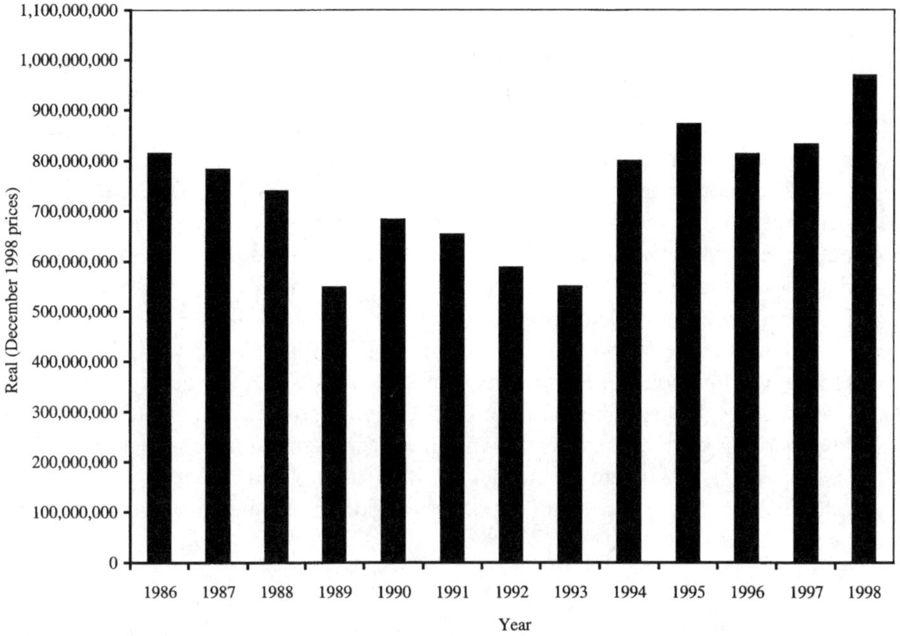

Source: Tribunal de Contas do Estado de Rio de Janeiro (1986–1999).

states, with roughly 30,000 persons participating out of a total force of 360,000 PMs. Four years later, the PM went on strike again in the northeastern states of Bahia, Alagoas, Paraná, and Tocantins, while threatening work stoppages in the state of São Paulo and ten others.

Although in Rio State threats of police strikes did not materialize, salaries were at the lower end of the spectrum, as shown in Table 8.1.[21] This table compares salaries of the lowest three ranks (corporal, soldier first class, and soldier second class) with the top three ranks (colonel, lieutenant colonel, major) across selected states.

As in Buenos Aires, low police salaries spawned myriad informal-sector activities, many of them illegal. In Rio, an estimated 90 percent of police officers were forced to seek a second job. The debate over secondary employment (the *lei do bico,* as it is known) goes back two decades: from the 1980s onward, second jobs have been alternatively sanctioned, outlawed, and sanctioned again. Whereas in Buenos Aires officers were hired through the PFA itself, in Rio they were hired directly by private security companies or by neighborhood shop owners and residents seeking extra protection. But as many private security companies were owned either by active and retired high-ranking police officers or by politicians, in a sense the state was competing with itself, given that panic over poor policing fed the need for private protection.

Long second shifts, moreover, further downgrade the efficiency of the police. Because controls over officers' activities as private security guards are even weaker than over their regular job, the temptation to use whatever methods are available in the course of duty runs high—especially because failure to apprehend thieves is punished by dismissal. Table 8.2 reveals the strikingly higher incidence of death and injury for police officers while off duty, presumably while working on second shifts, although some numbers may be a function of death squad activities, and others may have resulted from late night travel back home.

In an interview, one former chief of the PC expressed the view that the problem of low police wages persists not due to lack of funds but by design. Low salaries, he argued, guarantee that nearly all police will come from the lowest rungs of society, thus making the task of containing the poor seem less oppressive.[22] There is, further, another crucial advantage to keeping salaries low: they ensure that the police will continue to be receptive to elite

Table 8.1 Military Police Gross Salaries per Month, Selected States of Brazil and Federal District (August 1997 prices in US$)

	Rio de Janeiro	Amapá	Brasilia	São Paulo	Rio Grande do Sul
Top three ranks					
Colonel	2,323.23	3,813.85	3,567.89	5,219.37	7,817.10
Lieutenant colonel	2,021.59	3,450.84	3,265.59	4,779.25	7,394.71
Major	1,542.66	3,088.76	2,821.37	4,163.11	3,921.01
Bottom three ranks					
Corporal	535.96	679.60	705.23	825.22	483.97
Soldier first class	490.75	555.47	614.32	768.22	463.86
Soldier second class	295.00	530.86	441.06	642.65	434.87

Source: Conselho Nacional de Comandantes Gerais das Polícias Militares, cited in Garotinho et al. (1998: 83).

Table 8.2 Military Policemen Killed and Wounded in Rio State, 1991–April 1998

Killed while on duty	169
Killed while off duty	1,101
Wounded while on duty	3,082
Wounded while off duty	4,206

Source: PM of Rio State, cited in Garotinho et al. (1998: 77).

co-optation. Whether through bribery or the promise of political favors, the Brazilian police have often turned a blind eye to malfeasance in high places. And given the slippery slope between passive and active corruption, they have all too often been involved in criminal activity themselves. Transgressions ranging from extortion to prostitution to drugs, arms dealing, and even "rental" of police guns for criminal use add up to a network of corruption that has flourished in a climate of weak oversight.

Internal and External Controls

In countries where the traditional repressive role of the police has not been fully vanquished and corruption remains rampant, such as Argentina and Brazil, the need to impose systematic and enforceable civilian oversight is self-evident. Moreover, when the threat of violence comes not only from criminals but from rogue police elements as well, the need for internal controls is also imperative, since the police cannot expect to gain credibility until the rot is curtailed from within. But can Brazil's police become a model of probity and efficiency?

Self-Policing

As in many police institutions throughout the world, attempts by the Rio police to cleanse its own machinery have been complicated by custom and practice. The rigid hierarchical structure of the police discourages direct access to superiors; even when encouraged by a reform-minded chief to denounce misconduct, few police ever do, perhaps because lower-ranking officers are frequently turned into scapegoats while superior officers are rarely held accountable. Since the average tenure of a chief is very short, moreover, the benefits for a whistle-blower are transitory, while the risk of expulsion or revenge is considerable due to unwritten codes of silence. Table 8.3 provides a good illustration of these points.

In principle, officers in each PM battalion are required to conduct frequent car patrols to ensure that the "foot soldiers" are stationed at their posts and doing their job. In practice, however, there is wide latitude for discretionary activity. Although PMs are required to carry arms at all times (in addition to the official-issue gun, police typically carry their own weapon and buy their own bullets), filing a detailed report after a weapon is drawn or discharged is not a standard requirement.

Serious cases of police misconduct, many of which are brought to light by the media through a network of informants, are investigated by an internal affairs division (*corregedoria*), an institution whose role was formally strengthened in May 2000 under the Garotinho administration, which unified

Table 8.3 Expulsions from the Rio Military Police

	Officers	Lower-ranking Military Police
1994	0	96
1995	1	57
1996	1	61
1997	0	86
1998	0	81
1999	2	57

Source: Secretaría de Segurança Pública, RJ; published in "Policiais a Serviço do Crime," *O Globo,* July 2, 2000.

the internal affairs of the PM and PC.[23] Most instances of police misconduct are punished by light sanctions; when pressure becomes intense, officers are fined, temporarily imprisoned, or transferred to distant outposts in Rio State, where illegal activity can continue relatively undisturbed since oversight mechanisms are even more lax.

External Controls

As discussed in Chapter 5, the overarching framework for Brazil's police is determined by the 1988 constitution and by the federal penal and procedural codes, which assign operational responsibility for police performance to each individual state. Although all three branches of government are meant to exert oversight over the police, in most states it is the governor who exerts undisputed authority. Issues of power and control are magnified by jurisdictional and political disputes with city mayors, as is evidenced by the situation in Rio de Janeiro.[24]

State Secretariat of Public Security. Although the municipality of Rio represents less than 5 percent of the state's physical territory, more than 50 percent of crime in the state is concentrated here. There are roughly 23,400 police to patrol Rio and Rio State, with respective populations of 5.6 million and 13.8 million.[25] Institutionally, responsibility for control and oversight of the police in Rio State rests with the Secretariat of Public Security.[26] The secretariat advises the governor on appointments of police chiefs, develops crime-fighting strategies, establishes policy guidelines, coordinates the activities of both the PM and the PC, and monitors the Internal Affairs Division. Although all these functions are in principle accountable to civilian oversight, in the 1990s elements from the armed forces and the PM tended to predominate in secretariat ranks; experiments with civilian appointees have usually been derailed by opposition from both the PM and the PC.

As long as the secretary manages to work in tandem with both chiefs to prevent public security from becoming a political liability, governors tend to allow wide latitude to the position. More often than not, however, secretaries are fired summarily, as is also the case with police chiefs and other top security officials. A new personal style, new directives, and new standards arrive with each new appointee. This, coupled with ideological shifts at the gubernatorial level, is one of the main factors that have made depoliticization of the Rio police an extremely difficult process. These and related issues will be discussed in greater detail in Chapter 9.

State legislative and judicial oversight. As in Argentina, national public security was the sole domain of Brazil's military for so long that when democratic governance was resumed, few legislators and judges had the essential know-how required to guide the modernization of the police forces or exert forceful control. This applies even today, particularly at the state level, where a lack of public security specialists is further compounded by the governor's undue influence in the whole process. Legislative input in the budget process remains nominal; the Rio State Legislature, for example, rarely modifies the budget presented by the governor, of which security forms part; if interference should happen, the governor can later modify the budget by decree.[27] Thus, crucial decisions directly affecting the security and very lives of the citizenry continue to be made without informed scrutiny or debate.

Still, during the 1990s, the Rio State Legislature attempted to establish more control over security issues. It mandated that special commissions, both temporary and permanent, investigate egregious cases of police brutality or suspected involvement in drug trafficking and corruption. Permanent standing committees, such as the Commission for the Defense of Human Rights and Citizenship and the Commission of Public Security and Police Affairs, were charged with studying legal reform projects with other public servants and members of civil society, who were invited to air their concerns.[28]

As stated by the 1988 constitution, the judicial branch at the state level has a potentially stronger legal framework for control of the security forces, but this capacity has gone largely unrealized. According to the document, "no one shall be arrested unless *in flagrante delicto* or following a written and justified order of a competent judicial authority"[29] An individual arrested in flagrante can be held for only twenty-four hours before a provisional detention warrant is issued by a judge; after this period, a family member must also be notified of the arrest and of the location of the detainee.[30] In practice, however, the PM often continues to arrest and hold suspects outside of legal limits. According to an investigation by the Special Rapporteur to the UN Economic and Social Council on Questions of Torture and Detention, "There is a tendency to carry out arrests later classified as *in flagrante* even when the individual is not actually caught in the act, but is under strong suspicion that he/she took part in criminal activities." The Rapporteur added that in many cases, the police had "planted criminal evidence, such as weapons or narcotics, on persons allegedly arrested *in flagrante*" (UNCHR 2001: 34).

The persistence of such conduct is enabled by the poor quality of legal assistance available to most crime suspects. An estimated 85 percent of detainees cannot afford legal counsel; in fact, owing to backlogs in the public defender's office, most suspects do not meet with their lawyer until the day of the trial (US Department of State 1996: sec. E). The fact that Brazil is one of the few Latin American countries that have maintained the practice of a preliminary criminal investigation carried out by the police alone helps to foster this state of affairs (UNCHR 2001: 34). According to the National Code of Criminal Procedure (art. 5), whenever a judge, the Office of the Public Prosecutor,[31] a victim, or the police themselves become aware of any violation to the penal code, the PC must open a police inquiry (*inquêrito policial*) without delay. While it is the Office of the Public Prosecutor that determines whether sufficient evidence exists to warrant an indictment, the initial reconstruction of the truth is carried out by the PC *on its own* (Kant de Lima 1995). The flaws of this system are magnified by the fact that although judges dismiss numerous cases outright for insufficient evidence and/or procedural violations, there is no system of regular feedback to the police so they can take remedial action to avoid similar irregularities in the future. In addition, police accountability is compromised by the fact that the shifting nature of work assignments in the PC exempts a precinct head (*delegado*) from full responsibility for any given investigation.

In cases where there are allegations of torture or other serious misconduct by the police, the Office of the Public Prosecutor can open its own criminal inquiry. Unfortunately, judicial authorities typically experience significant difficulties in gathering evidence and identifying responsible parties because, fearing reprisals, witnesses often refuse to come forward. This fear is grounded on numerous assassination attempts on witnesses,[32] in spite of a witness protection program. Other factors, such as an underpaid and overworked staff, police codes of silence, and intimidation of forensic pathologists, further hinder the capacity of the Office of the Public Prosecutor to carry out independent investigations.[33] Therefore, except in high-profile cases where political pressure escalates, the office must usually rely upon the Internal Affairs Unit of the police to carry out corruption inquiries.

Conclusion

The Brazilian police's reliance on brutality and intimidation tactics can be traced back to their original role during the empire, when the court of the exiled Portuguese royal family gave them virtual free rein to contain slave revolts and maintain public order. In the twentieth century, during the Vargas era and later, the police were subsumed to the military and used for repressive purposes against political opponents and the civilian population at large, much in the same way as were the police in Argentina at different times in their history.

Following Brazil's transition from military rule to electoral democracy, the crucial questions of what new role the police should have and what methods they should use to combat rising drug trafficking and crime were not fully settled. The legislative branch lacked technical expertise on security issues and the strength to stand up to governors' political dominance. The judiciary was burdened by cumbersome procedures and entangled in a maze of constitutional and penal issues that could not be easily resolved. Internally, the control mechanisms of the police were rendered almost futile by codes of silence and by the practice of scapegoating low-ranking cadres instead of punishing their superior officers. In the absence of firm external direction and the added problem that the State Secretariat of Public Security was frequently a pawn of the governor, the pursuit of standardized professional codes for the police remained a casualty of political capriciousness. Beset by low levels of professionalism, a dual and antagonistic structure, inadequate pay scales, and a continuing culture of vigilantism, the police were regarded with fear and distrust by Brazilians of all social classes.

In the 1990s, when unprecedented levels of crime and drug trafficking were turning Rio into a virtual battleground, it became imperative to systematically address these complex and wide-ranging problems. But were government authorities up to the task of reform? The next chapter examines the successive strategies adopted.

Notes

1. Some large cities also have their own small municipal police forces, and at the federal level there is a relatively small FBI-style force, the Federal Police.

2. Formally, the top rank in the PM is known as the commander in chief (*commandante geral da Polícia Militar*), while the top job in the PC is chief of the Civil Police (*chefe da Polícia Civil*). For simplicity's sake, both will be referred to as chief.

3. It was the French, by way of Portugal, who introduced the institutional model of the intendency in the mid-1700s. But unlike the French, the Portuguese organized the police not as a national force but as a state force, as in Rio de Janeiro when the city was the capital of the empire. In 1832, the intendent became the chief of police. The 1871 judicial reform, however, eliminated the judicial powers of the police. Police chiefs and *delegados* (precinct heads) were still required to gather evidence to build a case against suspects, but formal prosecution, evaluation, and sentencing decisions were handed over to public prosecutors or judges. See Holloway (1993: 32, 247) and Bretas (1997: 40–42).

4. Constitution of Brazil, ch. 3, art. 144, para. 4, sec 5.

5. See IBGE (2000, 2002).

6. Author interview, June 9, 2001.

7. This Weberian concept was one of the first things cited in many interviews with police officers.

8. Since the early 1990s, various tour operators have obtained permission from drug traffickers for organized jaunts into Rocinha and other Southern Zone *favelas.*

9. See "A Explosão de Droga Nos Guetos do Rio," *Isto É,* September 2, 1987.

10. See "Vazio de Poder," *Isto É,* April 21, 2004.

11. "Tráfico Tem 10 Mil Homens," *Extra,* May 28, 2002.

12. Author interview, July 11, 2001.

13. "Narcoditadura, o Poder Cada Vez Menos Paralelo no Rio," *O Globo,* June 25, 2002.

14. See "Treinamento de PM Consiste em 50 Tiros," *Jornal do Brasil,* August 4, 1996.

15. Interview with Captain Rodrigo Pimentel, "Entrevista com Capitão Rodrigo Pimentel," *Jornal do Brasil,* November 28, 1999.

16. Author interview, July 12, 2001.

17. This is perhaps a function of the fact that the process of democratic transition in Brazil lasted much longer and was efficiently controlled by the military. In contrast, in Argentina the dictatorship ended swiftly, and with a military much derided for its defeat in the Falkland Islands War in addition to its seven years of failed economic policies and fierce state repression.

18. Author interview, July 25, 2001.

19. Had data been available for the number of police officers killed in Rio City as opposed to the Rio State as a whole, the author of the study believed that this ratio would have been even higher, as he estimates that many of the police casualties occurred outside the city in the surrounding metropolitan area.

20. Interview with Josias Quintal, secretary of Public Security, "Entrevista com Josias Quintal," *Jornal do Brasil,* August 23, 1999.

21. By comparison, an entry-level officer in the New York Police Department in 1997 had a monthly base salary of US$2,319.83; those in the middle rank earned $4,106.25, and those in the top rank $11,083.33. See Bureau of Justice Statistics (1997).

22. Author interview, June 19, 2001.

23. Lei 3403 (Corregedoria Geral Unificada), Assembléia Legislativa do Estado do Rio de Janeiro, May 15, 2000.

24. Some of Brazil's larger cities, such as Rio and São Paulo, have control over the Municipal Guard, a relatively small force whose functions are limited by the constitution to the protection of public buildings, property, and installations. See 1988 constitution, ch. 3, art. 144, sec. 8. In Rio this force has existed only since 1993, has fewer than 5,500 members, and does not carry firearms.

25. These are 1999 statistics from CIDE (2001). If the municipalities surrounding Rio are considered, the size of the Rio metropolitan area is 10.3 million or roughly 76 percent of the state. Rio is the second largest Brazilian city after São Paulo.

26. The Secretaria de Segurança Pública was created during the government of Marcello Alencar by Decree 21.258 on January 1, 1995. Although a similar institution had previously existed, Governor Brizola abolished it upon assuming office in 1983, perceiving it as a vestige of the military regime. The institution was subsequently separated into two distinct secretariats, one for the PM and one for the PC, until eventually it was unified again.

27. In 2000, the Rio State Legislature added an amendment to the budget prohibiting the transfer of resources from health, education, sanitation, and public security to other sectors, although the governor could still make changes of up to 20 percent of the total budget in other areas without consulting the legislature. A year later, however, the governor initiated a bill that would enable him to make changes to at least 10 percent of the funds allocated to the restricted categories—which the legislature also approved.

28. The Comissão de Defesa dos Direitos Humanos e Cidadania and Comissão de Segurança Pública e Assuntos de Polícia, respectively. The former was tied to left-leaning representatives, while the latter was identified with police interests.

29. Constitution of Brazil, ch. 1, art. 5, sec. 61.

30. Ibid., art. 5, sec. 62.

31. The Office of the Public Prosecutor (Ministério Público) is the primary state prosecution agency. It is staffed by prosecutors (*promotores*), who, inter alia, are charged with exercising external control of the police. See arts. 127–129 of the constitution.

32. In 1993, the key witness in the notorious Candelária Church case (where eight street children were executed by the police while sleeping at the foot of its steps) was shot twice in the head while under the protection of the state-run Witness Safe House (Casa de Testemunha). The witness survived but was forced to flee to Switzerland under the protection of Amnesty International.

33. The Forensic Medical Institute (IML) is subordinated to the State Secretariat of Public Security, which, as previously mentioned, is typically staffed with personnel from police circles. Many human rights reports have alleged that the PC unduly influences IML reports (UNCHR 2001: 49). In a controversial case, a judge ordered the exhumation of seventeen out of twenty-one victims of the Vigário Geral massacre, in which more than fifty police officers had been implicated, because of forensic irregularities.

CHAPTER 9

Reform the Brazilian Way

In the 1990s, the public security situation in Brazil's largest cities had deteriorated to such a point that it consistently ranked at the top of public concerns; in Rio de Janeiro, every gubernatorial campaign hinged on promises to improve it. Proposals to crack down on police corruption and human rights abuses and plans to modernize the institution and strengthen its controls were not in short supply at either the federal or state level. This chapter will survey these proposals. Unfortunately, however, the reform process was carried out in such an inconstant and disjointed way that the commitment and intentions of government authorities must be scrutinized anew. Nowhere was this more evident that in Rio de Janeiro, where over the course of the 1990s, four different governors adopted policies that reversed or suspended the efforts of their predecessors.

The Federal Level: Plans, Laws, and New Institutions

As previously noted, the federal government is responsible for the broad constitutional and legal framework of the Brazilian police, although the onus of implementing these laws and overseeing the police lies with each state. This power-sharing arrangement has created frequent conflict between the federal and state governments, which regularly trade blame whenever a serious security crisis erupts. In the 1990s, the federal government was prodded into adopting a more proactive role, as a series of human rights scandals brought scathing criticism from the international community, tearing at Brazil's self-image as an emerging economic power and racial haven. In the aftermath of media broadcasts showcasing a litany of unpunished abuses—such as indebted peonage, exploitation of minors, police extermination of street children, and contract killings—the federal government obtained quick legislative approval for new programs designed to improve its record and its

125

negative image abroad. Respected agencies such as Amnesty International, the International Commission of the Red Cross, and Scotland Yard were invited to come to Brazil to provide human rights training.

As was the case in Argentina, much of the legislation was initiated as a political response to a specific crisis, rather than as part of extensive and considered public policy deliberations regarding public security and police reform. Over time, the sustainability of such programs was decreased by the fact that in some cases states' compliance was left conditional and elective. Programs were also launched without adequate institutional frameworks to allow viable monitoring by federal authorities. Other programs, while loaded with good intentions, showed a notable disconnect with local realities. Two of the most heralded federal initiatives, the Statute of the Child and Adolescent and the National Human Rights Program, are cases in point.

The Statute of the Child and Adolescent

In April 1990, less than one month after assuming office, President Fernando Collor de Mello[1] launched his National Plan for the Prevention and Reduction of Violence Against Street Children. Following intensive lobbying by human rights organizations in the aftermath of scandals involving police violence against street children in Brazil's largest urban centers, he also signed into law a highly progressive piece of legislation for children's rights, known as the Statute of the Child and Adolescent (ECA).[2]

The ECA calls for the "comprehensive protection" of the civil, economic, and social rights of children. It contains specific articles on due process for minors (children under eighteen), specifying conditions under which they can be detained and imprisoned (up to three years), and establishing the separation of inmates by sex, age, physical size, and nature of the offense. The ECA also mandates that young offenders be provided with opportunities for resocialization, leisure, work, interaction with their community, and medical and psychological treatment.[3]

At the time of launching, the ECA was hailed as one of the most encompassing pieces of child legislation in the world. It has, nevertheless, been "routinely disregarded since its inception," according to several human rights monitors (Human Rights Watch 1994: 20)—which is hardly surprising, since the conditions and standards it set for children's rights were profoundly dissonant with the deep poverty and inequality that continues to afflict much of Brazil. In 1999, almost 35 percent of all Brazilian children and adolescents—more than 20 million—were estimated to be living in poverty. In the same year more than 2.9 million children aged fourteen and under were believed to be working with their parents under conditions akin to debt bondage or forced labor, even as thirty-three programs within five government ministries were devoted to fighting child labor. Child prostitution remained a

significant social problem, even though as of 1999 there were forty programs run by national and international NGOs and government agencies
designed to combat the phenomenon (US Department of State 2000: sec.
4, and 2002: sec. 4).

More than a decade after its enactment, many ECA stipulations remain
unfamiliar to criminal justice system institutions, which are still governed by
old stereotypes and misconceptions about the treatment of young offenders.
Abuse and illegal imprisonment of street children by police continue
throughout the country; gross overcrowding is the norm in most juvenile
detention centers, most of which have scarce or nonexistent rehabilitation
and counseling opportunities. Opponents of the ECA have called for its re-
peal, based on the perception that "soft" punishment of minors has encouraged drug dealers to exploit them. Some have even claimed that the
ECA's "permissiveness" has actually spurred extrajudicial executions by
police who believed that otherwise young criminals would escape punishment.[4] In the meantime, homicide has become the leading cause of death for
children aged ten to fourteen (US Department of State 2002: sec. 4).

National Human Rights Plan

When President Collor resigned to avoid impeachment for corruption, Itamar Franco assumed an interim presidency (1992–1995), declaring that his
main focus in office would be to restore Brazil's flagging economy and control hyperinflation. On the very day he was sworn in, however, his attention
was diverted from economic issues. On October 2, 2002, the São Paulo PM
stormed Carandirú Prison[5] to quell an inmate riot, killing 111 prisoners. It
was the worst prison massacre in Brazilian history, and the investigation
would continue for more than nine years.[6] Determined to avoid a similar
entanglement, Franco's finance minister and successor, Fernando Henrique
Cardoso (1995–2002), declared shortly after assuming office, "The time has
come for us to demonstrate in practice and at the national level that we will
put an end to impunity, and that we are going to fight to ensure that human
rights are respected" (quoted in Pinheiro 1999: 45). As a noted sociologist
with several published books, President Cardoso had credentials in this area
that were impeccable. Nevertheless, he was dogged by human rights scandals throughout both his administrations, many involving violent confrontations between the police and the increasingly militant Movement of Landless Rural Workers (MST). In the northern state of Pará, for example, after
failing to disperse a protest by landless peasants with tear gas, the police
killed nineteen protesters. Although the police claimed they were attacked
first, autopsy reports showed that at least ten of the victims were summarily executed: seven were killed with knives and sickles, and three were shot
at point-blank range.[7]

One month later, President Cardoso launched a National Human Rights Program, hailing it as the first of its kind in Latin America. Devised by the Ministry of Justice in conjunction with civil society, the ambitious program included more than 200 measures that were to be implemented by a National Secretariat of Human Rights set up within the ministry. Concurrently, a ministerial working group was appointed to review the status of public security nationwide and draft a comprehensive plan for police reform. Following a period of consultation with ombudsmen, human rights groups, and police and bar associations, a series of sweeping recommendations were drafted, including salary increases for the police, increased human rights training, modernization of police equipment, greater coordination of crime data between the PM and the PC, establishment of ombudsman offices in every state, and community safety councils in all municipalities.

An important corollary to the work of the National Human Rights Program was the 1996 Bicudo Law, which shifted jurisdiction for crimes of "intentional homicide" committed by PM officers from military to civilian courts.[8] Under the previous system, crimes committed by PMs had been tried by a special military tribunal composed of four high-ranking PM officers and one civilian judge, all of which guaranteed accused officers some level of impunity (Pinheiro 1991: 169). The system not only was notoriously overburdened[9] but was also tilted toward exoneration, since most instances of police abuse were classified as administrative errors or "excesses" and thus subject to relatively light sanctions. Thus, shifting cases of intentional police homicide against civilians to regular courts was a milestone in the annals of police reform, albeit a minor one, since under the Bicudo Law, the police still handled the initial inquiry, determined whether the homicide was intentional, and decided if the case should go to trial. In this way, the police retained numerous avenues through which to short-circuit an investigation and prosecution, particularly as the average case took eight years. Compounding this continued lack of accountability, cases involving other crimes such as torture, kidnapping, illegal imprisonment, battery, and extortion remained under the jurisdiction of the military police court system.

Another important legal initiative was a 1997 law that typified the crime of torture, thereby seeking to codify the precepts of the UN Convention Against Torture. This law was initially embraced by human rights groups as an important step toward ending police violence; three years later, however, the UN Special Rapporteur on Torture determined that the law had been "virtually ignored," noting that no convictions had taken place between 1997 (when the law was passed) and March 2000, and confirming that torture was still very prevalent in

> all phases of detention: arrest, preliminary detention, other provisional detention, and in penitentiaries and institutions for juvenile officers. It does not happen to all or everywhere; mainly it happens to the poor, black common

criminals involved in petty crimes or small-scale drug distribution. And it happens in the police stations and custodial institutions through which these types of offenders pass. The purposes range from obtaining information and confessions to the lubrication of systems of financial extortion. (UNCHR 2001: 53–55)

The laws and programs launched under President Cardoso did indeed fill a much-needed vacuum. Nevertheless, as was the case in Argentina, their impact was often more nominal than effective, since instead of evolving out of a systematic evaluation process, they were hastily launched in the aftermath of scandals and contained intrinsic design flaws that virtually guaranteed failure of implementation. The National Human Rights Program, for example, contained dozens of clauses that were not legally mandatory; governors had leeway to select which to comply with and which to ignore. Indeed all parties were keenly aware that the 1988 constitution, which cemented gubernatorial control over local policing, had failed to institutionalize federal oversight of police conduct across the country.

The State Level:
A Cycle of Shifting Standards, Resources, and Priorities

Although state governors were bound by the 1988 constitution to maintain the dual nature of the PM and the PC, they nevertheless had substantial scope to reform and improve existing structures and performance. Instead, successive Rio State governors in the 1990s spent most of their time and resources on an incessant cycle of partial approaches that veered off course even as the drug traffic steadied its hold.

Restraining the Police and Other Civilianizing Attempts: Leonel Brizola (1983–1987, 1991–1994) and Nilo Batista (1994–1995)

As previously mentioned, Leonel Brizola's tenure as the first elected governor of Rio State (1983–1987) was marked by the disastrous outcome of his liberalizing public security policies. But at least these policies constituted a revolution of sorts: by seeking to end police repression as a means to contain the effects of inadequate social policies, Brizola attempted nothing less than a reengineering of the social dynamic. In his Action Plan for the Economic and Social Development of the State of Rio de Janeiro, 1984–1987, Brizola had written of seeking to create "a consciousness among the population that would end the arbitrary nature and impunity with which state authorities operate. The citizen should not have to fear the police, who will be directed to protect rather than repress" (quoted in Cerqueira 2001: 165).

During his first term, Brizola took a series of measures that would eventually wreak havoc with his presidential aspirations and with Rio's public security situation. Determined to prove that a more humane approach to crime fighting could prevail, he sought to dismantle the death squads—which were most active in the *favelas*, where state penetration was low—and ordered a halt to "blitzes" (roadblocks accompanied by spot searches), in which racial profiling was widely used. But it was his order barring the police from "kicking down the doors of shacks" and "arresting and searching suspicious people without judicial authorization" (Cerqueira 2001: 166) that most polarized the city. The powerful media conglomerate Globo almost immediately launched a relentless campaign to ridicule Brizola's security policies, with devastating impact.

Not only was the governor's handpicked candidate for his successor soundly defeated, but the next governor, Wellington Moreira Franco (1987–1991), abandoned Brizola's programs altogether and ordered the resumption of many of the repressive police tactics employed during the military era. By now, however, drug traffickers had powerful connections as well as arsenals; the enormous profits of their trade allowed them to control attempts to subdue them. Having made no significant dent on crime, Moreira Franco's policies failed and directly led to the reelection of Leonel Brizola.

In March 1991, as soon as he assumed office, Brizola reappointed as chief of the PM and state secretary for public security the same Colonel Carlos Magno Nazareth Cerqueira who had served as chief of the PM in Brizola's first gubernatorial term (he was also the first Afro-Brazilian police chief in the country). The vice governor, Nilo Batista (a well-known human rights activist and expert in penal law), was asked to coordinate justice policies statewide. The trio set out to reinstate and expand the humanistic policies that had been blamed for the escalation of crime in Rio during the 1980s. Among other initiatives, they formed Citizen Advisory Committees, made up of representatives from housing associations, churches, schools, and business; created a Central de Denúncias, a predecessor to the ombudsman's office, where citizens could lodge complaints against the police; and established a variant of the US DARE (Drug Abuse and Resistance Education) program to teach school children aged nine to ten to say no to drugs. In the affluent neighborhoods of Leme and Copacabana, they launched a pilot community policing program in conjunction with Viva Rio, a well-known NGO; in the *favelas,* Centers for the Defense of Citizenship (CCDCs) were set up to assist residents with simple legal services.

As had occurred in his first administration, Brizola's policies met with widespread opposition, leading again to his excoriation by the media and the derailment of his second presidential campaign. By giving carte blanche to criminals to violate society's norms, the media alleged, the governor was holding all of Rio hostage to fear. When I asked what had happened the second time around, a former high-ranking aide to Governor Brizola responded that since "everything passes through the federal government and the state government has very little power," all the Brizola team could do was adopt "surface measures" that barely scratched the face of an unjust social order. But, he maintained, at least they kept the police from "running loose" in the *favelas*.[10]

A worsening economic crisis was also laid at Governor Brizola's door, since due to the rise in criminality, industry had embarked on a massive exodus from the convulsed city into calmer pastures, causing unemployment to rise. In early 1992, a few months before Rio was to host the UN-sponsored International Earth Summit, Governor Brizola was forced to ask President Collor for federal troops to guarantee the safety of hundreds of expected foreign visitors. Although the summit took place in an atmosphere of relative calm, the army's presence provided only a temporary palliative. One year later, in the early hours of July 23, 1993, a band of persons suspected of being police officers killed eight street children who were sleeping on the footsteps of the Candelária Church. The following month, a heavily armed police contingent stormed the Vigário Geral *favela* to avenge the death of four of its men, killing twenty-one people.[11]

Once again, the media declared that Rio was in a state of anarchy. Scenes of gangs armed with hand-held rocket launchers and of roving half-naked youths sweeping beaches and other public spaces "like a tidal wave" were relentlessly televised. TV cameras were taken into *bailes funk* (youth dances held mostly in *favelas*, which were increasingly attracting a more affluent clientele), with reporters claiming that they often degenerated into "orgies of sex and violence." Middle-class alarm escalated further when the press revealed that girls were being "scalped" by young criminals using razor blades so their hair could be sold for wigs.

Unable to control traffickers, rogue policemen, or frenzied youth, interim governor Nilo Batista (who succeeded Brizola when the governor stepped down early to campaign for the presidency) signed an accord with interim president Itamar Franco to launch an all-out military operation to rid *favelas* of gangs, drug traffickers, and guns. Dubbed Operation Rio, the campaign lasted from November 1 to December 30, 1994. Under the protection of helicopters, tanks, heavy artillery, and specially trained dogs, thousands of army soldiers and federal police officers, joined by the state PM and PC freshly placed under military command, simultaneously raided several dozen *favelas*, storming houses without warrant and arbitrarily detaining scores of residents (together with some residents of middle-class neighborhoods). To defuse criticism by human rights groups, it was announced that Operation Rio would also implement public works projects (Hunter 1996: ch. 3; Resende 1995). Operation Rio arrested more than 500 people, captured 300 firearms, and confiscated more than 7 kilos of cocaine and 74 kilos of marijuana (Human Rights Watch 1996: 3). In its aftermath, support for the military as an institution ran very high, in stark contrast to interim governor Nilo Batista, who left office with the lowest ratings of any Brazilian governor in the same period.

Later, writing on Operation Rio and the remilitarization of public security that it brought, the former state secretary of security lamented, "We failed to implement and consolidate the democratic model that we defended. . . . We didn't know how to make the police investigate before an arrest; we didn't know how to make the police understand that their main task was to arrest instead of kill" (Cerqueira 2001: 50).

Confrontation or Repression?
Marcello Alencar (1995–1998)

With the "humanitarian" approach to public security once again discredited, Rio voted out the Brizola-backed candidate in favor of Marcello Alencar, who had pledged a complete break with Brizola's policies. His views on the public security situation were made clear in an interview just prior to assuming office:

> The security forces of the state are completely disorganized. . . . There is total anarchy, the police lost all credibility, and the popular classes see them more as criminals than as help. . . . When the police go into the *favelas,* they go to extort and to kill. The local population goes for help to the local criminal boss rather than complain to police precincts. The government has lost control.[12]

A hard-line appointment. Governor Alencar moved swiftly to establish control; leaving nothing to chance, he immediately requested that the federal government again send army troops to patrol the *favelas.* Unhappy with his first secretary of public security, Alencar fired him after barely three months on the job, appointing in his place retired army general Nilton Cerqueira.[13] General Cerqueira had first gained notoriety in the 1970s as the head of an intelligence unit that captured and killed a well-known guerrilla leader in Bahia.[14] Human rights organizations immediately denounced his appointment, calling him a throwback to the repressive military era; in military and police circles, however, General Cerqueira was perceived as a nationalistic and incorruptible hard-liner with intimate knowledge of the police institution, acquired during his term as chief of the Rio PM during the final years of the dictatorship. Having been elected to the national legislature, he resigned his seat following the call by Governor Alencar.

As secretary of public security, General Cerqueira immediately halted Brizola's community policing programs, terming them unsuitable and "elitist" forms of policing that would be incapable of making a dent in the stark

Brazilian reality. "Soldiers of the law and heads of households cannot allow themselves to be killed by criminals," he said, adding that in confrontations "the police, not the criminal, needs to fire the first shot and ask questions later."[15] At the same time, General Cerqueira warned the police that involvement in crime or corruption would not be tolerated. He set up a quota system for apprehension of criminals, drugs, and armaments and reinstated random "blitzes" at key entry points to the city—a move welcomed by the middle class and resented by many dark-skinned *cariocas* who protested that they were being unduly harassed.

Bravery points. The general reintroduced an obscure policy known as "bravery promotions," which had first been codified in 1975. While this policy required the testimony of two impartial witnesses to demonstrate that "limitless courage" had been employed in confrontations with criminals, Human Rights Watch would reveal in a later study that 80.4 percent of promotions had been granted without such testimony (1997: 34–35). Pay increases of between 50 and 150 percent were also authorized for any PM, PC, or firefighter who demonstrated "special merit." It is estimated that between November 1995 and March 1996, 257 officers received bravery promotions. One such officer was the commander of the Ninth Battalion, who was promoted to the top rank of colonel[16] after his battalion claimed seventy-five deaths while battling drug gangs between August 1995 and February 1996—a figure four times higher than the number of civilians killed in the whole of New York City during a comparable period (Human Rights Watch 1997: 15).[17]

Overall, according to Human Rights Watch, General Cerqueira's tenure was characterized by a sixfold increase in the number of civilians killed by the PM, from 3.2 per month to 20.55 (Human Rights Watch 1997: 14). Other sources, however, were quick to defend General Cerqueira's record, arguing that his decision to get the police out of their barracks and into the streets had led to a higher number of confrontations with criminals, inevitably resulting in more injuries and fatalities. In the words of a former high-ranking security official,

> Until General Cerqueira came, police officers had simply stopped trying to penetrate the areas where the bandits hid because of Governor Brizola's prohibition. But whether they went in or not, the police kept getting blasted for everything in the media anyway. As a result, police officers had become so demoralized that they would just stay in their precincts and barracks rather than chase crime out in the streets.[18]

The official defined the system of bravery rewards and promotions as nothing more than "a human resources management technique used . . . in order to try to recover the productivity of the police." During the Brizola-Batista era,

PMs had been reluctant to bring suspects into a precinct, as they were required to remain on hand for as long as it took the PC to file a crime report. Since the process usually took between four and five hours, this period was viewed by the PM as wasted time. General Cerqueira's policies, on the other hand, "made it worthwhile for the PM to make arrests, because it brought them salary increases, and even a widow's compensation in case of death, plus a great deal of symbolic prestige."

One PM officer, who had been promoted for bravery under General Cerqueira's program, maintained in an interview, "Crime will go up if you don't fight it where criminals are; criminals spend their whole lives plotting. You have to make their life hell so they don't come down from the hills."[19] He added, "I didn't allow the bandit [*marginal da lei*] to leave the hills for the asphalt. I would corral him so that he could not get out. . . . I would go after traffickers daily. We worked a lot at night and had many armed confrontations because we were more prepared to operate in the dark than they were."

Still, the official acknowledged that they had been really playing a game of cat and mouse, since dealers simply migrated elsewhere when the pressure was too high. Had the police continued to receive firm support and guidance, they could have managed to occupy the critical points in a slum *before* traffickers settled in and intimidated residents, most of whom, he added, were honest folk who did not want the traffickers there. It was imperative that this process be undertaken early on, because "if you don't arrive in time, the drug traffickers will set up their own forms of counter-intelligence to try to turn the population against the police. They provide a few health services and convince residents to go to the media and complain." Later, when I asked how the police differentiate among hardened criminals, petty crooks, and honest residents, he said,

> The police know how to tell. . . . Criminals shouldn't have human rights; you can't imagine how horrible these people are. Some of these traffickers kill and burn people, and then pigs eat the corpses so that there is nothing left. Human rights are for decent people. Criminals are completely different from decent folk, but it is true you need to be able to differentiate between a small-time crook and a really big one, though it is also true that sometimes you have to use violence to deter a small-time crook from becoming even more violent.

Human rights groups bitterly complained against this mindset, blasted General Cerqueira for sanctioning police violence, and went so far as to call Governor Alencar a "criminal" for hiring such an "assassin."[20] General Cerqueira countered with his own critique of NGOs, denigrating their cushy salaries and saying that they "gave the distinct impression of living on another planet, rather than in the city."[21] He made a practice of referring to the prominent NGO Viva Rio (Long Live Rio) as Viva Rico (Long Live the Rich) and suggested that his two most outspoken human rights critics, both of whom were foreigners,[22] return home quickly since they understood so little about Brazil and the problems the police faced. He wondered how prisons in Brazil could meet standards advocated by the United Nations when the national fight against crime was being carried out on a "rudimentary" level and the monthly expense to maintain an inmate would exceed the salary paid by the state to the average policeman.[23]

A crackdown on corruption from the left. On May 30, 1995, in a move that astonished not only his detractors but his supporters as well, General Cerqueira brought in Hélio Luz to head the Antikidnapping Division (DAS) of the PC. Luz had gained a rare reputation for efficiency, intelligence, and personal integrity while serving in the interior of Rio State and later in the Baixada Fluminense, a district with high crime rates. But as a vocal card-carrying member of the leftist Workers Party, Luz was squarely on the opposite side of the political spectrum to both General Cerqueira and Governor Alencar. Upon assuming office, he proclaimed that "hereafter the police will not kidnap any longer"—a startling admission by a high-ranking insider.[24]

Barely a month later, Luz was promoted to chief of the PC. With characteristic bluntness, he declared that the whole criminal justice system was in critical condition: "Lawyers go to police precincts to bribe, prison guards don't guard, detectives don't investigate, police stenographers can't type, and coroners are afraid of the corpses."[25] After warning the PC that complicity in drug trafficking, kidnapping, extortion, and other serious crimes would not be tolerated, he quickly set out to expand the internal affairs division, taking personal control of police transfers, a process so murky that it had functioned primarily as a means to assemble crime rings.

At the same time, Luz recognized that certain forms of petty corruption would be impossible to root out. In a controversial decision, he made a pact with the Grupo Astra—a clandestine and powerful group of detectives—setting the limits of what he would tolerate. He promised to personally see to their expulsion if they crossed the line, while assuring them of his support in the fight for better salaries if they put their expertise and vast informant network at the service of good policing.

Luz also harnessed the private sector to assist in the fight against crime. He linked the intelligence services of the Secretariat of Public Security to the Disque Denúncia (Dial-a-Crime) hotline. This program had been established by the Federation of Industry Owners of Rio de Janeiro State (FIRJAN) in 1995 amid a wave of kidnappings so that callers could provide anonymous tips; if a tip led to an arrest, callers could then use a previously arranged secret code to claim rewards of US$130–4,300, or up to US$8,600 for high-profile cases. Because of its private-sector funding, Disque Denúncia survived different administrations. It played an important role in reducing kidnappings, from 235 in the state in 1995 to 9 in 2001.[26]

In spite of making some of the biggest drug busts in Rio's history—including the capture of eight major traffickers and kidnapping ring bosses[27]—Hélio Luz's chances at deeper reform of the PC were cut short due to lack of support from Governor Alencar. The governor halted Luz's attempts to improve PC training through a specialized course at the State University of Rio de Janeiro (UERJ) and reneged on a pledge to increase the salaries of the PC by 53 percent despite having heralded it as a fait accompli (Benjamin 1998: 133). Luz resigned, but then he agreed to stay after a hundred PCs and members of civil society demonstrated on his behalf. Only a few months later, however, Governor Alencar dismissed him for good, declaring, "He has many virtues, but he has a . . . compulsion to publicize his beliefs."[28] Others would say that the governor tired of Luz's proclamations that corruption webs were not limited to police patrimony but ran throughout the state and elites of Rio de Janeiro.[29]

Even though the tenure of General Cerqueira and Luz was characterized by extreme controversy, they accomplished some quantifiable gains in reducing the crime rate in Rio between 1995 and 1998 as Figures 9.1 and 9.2 show. Human rights advocates and other detractors, however, maintained that these gains paled when measured against the sixfold increase in civilian deaths recorded during the period. During the subsequent gubernatorial campaign, candidates also ridiculed the crime reduction claims, alleging that Alencar's team had distorted statistics for political gain.

A Third Way?
Anthony Garotinho (1999–2001)

With the victory of Anthony Garotinho over Marcello Alencar's chosen candidate in the October 1998 gubernatorial elections, the standards and codes by which the police were judged, promoted, and evaluated were again turned on their head. Many of the officers who had been promoted as heroes under General Cerqueira's "bravery promotions" program were demoted[30] and their salaries and pension increases rescinded. Upon assuming office in January 1999, Governor Garotinho, a self-proclaimed left-of-center evangelical Christian, appointed Luiz Eduardo Soares as undersecretary of research and citizenship in the Secretariat of Public Security. A noted sociologist and architect of the new administration's security policy, Soares had devised a reform philosophy meant to bridge the opposing approaches to public security espoused by previous governments: his "third way" would modernize the Rio police and increase their crime-fighting abilities while simultaneously respecting human rights.

**Figure 9.1 Number of Recorded Kidnappings,
State and City of Rio de Janeiro, 1995–1998**

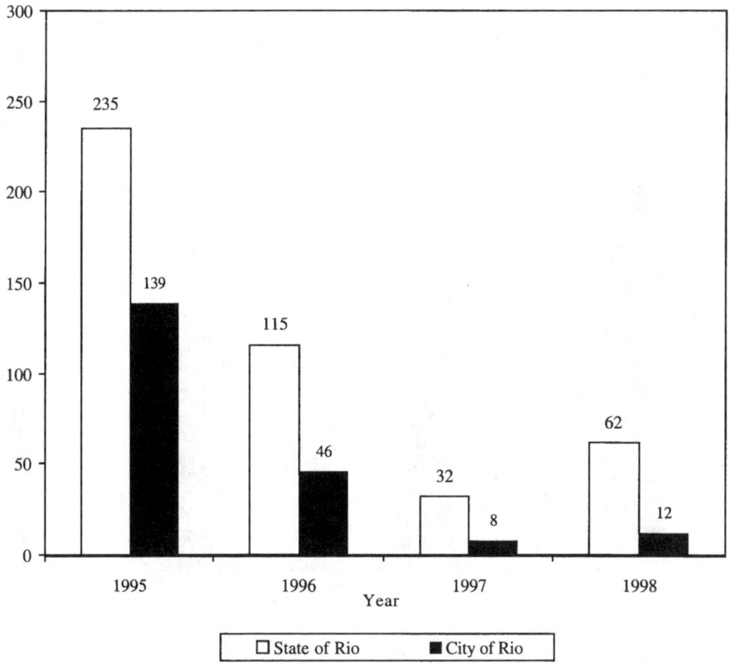

Source: Polícia Civil, cited in NECVU/UFRJ (2001).

Based on the lessons of past administrations, Soares launched the most ambitious multipronged approach undertaken in the 1990s. His program was backed by an injection of US$20 million in 1999, with US$50 million more promised for 2000. Beyond much-needed upgrading of matériel, Soares set out to raise the value and the standing of the police profession through improved training and salaries. Communities would be able to participate in security decisions that directly affected them, and increased use of information technology would improve management and enable a more targeted and streamlined approach to policing (Soares 1999).

The Delegacia Legal, or Clean Precinct. The pillar of Soares's plan was the Delegacia Legal[31] or Clean Precinct project. The project envisioned a holistic approach, aiming to transform the 121 existing PC precincts (and 30 additional specialized ones) from centers of intimidation to centers of professionalism. Aggressive, shabbily dressed policemen staffed most PC precincts in Rio; they treated complainants rudely and often asked for

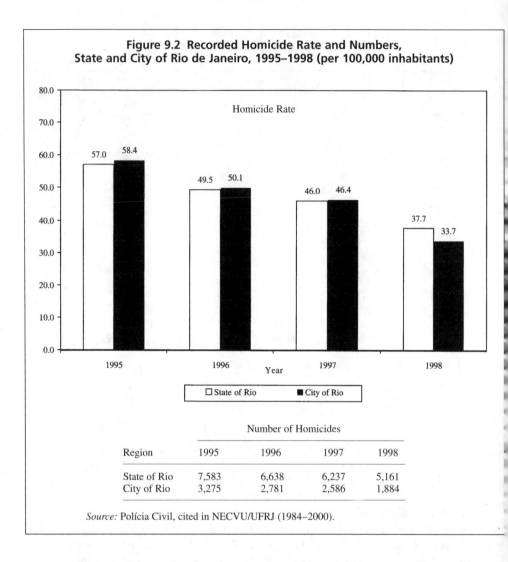

Figure 9.2 Recorded Homicide Rate and Numbers,
State and City of Rio de Janeiro, 1995–1998 (per 100,000 inhabitants)

Number of Homicides

Region	1995	1996	1997	1998
State of Rio	7,583	6,638	6,237	5,161
City of Rio	3,275	2,781	2,586	1,884

Source: Polícia Civil, cited in NECVU/UFRJ (1984–2000).

bribes to process a crime report, particularly if an insurance claim was involved. Alternatively, if prospects for solving the crime looked poor, the complainant was often discouraged from filing a report so as not to bring down precinct statistics. If a complainant was obdurate, he or she would be forced to wait for hours; the process was so bureaucratic and cumbersome that it could take more than a week. After an initial evaluation, Soares had concluded that "if the police were a private enterprise, they would have been forced to close their doors in twenty-four hours, such was the extent of the organizational irrationality we saw" (Soares 1999: 4). Governor Garotinho himself was aghast after a surprise tour of the city's main police precincts, exclaiming, "The police precincts were like something out of a horror movie. I saw rats running through the halls, crumpled police reports on the floor, typewriters with no keys, and cops working with no shirt on. . . . Marcello Alencar should be ashamed of the situation in which he left the public security situation."[32]

Plans were laid to remodel the ramshackle precincts using modern architectural design. Holding cells would be removed, as Soares argued (as had Hélio Luz a few years earlier) that the PC was unduly preoccupied with guarding prisoners—up to 400 at any given time. In cases when remodeling was not feasible, new precincts were to be built, and their reception areas would be staffed by female university students or other civilian personnel to free police officers from performing administrative tasks. Criminal reports would no longer be filled manually but using a computer program designed in conjunction with one of Brazil's top university engineering departments. A statewide crime database would enable police managers to ascertain crime hot spots, monitor progress of any given case, and better target police activities. Where "organized negligence" previously reigned, transparency and public service would take over.[33]

Integrated Public Security Zones. Linked to the Clean Precinct project was a project known as the Integrated Public Security Zones (Areas Integradas de Segurança Pública).[34] The project foresaw the rationalization of PM battalions and PC precincts into thirty-four administrative zones, so that the two forces could finally attempt to work in unison. As previously discussed, lack of jurisdictional convergence between the two forces had increased statistical discrepancies and further hampered coordination efforts; in addition, jurisdictions did not correspond to the boundaries of either local neighborhoods or local councils (*regiões administrativas*), turning most planning efforts into a logistical nightmare. Because PMs outnumbered PCs, each Integrated Public Security Zone consisted of two PM battalions for each PC precinct. In addition, Community Security Councils (Conselhos Comunitarios de Segurança) were set up to ensure that citizens' concerns would be heard regularly by the PM commanders, the PC precinct chief, and urban planning authorities.

Training. As part of Soares's overall strategy, numerous projects were designed to improve police capacity, including specialized training for members of new units that would provide assistance to tourists, control traffic (including roadside searches), and monitor security in soccer stadiums. In contrast with the PFA in Buenos Aires, who administered their own university, lower-ranking police officers in Rio were sent to the UERJ so they could interact in a civilian setting with academics, guest lecturers, and other students. The evening program, launched in 1999, was originally designed to last eight months (although it was later shortened to four), with a coursework covering such topics as modern Brazilian history and politics, citizenship, justice, and human rights. About fifty-five to sixty police officers from the PM and PC, firefighters, prison guards, and NGO representatives were enrolled at any given time.

This initiative was loosely modeled on a separate program for high-ranking officers at the Fluminense Federal University (UFF). In 1998, a group of officers had approached Roberto Kant de Lima, a distinguished anthropologist at the UFF and expert on criminal justice, to replicate a specialized course he had given to police forces in other states. Professor Kant's curriculum, based on the principle that a better educated and more open-minded police leadership would eventually increase the likelihood of change from within, soon attracted the attention of the Ford Foundation, which decided to cofinance the program. Many well-known Brazilian intellectuals were invited to lecture on sociology, race relations, criminology, media studies, and the like. The course was expanded to one year, becoming a prerequisite for promotion to the highest tier of the PM.

New institutions of accountability. To complement the technocratic and structural innovations discussed above, Soares's team also sought to expand civil society's involvement in public security issues, a role that had hitherto been largely confined to a few activist NGOs. In January 1999,[35] an ombudsman's office was set up to encourage the public to report complaints about police misconduct and abuse of authority. While the office's mandate precluded it from carrying out investigations, it endeavored to ascertain the veracity of complaints and to accompany the investigation process carried out by the PC or the Office of the Public Prosecutor to ensure appropriate redress. A prominent expert on human rights and the criminal justice system was appointed ombudsman.

In conjunction with the Ombudsman's Office, Citizenship Referral Centers were established to reach out to the gay community and to *favela* residents and to fight racism, anti-Semitism, and domestic violence. Leaders in the affected communities were selected to head the centers, which, following on Disque Denúncia's footsteps, were outfitted with telephone hotlines to allow citizens to report discrimination and hate crimes.

In December 1999, the Institute of Public Security[36] (ISP) was created to orchestrate these policies. The ISP, which many regarded as a supra–Secretariat of Public Security, was charged with yet another crucial task: to oversee the gradual hiring of 8,000 new PMs and 2,000 PCs who would eventually form part of the New Police Force, a parallel structure that was being planned to circumvent the constitution's restrictions on unification of the PM and PC. A bizarre set of legal loopholes was unearthed so that New

Police Force personnel could retain their original affiliation without infringing on the constitution. At the top, the force was designed to operate with a unified command structure; its career ladder was significantly shortened, and significantly higher pay and benefits were envisaged. Although recruits would be drawn from PM and PC ranks (albeit under a strict selection and training process designed to weed out police officers lacking clean records), the New Police would have new uniforms, logos, cars, and weaponry.

Projects to improve police relations with favela residents. Complementary to the above initiatives, Soares and his team launched various projects to improve the tense relationship between police and *favela* residents. Two of the most notable were the Peace Reserves (Reservistas da Paz) and a program in the Pavão-Pavãozinho *favela*.

The Peace Reserves project was designed to provide state-funded internships in the PM for close to 500 youngsters aged eighteen to twenty-three.[37] The project aimed at keeping poor youngsters off the streets, exposing them to a source of potential employment, and more generally, teaching them discipline and self-esteem. Equally important, the project was designed to diminish the prevailing mistrust between the police and *favela* residents through close contact in a positive environment. In the words of one of the project's creators, "Both groups have traditionally viewed each other with mistrust and often as enemies, but when they work side by side, they see each other for what they are: people with families, dreams, and values."[38]

Each participating PM battalion appointed a project coordinator, who was sent for training in community relations to a local Catholic university. Peace Reserves candidates had to pass a written examination and submit to an interview, after which those who were selected were trained in first aid, given civic lessons, and put through a vigorous physical exercise regimen. Those who did not drop out were given apprenticeships with the PM in tasks such as mechanics, nutrition, cooking, filing, dictation, and computing. Their salary, for half-day shifts, was twice the minimum wage, plus a food and transport voucher.[39] The Peace Reserves project, according to one PM, "helped us break down negative stereotypes of the police. . . . It allowed us to teach youngsters discipline and good values. . . . By the time they finished, they were more orderly, respectful, and disciplined."[40]

The second model project was a joint venture by Viva Rio, the PM, and the Secretariat of Public Security. Launched in September 2000 in the Pavão-Pavãozinho *favela*, it was a local adaptation of various community policing and disarmament projects that had been carried out in poor neighborhoods of Boston and San Diego. The community policing project sought to replace "periodic intrusions" into the *favela* with a more constant and interactive form of policing whereby residents would be consulted on their needs and encouraged to participate in monitoring and follow-through.[41] One hundred specially trained PMs from a new unit called the Special Areas Policing Squad (GPAE) were deployed, with roughly ten present at any given time. After consultation with community leaders, it was agreed that the two most urgent objectives of the project should be to rid the *favela* of guns and corrupt police officers and to end children's involvement as lookouts and messengers for the drug traffickers. A tacit pact was made between the police and drug gang leaders: if the gangs stopped patrolling with openly displayed weapons, negotiated their deals in private, and stopped involving children in the trade, the police would in essence leave them alone in the interest of bringing violence down and making the community more livable.

In the words of one Viva Rio representative, this project was extremely important, because "without the police, the presence of the drug traffickers inhibits public officials from entering the *favelas*. Without adequate policing the population lives in constant fear—of coming and going, of speaking out, of forming legitimate associations, all of which hampers their ability to achieve voice and representation in Rio."[42]

The Impact of the "Third Way"

The tenure of Luis Eduardo Soares as undersecretary of public security was the first time a public security reform policy was systematically and comprehensively designed for Rio de Janeiro. As the above survey shows, the "third way" sought to target many of the structural problems that beset the Rio police. Whether this approach correlated to local reality is open to debate; what is unarguable, however, is that no sooner had Soares's policies been launched than a belligerent reaction set in to stymie their success.

It was his own patron, Governor Garotinho, who most undermined Soares's reforms: he appointed as head of the Secretariat of Public Security an army general who had been a close associate of General Nilton Cerqueira, the former hard-line secretary, whom Soares considered the "arch enemy of those of us who defend human rights" (Soares 2000: 53). The new secretary lasted only four months, but Governor Garotinho replaced him with another official with ties to military repression, Josias Quintal. Soares refused to report to Quintal and requested direct access to the governor.[43] By twice installing such diverging currents within the secretariat, Governor Garotinho was deliberately sending an ambiguous message to the police and to the public.

Many sectors within the police staunchly opposed Soares, distrusting his outsider status and resenting his use of the media to constantly criticize them. Matters were not helped when Soares's wife was appointed to head a commission charged with investigation of the bravery awards under the

Alencar administration. Others were incensed by Soares's recommendations for chiefs of the PM and PC, regarding them as privileged young officers who, owing to their connections, had never had to dirty their hands in the streets. Although Governor Garotinho accepted Soares's recommendations, both chiefs lasted less than a year in office. They were replaced by others whom Soares considered hostile to his reforms—in particular the chief of the PC, whose record was tainted by allegations of corruption and links to drug traffickers.

The rift between Governor Garotinho and Soares finally came to a head after the ombudsman, a close Soares ally, called a press conference to make serious charges of police impunity. The ombudsman alleged that between March 15 and December 15, 1999, only 117 policemen (112 of them PMs) had been punished out of a total of 1,586 complaints forwarded by her office; none were suspended or fired even though several officers had been caught in flagrante delicto and one case involved the decapitation of a young girl. Three months later, the situation had not improved. As stated in the ombudsman's annual report, during this period sixty-nine additional cases were brought against *delegados* (the PC officers in charge of precincts), with none punished; in the case of the PM, out of the ninety-four charges against high-ranking police officers, only six had been punished (Ouvidoria RJ 1999: tables 3–7).

The police, however, were reluctant to investigate. Denouncing the presence of a "rotten gang" (*banda podre*) in the police, the ombudsman and Soares then appealed directly to the Office of the Public Prosecutor. Incensed, the governor fired Soares on live television on March 17, 2000,[44] after which Soares's entire security team resigned in protest. After receiving death threats, Soares and his family were forced into exile in New York, where he would write a book on the affair.

Mindful of the crucial importance that a successful "third way" could have for his 2002 presidential ambitions, however, Governor Garotinho replaced Soares with a progressive former PM official. Jorge da Silva, whose master's thesis had dwelled on the relationship between racism and police violence, had thirty-three years' experience in the force, an advantage that was expected to put his working relationship with the secretary of public security and with the chiefs of the PM and PC on more solid footing. The new team soon released a Public Policy Action Plan for Security, Justice, and Citizenship. The 200-page plan contained some projects that had been initiated by Soares, others that were revived from the Brizola administration (such as the Community Centers for the Defense of Citizenship and the local variant of the US DARE program), and some new approaches. The latter were heavily focused on improving social assistance networks for the poor, including soup kitchens and food vouchers, and on increasing police capacity to fight drug trafficking.

In the meantime, the governor established a Clean Hands Commission to investigate Soares's rotten gang accusations, which had received extensive media coverage.[45] While the investigation was being carried out, Governor Garotinho unilaterally suspended 124 PMs and 228 PCs suspected of criminal activity. Six months later, the Rio State Superior Court ruled their suspensions unconstitutional and ordered the governor to reinstate them. None of these men, nor any of those indicted after the Clean Hands Commission finished its investigation, were among those named by Soares as members of the rotten gang.[46]

The implementation of the police reform agenda had been in jeopardy even before the departure of Soares and his team. The Clean Precinct project, for instance, had been sabotaged by PC elements who had long benefited from the status quo. Once a PC completed the requisite two months' training in the new computer software, the officer was deliberately transferred to an "old" precinct, so that the whole training process would need to be repeated again; this rendered the software virtually inoperable in the meantime and caused severe delays in processing crime reports. The delays were then offered to the media as proof that the Clean Precinct initiative had misfired—accusations that were mirrored in subsequent newspaper editorials urging Governor Garotinho to reevaluate the idea.

Notwithstanding these setbacks, some precincts did benefit from an overdue makeover, although cosmetic changes were obviously not the paramount goal of the program. At the time of Soares's dismissal, only 6 out of 120 precincts scheduled for reform had been modernized.[47] Later the project was overseen by a chief of the PC whom the governor had appointed even though Soares had identified him as having links to drug trafficking; it was only after new accusations of corruption surfaced against the chief[48] that Governor Garotinho fired him. Similarly, the Integrated Public Security Zones project, whose defining benchmark was strategic interaction between the PM and the PC, lost its momentum following Soares's departure. Since no systematic monitoring mechanism had been set in place, the project's success relied too heavily on individual goodwill. Where none existed, interaction among the PM, PC, the community, and urban authorities remained virtually nonexistent.

As far as higher education for the police was concerned, financial support by the Ford Foundation ensured the continuation of the university course for higher-ranking officers. However, attendance at the course designed for lower-ranking police officers and firefighters dropped by 30 percent when students found out that their superiors would not recognize their efforts. Despite protestations by many academics, the decision stood. One of the professors who participated in the course told me, "The government tries to show everybody that they are investing in particular areas, but because there is no follow up, no one really benefits from their investment.

. . . As a result, the whole thing is a waste of effort and resources."[49] The governor's overall commitment to improving the educational standards of the police was further called into question when in April 2001 he forwarded a bill to the Rio State Legislature (subsequently approved) reducing the entry-level requirements to the PC from the required advanced diploma to a high school degree.[50]

In terms of the creation of the New Police Force, the legal obstacles set by the constitution to the dismemberment of the PM and PC could not be cavalierly dismissed. After Soares's departure, the project lost momentum, and only a small percentage of New Police members benefited from either improved training or higher pay scales. It was soon apparent that in spite of the redesigned uniforms and logos, it would take a great leap of faith to differentiate the New Police from the old.

Still, implementation of projects aimed at improving policing for the urban poor continued after Soares's exit. The Peace Reserve Project, for instance, was championed faithfully by Soares's replacement, da Silva. The project managed to accomplish its modest objectives mostly in those cases where it benefited from the individual commitment of a PM battalion chief. At the same time, as revealed in an interview, some of the young Peace Reserve participants grew weary at the Garotinho administration's insistence that they appear at televised political events and rallies, since it added to the perception that the Peace Reserve program was being politically exploited.[51] In addition, many youngsters were apprehensive about appearing jointly with the police, for fear of repercussions in their *favela* neighborhoods.

The view that the governor's commitment to socially responsible projects was nothing more than a campaign strategy to expand his populist support base in time for the presidential elections of 2002, for which it was expected he would be a candidate, was shared by many. A new program, Citizenship Check (Cheque Cidadão), came under particular suspicion. Through this initiative, low-income families that kept their children in school received checks for up to US$40 per month from the State Secretariat of Social Action and Citizenship—headed by none other than the governor's wife, "Rosinha" Matheus de Oliveira. Accusations of favoritism also dogged the program from the start because, according to an investigative report published in a prominent newsdaily, 214 of the 250 organizations involved in selecting deserving families (more than 42,000 a month) were evangelical churches, the group that formed the governor's main support base.[52]

The community-policing project in Pavão-Pavãozinho, for its part, started attracting international attention for having "rid the *favelas* of serious violence" within two months of its launching.[53] Some at home were more cautious. A year after the project began, one active participant stated in an interview that he feared the situation in the *favela* would likely revert to its original state as soon as Viva Rio, the force behind the project, moved on. By virtue of its links to Soares, the project was regarded with disdain by the PM high command. One well-connected police source confided that, in fact, some of the worst performers in the PM had initially been sent to the specialist unit in the *favela* as part of a purposeful strategy to thwart the project's success. Indeed, more than 40 percent of those initially sent to police the *favela* had to be transferred out for truculence and corruption.

Nevertheless, the project managed to survive after Soares's premature exit—perhaps aided by high-profile visits from foreign dignitaries including representatives of international NGOs, World Bank representatives, and Britain's Prince Charles. The transfer of the Pavão-Pavãozinho pilot project to the more than 600 other *favelas* in Rio was a more uncertain proposition, for several reasons. Pavão-Pavãozinho is a small *favela,* with only about 15,000 residents,[54] and is therefore relatively easy to manage. Because of its breathtaking panoramic views, it is more photogenic and media friendly than the more remote and insalubrious slums of the Northern Zone and the western parts of the city. More important, as Pavão-Pavãozinho is located on a hill straddling Copacabana and Ipanema, whatever happens on top reverberates in the wealthy beachfront neighborhoods below. Accordingly, Pavão-Pavãozinho has been frequently selected for pilot programs,[55] many of which were later abandoned. To expand the community-policing program to the more than one million residents living in Rio's more distant and grimmer slums would have required a level of commitment and continuity that, as shown in previous chapters, was sorely absent.

Conclusion

To summarize, the police in Rio in the 1990s were confronted with the nearly impossible task of combating high levels of violent crime and drug trafficking in a political environment riddled with contradictory messages and pressures. Substantial structural problems affected not just the Rio police but the institution in Brazil as a whole, requiring a concerted effort by both the state government and federal authorities. Yet the federal authorities fell far short of providing the strong leadership required for police reform, even as Brazil's international image deteriorated due to police corruption and brutality; it was therefore largely left to individual states to undertake whatever measures they deemed most expedient. In the case of Rio State, successive governors, whether on the left or right or in the center, shared a common failure: they all failed to extricate the police from the whims and vagaries of extreme political manipulation, as they dismissed and replaced police chiefs and state security officials with such dizzying frequency that the chances for any reform measure to take root were minimized.

In contrast, in countries such as England, the chief constable (chief officer) of all provincial police forces is chosen by independent standing regional commissions, or police authorities as they are called, composed of elected officials, magistrates, and community leaders, following a competition among candidates from police forces across the country.[56] The term of chief officers normally lasts from four to seven years, with the possibility of extension, and is not tied to the term of the mayor or city council in question. Removal of a chief constable occurs only under exceptional circumstances and can proceed only if authorized by the central government via the home secretary (Reiner 2000b: 188–189). In the case of England's largest force, the London Metropolitan Police (with more than 26,000 officers), the chief commissioner (chief officer)—who is chosen by the Home Office—changed only five times between March 13, 1977, and 2000. Outside the capital, for example, in the twenty-six-year period between April 1974 and 2000 the chief constable of the Greater Manchester police changed only three times (Wall 1998).

In large US cities, police chiefs change more frequently than in the United Kingdom, as elected mayors rather than standing commissions typically appoint them. Despite this, a basic degree of continuity in standards, codes of conduct, and personnel is maintained. In Brazil's largest states, it is not uncommon for the police chief to change three times during the four years of a governor's tenure—and more when governors resign to run for higher office. A combination of low levels of professionalism, weak democratic controls, and extremely low salaries perpetuates an extreme politicization of police governance. In such a climate, crackdowns on police corruption are short lived, since rogue police elements can be fairly confident that if they tone down their activities until a new authority is appointed, the cycle of corruption can resume again. The arrested development of the reform process not only brings stress and demoralization to a poorly remunerated police but also perpetuates their lack of professionalism. Unable to rid themselves of the remnants of their violent legacy, used by the elites as a hedge between rich and poor, the police remain a highly volatile institution lacking in both capacity and credibility.

Given the critical need to confront the problems described, why have responses been so consistently inadequate? The following two chapters address this question.

Notes

1. Collor de Mello was the second civilian president since the restoration of democracy in 1985, and the first elected by popular vote instead of by the electoral college.
2. Lei 8.069 (Estatuto da Criança e do Adolescente, ECA), Congresso Nacional, July 13, 1990.
3. See ibid., bk. 1, title 1, arts. 1–4; bk. 2, title 3, ch. 3., art. 111; and sec. 7, art. 121, para. 3, arts. 122–124.

4. Indeed, the perception that the ECA affords impunity to minors has contributed to popular support for such police actions. Following the murder of eight street children at the Candelária Church in the business sector of Rio by off-duty police officers, the police hotline was so swamped by calls voicing approval for this action that it had to be disconnected. See Prillaman (2000: 96).

5. Carandirú was the largest prison in Latin America; at the time of the massacre it held more than 7,000 prisoners despite capacity for only 3,300. It closed September 15, 2002, in the aftermath of a multiprison uprising in 2001 that affected twenty-nine prisons at once and involved over 30,000 inmates, who took 7,000 hostages.

6. In June 2001, almost nine years after the Carandirú massacre, a court convicted a retired chief of the PM, Colonel Ubiratan Guimarães, sentencing him to 632 years (although the constitution sets a maximum prison term of thirty years). This marked the first time since the enactment of the Bicudo Law that a PM with the rank of colonel faced a civilian jury. (The Bicudo Law, passed in 1996, is discussed later in this chapter.) The trial took place only after Guimarães lost his reelection bid to the São Paulo State Assembly, a position that had offered him parliamentary immunity. He was, however, immediately released on appeal. The remaining eighty-five PMs indicted still awaited trial at the end of 2005.

7. Initially, all 157 police officers that had been charged and tried for intentional homicide were acquitted in 1999. But in April 2000, the Supreme Court of the State of Pará annulled the trial and judgement, citing numerous irregularities. After a new presiding judge was appointed and subsequently changed five times, the retrial was held in April 2002 and resulted in the conviction of the two commanding officers. Major Jose Oliveira was sentenced to 158 years in prison and Lieutenant Colonel Mario Pantoja to 228 years. The 144 other police officers who remained living and fit for trial were absolved, a ruling sharply criticized by Amnesty International. After serving a brief period in prison, the two convicted commanding officers were both set free in October 2005 pending appeal.

8. Lei 9.299 (Bicudo Law), Congresso Nacional, August 7, 1996.

9. To provide an indication of some of the problems faced by this system, at the close of 1992 the Military Police court system in São Paulo had roughly 14,000 cases pending in four courts, each court having only one prosecutor. Sixty-four percent of the 2,359 cases against police officers that were sent to military tribunals in the São Paulo State between January and October 1998 were withdrawn without a court hearing for reasons of insufficient evidence. A human rights group in Brazil's northeast studying police crimes found that between 1970 and 1991, 92 percent of the cases tried in police courts were absolved. See Human Rights Watch (1994: 41) and US Department of State (1999: sec. 1a).

10. Author interview, June 12, 2001.

11. Fifty-two policemen were charged in the crime. One of the former officers accused was at the time serving as a member of the Rio State Legislature and thus could not be arrested without a revocation of his parliamentary immunity. For more on the Candelária and Vigário Geral massacres, see Amnesty International (2003).

12. "Entrevista: Marcello Alencar," *Jornal do Brasil,* November 17, 1994.

13. General Nilton Cerqueira is not to be confused with Colonel Nazareth Cerqueira, who, as previously discussed, served as chief of the PM and state secretary of security under Brizola.

14. This intelligence unit, the DOI-Codi, was also accused by Human Rights Watch of causing the disappearance of 152 persons and the death of 269 more in addition to substantial torture of prisoners. General Cerqueira emphatically denied his involvement in these activities.

15. See "Secretário Defende Que Polícia Atire Primeiro," *Folha de São Paulo,* May 20, 1995, and "Especialista Vê Incentivo ao Extermínio," *Jornal do Brasil,* April 22, 1996.

16. The next gubernatorial administration stripped the commander of the Ninth Batallion, Colonel Marcos Paes, of his status as decorated hero, demonized him as a public scourge, and forced him to resign.

17. By comparison, previous commanders of the same Ninth Battalion over a period of two and a half years, from January 1993 to July 1995, were blamed for the deaths of thirty-five civilians. See Cano (1997: 48).

18. Author interview, June 9, 2001.

19. Author interview, June 20, 2001.

20. Author interview with a prominent human rights activist in Rio, July 25, 2001.

21. "Nota aos Policiólogos," *Jornal do Brasil,* May 6, 1996. See also the 1996 presentation by General Nilton Cerqueira at the Federação das Indústrias do Estado de São Paulo (in Cerqueira 1996).

22. These outspoken critics of General Cerqueira's policies were from the United States and Spain, respectively. Each had published studies showing the escalation in police violence and the loose standards with which bravery was judged, and revealing that forensic data suggested that many suspects had been shot in the back. See Human Rights Watch (1997) and Cano (1997), respectively.

23. "Secretário Defende."

24. "Hélio Luz," *Jornal do Brasil,* March 8, 1996.

25. Ibid.

26. Kidnapping data from NECVU/UFRJ (2001).

27. "Cerqueira Diz Que Resolveu Segurança," *Jornal do Brasil,* January 8, 1997.

28. "Rio Police Chief Fired for Speaking Out," *Reuters Business Briefing,* September 1, 1997.

29. As part of the PT (Workers' Party), Luz subsequently won election to the Rio State Legislature, where he continued to denounce corruption in the government.

30. Colonel Marcos Paes of the Ninth Batallion, for example, heralded as a hero under Alencar and demonized under Garotinho, was forced to resign. However, the mayor of Rio, a political opponent of the governor, later hired Paes as an adviser on security matters.

31. The word *legal* in Brazilian Portuguese has a dual meaning: one is the same meaning as the English word, while the other is "good," "clean," or "friendly."

32. "Garotinho Fica Chocado com Delegacias," *Jornal do Brasil,* January 23, 1999.

33. Oral presentation by Soares (2001).

34. Passed by an administrative order on July 26, 1999 (Resolução SESP n 263).

35. An office that has existed in São Paulo since 1995.

36. The Instituto de Segurança Pública was established by Law 3.329, December 28, 1999.

37. Governo do Estado do Rio de Janeiro (2000: 37).

38. Author interview, June 25, 2001.

39. The total amount was about BRL404 per month—about US$221 per the average interbank exchange rate for 2000.

40. Author interview with a midlevel PM in charge of supervising the Peace Reserves in his batallion, July 11, 2001.

41. Author interview with a high-ranking official of the PM involved in state community policing programs, July 20, 2001.

42. Author interview, July 18, 2001.

43. Particularly after Soares was promoted in October 1999 to the position of coordinator of security, justice, civil defense, and citizenship (*coordenador de segurança, justiça, defesa civil e cidadania*), a position technically above Secretary Quintal.

44. News crews, quick to zero in on cheers and hugs traded between police officers in various Rio precincts after this event, renamed the "rotten gang" the "happy gang."

45. The commission also promptly began investigating Soares.

46. Forty-two other accusations were made, and twenty-seven other PMs and PCs were formally indicted. "'Comissão Mãos Limpas' Que Investigou 'Banda Podre' da Policia Propõe Inquerito Contra Luiz Eduardo Soares Que Fez Denúncia," *Folha de São Paulo,* November 1, 2000.

47. "Entrevista com Luiz Eduardo Soares: Ex-assessor de Garotinho Defende 3a Via Contra Crime," *Folha de São Paulo,* December 2, 2000.

48. The chief, Raffik Louzada, was later indicted by the federal government for involvement in drug trafficking.

49. Author interview, June 13, 2001.

50. Lei 3545 (Altera a Lei 2990 de 23 de Junho de 1998, Plano de Cargos da PC), Assembléia Legislativa do Estado do Rio de Janeiro, April 2, 2001.

51. Author interview with four Peace Reserve participants, July 11, 2001.

52. See "Cheque Cidadão em Branco," *O Globo,* June 8, 2001.

53. See "Taking Boston's Lead, Police in Rio Lighten Up," *Christian Science Monitor,* November 8, 2000, and "Nice Cops, Nasty Cops," *Economist,* September 6, 2001.

54. "Invasão Pacífica," *Veja Rio,* April 18, 2001.

55. The Brizola administration constructed one of its first Centers for the Defense of Citizenship and Security in this same *favela.*

56. For more on the role and evolution of local police authorities in Britain, oversight of the police, selection of the forty-one provincial chief constables, and debates over police accountability in Britain more generally, see Reiner (1991) and Jones and Newburn (1997).

CHAPTER 10

Threats and Priorities

There could have been few cities in the 1990s that were in more dire need of police reform than Rio de Janeiro. Yet even as the public security situation continued to deteriorate, neither state nor federal officials showed sustained commitment to a task whose magnitude required their concerted effort. Echoing their Argentine counterparts, conventional wisdom among many Brazilian specialists pointed in two directions to explain this vacillation: they held that entrenched police opposition short-changed reform and/or that getting the struggling economy back on its feet was the foremost item on the national agenda.

This chapter examines both arguments. It arrives at the conclusion that while police resistance to reform was substantial, often taking on an ominous character, it could not by itself have derailed genuine reform efforts; similarly, the federal government had enough breathing room to address key domestic priorities beyond its paramount economic concerns. Even in the absence of federal leadership, moreover, state governments had enough autonomy to meaningfully address an issue whose impact was so deleterious to vast segments of the population—not to mention to its own prosperity. Closer analysis shows that neither one of these factors, individually or combined, could have impeded the world's eighth largest economy from restructuring an institution so crucial to the legitimacy of the state and its laws.

Lobbies, Strikes, and Boycotts

As was the case in Buenos Aires, many policy experts interviewed in Rio were quick to advance the hypothesis that police reform would have been accomplished had the police not been so effective in organizing against it. One of the main reasons the police resisted, it was argued, was that the status

151

quo enables the police hierarchy to enjoy privileges and benefits disproportionately higher than would be the case if systemic reform were carried out.

A related argument held that the constitutional dichotomy in the structure of the police made both the PM and the PC resist new initiatives out of fear that the other would gain advantage in the process. Others interviewed advanced a less conspiratorial viewpoint, arguing that the weight of history and tradition on the police were simply too great to overcome. Regardless of which of these perspectives has greater merit, there is little doubt that some elements within the PM and PC had several avenues at their disposal, if not the will, to resist reform.

In Rio, both the PM and the PC formed associations representing their respective interests. The PM officer class had the Officers Club and the subofficer class the Association of Corporals and Soldiers; for its part, the PC had the Association of Chief Detectives (ADEPOL) and the Civil Police Union. All four were linked to similar associations in other Brazilian states.[1] Both the Officers Club of the PM and ADEPOL filed lawsuits in Rio State to stop implementation of Governor Garotinho's New Police Force or Nova Policia,[2] which, as noted in the previous chapter, was an attempt to bypass the constitutional ban on unification of the PM and PC. They also sued successfully to force Governor Garotinho to reintegrate hundreds of PMs and PCs he had suspended while charges of corruption and excessive violence against them were still pending.

Because police associations also lobbied internally to ensure support for specific political candidates, they constituted an important source of votes—one that savvy politicians took great care not to alienate. It was not just career politicians who courted police associations. There were also significant contingents of former police officers running for office, since serving in elected positions ensured continued representation of police interests at both the state and federal levels.[3] To name but a few:

- Hélio Luz, former chief of the PC, was elected to the Rio State Assembly.
- General Nilton Cerqueira, chief of the PM during the dictatorship, was serving in Congress when Governor Alencar appointed him secretary of public security.
- José Guilherme Godino "Sivuca" Ferreira, a former PC high official, whose campaign slogan was "A good criminal is a dead one," was elected in 1998 for a third consecutive term to the Rio State Assembly.
- Colonel Josias Quintal, a former police officer who was secretary of public security under Anthony Garotinho, won election to Congress in October 2002.
- Álvaro Lins, chief of the PC under Anthony Garotinho, ran unsuccessfully for the Rio State Assembly.

The police often resorted to more drastic methods, however, to make their voices heard. While the PM did not have, unlike the PC, a legal right to unionize or strike,[4] in 1997 thousands of PMs nevertheless went on strike in seventeen states simultaneously to demand better pay. Some donned black hoods to disguise their identity, while others took their chances in the open, facing the risk of imprisonment and expulsion from the force. Police strikes inevitably produced public chaos, sending governors and their aides rushing to the negotiating table—in some cases, under armed protection and wearing bulletproof vests. In a number of states, widespread looting and other crimes forced governors to ask for army troops. In the small state of Alagoas, a panicked population rose up to demand the resignation of the governor following shootouts between the police and the army; four years later, in 2001, when simultaneous police strikes shook Brazil again, President Cardoso issued a decree granting police powers to the military.

Even where police strikes were averted, as was the case in Rio State in the 1990s, the power balance between the police and the government was in a perpetual state of flux. Officials across the political spectrum were keenly aware that the police usually reacted to perceived threats to their interests with latent threats of their own. The chief of the PC during the hard-line administration of Governor Alencar, Hélio Luz, was widely believed to have forged a mutual "nonintervention" pact with the Grupo Astra—a clandestine police band that used illegal methods to solve crimes—in order to avoid a boycott of his initiatives. During the centrist government of Anthony Garotinho, as previously noted, Luiz Eduardo Soares's reform efforts were sidetracked by opposition from retrograde police elements, who waged an intimidation campaign against his "third way" proposals that included work slowdowns, virulent misinformation, and anonymous threats against Soares's supporters, friends, and family.

If a case can be made that police resistance was a significant obstacle to reform at the state level, the tenacity that police lobbies and officers-turned-legislators showed in promoting their own interests at the federal level was also substantial. As examined in the previous chapter, in the 1990s the federal government launched ambitious public security and human rights programs to combat crime and police abuses at the national level; their numerous clauses and provisos, however, could not hide the fact that mandatory compliance by the states was not required and that monitoring by federal agencies would be selective. Since the 1988 constitution had confirmed not only the dual nature of the police but also states' autonomy over their own forces, a constitutional amendment would be required to fundamentally alter the status quo. However, although between 1988 and 2001 federal legislators managed to enact a staggering thirty-five constitutional amendments on a wide array of issues, they failed to approve an amendment that would have allowed the states to modify the police structure to suit their local needs or to eliminate the PM's status as a reserve force of the national army.

A Preoccupation with Economic Destiny

A second rationale, that economic priorities eclipsed other policy issues from the government's agenda, de facto dooming the police reform effort from the start, was also strongly advanced in Brazil. Although, as noted in Chapter 5, an intense preoccupation with the economy was also present in Argentina, in Brazil this obsession emanated less from perennial economic crisis than from a collective feeling of "manifest destiny": Brazil is meant to become a world power (*grande potência*) equal to, if not greater than, the industrialized nations of the north.[5] According to former president José Sarney, Brazilian self-confidence has long been fueled by such common patriotic sayings as "God is Brazilian" and "The future belongs to Brazil" (1986: 101). Of the words inscribed on the Brazilian flag, "Order and Progress," the second has the deeper resonance. In Brazil, "economic growth is so highly valued that it usually trumps other policy goals: low inflation, balance in external accounts, high employment, improvements in social welfare, and so forth" (Kearney 2001: 19–20).

As reviewed in Chapter 7, in contrast to the economic mismanagement of the last military dictatorship in Argentina, the Brazilian military were credited with launching an "economic miracle" between 1968 and 1973, a period that saw a huge expansion of the industrial sector and overall growth rates of 11 percent annually. For the rest of the 1970s, average annual growth overall remained at a still impressive 7 percent, with industry growing at around 7.5 percent (Baer 1990: 44–45). After the first oil shock of 1973, Brazil was the first country in the world to develop the technology to run automobiles on sugarcane alcohol fuel. To further diversify its energy supply, Brazil also undertook the construction of the world's largest hydroelectric dam, at Itaipú on the border with Paraguay.[6] By 1983, however, a combination of oil shocks, heavy borrowing, rising US interest rates, and the ripple effect of Mexico's debt moratorium caused a sharp economic downturn. Like its neighbors, Brazil was plagued by balance of payments crises, stiff debt-servicing requirements, capital flight, and steep inflation. With foreign debt spiraling out of control, in February 1987 the government declared a partial moratorium on debt interest payments (Schneider 1996: 162–165).

These events set off a long period during which preoccupation with restoring economic growth was paramount. Between 1986 and 1994, seven major economic plans were launched to stabilize the economy; the failure of the first four plans, implemented under President Sarney between 1985 and 1990, together with mounting inflation and economic contraction, paved the way for the election of populist Fernando Collor de Mello in 1990. On inauguration day, President Collor froze Brazil's financial assets and prices, introduced a new currency, and laid plans to shrink the public sector through massive layoffs. By 1992, however, neither these draconian measures nor a second economic plan had managed to get the economy back on track (Baer and Paiva 1998: 111).

By the time interim president Itamar Franco appointed Senator Fernando Henrique Cardoso as finance minister in 1993, several other economic plans had also failed to resuscitate the economy. Rather than quickly push through another package of shock measures, Cardoso negotiated with Congress for ten months to secure approval for his anti-inflation Real Plan. The centerpiece of this plan was the conversion of all prices, salaries, and contracts into another new currency, the *real* (the country's fifth currency since 1986)—a process designed to take place in stages (Kearney 2001: 17–18). In the first six weeks áfter the introduction of the new currency, the hyperinflation that had eroded savings and earnings decreased so drastically that Cardoso became a national hero, and he was catapulted to the presidency in October 1994.[7] Throughout both his terms, efforts to bring about fiscal reform, privatize industry, and weather the effects of various international financial crises dominated the national agenda.

A Closer Look

The argument that the Rio police thwarted their own reform, not only because of their conservative culture but because they had enough formal and informal tools at their disposal, is powerful. The most extreme police elements gained considerable leverage over politicians or would-be reformers by using the threat of strikes, by staging high-profile crimes, or by inflicting bodily harm; more moderate factions used police lobbies to the same effect. Although in Buenos Aires the PFA could activate a vast intelligence network whenever a political threat was imminent, the police did not go on strike or routinely run for office. In Rio, on the other hand, many former police officers metamorphosed into legislators, a position from which they could help shape public policy and defend their interests.

But even if the police did their best to thwart reform, intransigence alone cannot account for the oscillations of the reform process itself. It is a fallacy to think that the police constituted a monolith wielding immense power over the political elites. There were sharp divisions between the police officer class and the suboffice corps that would have prevented uniform opposition to change and that politicians could have used to their advantage in promoting reform. Even the police officers who held elected legislative offices varied in their political party and ideological affiliations.

Perhaps more important is that there were progressive, reform-minded police factions with which a government that was firmly committed to reform could have allied, particularly as there was at least basic agreement on two necessities: the force as a whole was in desperate need of better salaries and of a professional set of standards that would increase officers' competence and standing. Factors other than police resistance to reform must therefore have been at work.

It is true that the Brazilian government's relentless pursuit of economic growth dwarfed many other issues on the political agenda. Nevertheless, if this argument was not fully convincing to explain the lack of progress on police reform in Argentina, it is even less applicable to the Brazilian case, for several reasons. Even though income inequality and poverty remain high, Brazil's aggregate economic performance has far outdistanced that of other developing countries. During the period 1950–1988, in fact, Brazil's economic expansion in GDP terms was exceeded only by that of Japan and South Korea.[8] By 2001, Brazil had the eighth largest economy in the world, and 32 percent of the Latin American GDP relative to Argentina's share of 10 percent.[9] In addition, the country boasted forty-one of the hundred largest Latin American companies (Argentina had just eight), according to the *Financial Times* 2001 global ranking.[10] Brazil's huge internal market, technologically sophisticated industry,[11] and strong export sector have lent its successive administrations a much higher degree of control over domestic priorities than is the case in Argentina.

During the 1990s, both countries' economic policies were influenced by the Washington Consensus agenda; but whereas privatization in Argentina was swift and extensive (with the overwhelming majority of state enterprises sold to foreign concerns), in Brazil the process was more deliberate and controlled. Despite the large aggregate numbers of industries that were privatized, many key sectors of the economy remained in state hands. On the whole, Brazil set in place conditions and regulations that favored national firms, although in frequent partnership with banks and foreign multinationals.[12] Given this, Brazil retained far greater control over its state assets and funds than Argentina did.

Even during its worst economic troubles, Brazil managed to maintain the confidence of IFIs and investors. Between 1982 and March 2000, for example, while Argentina was forced to negotiate eight different loan packages with the IMF, Brazil required only three. Moreover, according to IMF data, Brazilian compliance with the conditions of these loans was so low that only 36 percent of funds were actually disbursed before expiration, compared to 62 percent in Argentina (Kearney 2001: 7–8). In a widely reprinted article, Joseph Stiglitz, Nobel Prize–winning economist and former World Bank vice president, praised Brazil for its "extraordinary human and material resources" and its capacity to take "advantage of its opportunities while at the same time facing up to tough realities, be it deficiencies in education, land issues or AIDS. At the root of its brilliant trajectory lies Brazil's capacity for creation of an ample national consensus. . . . The creativity of its winning [soccer] team reveals much about the winning spirit of the country."[13]

In stark contrast to the World Bank's pessimistic millennium outlook for Argentina, its Country Assistance Strategy Progress Report praised Brazil's performance over the 1990s on nearly all fronts. It lauded, inter alia, "its solid record of social and economic progress," "the government's credibility and its proven and tested risk management capacity," the "implementation of institutional reforms," and "its resolve and capacity to respond adequately to new macroeconomic shocks" (World Bank 2002: 1–7).

Why then should such a country include police forces that have been only superficially modernized since the nineteenth century? Why would a federal government capable of significant economic accomplishment fail to show the leadership essential to addressing head on an issue so crucial to democratic legitimacy? And what about the states themselves? Even without federal intervention, or a constitutional amendment, state governors had ample formal powers over their own police forces. Public security, moreover, was the main galvanizing local issue in Rio: every gubernatorial election since 1983 had hinged on issues of crime, violence, and policing. If the cycle of crime and violence extracted an obvious cost in terms of the quality of life in the city, it also posed an inordinate burden on public health services, disrupting commerce and causing millions in lost revenue. Hostage taking, shootouts, and assaults also dimmed the city's cultural and night life, since many *cariocas* stayed home rather than risk walking or driving the streets at night.[14] Rio's immense tourist potential remained underexploited: deterred by the city's reputation for violent crime and the unsettling presence of army troops patrolling the streets, many international tourists chose to go elsewhere.[15]

The implications for political life were equally stark. What kind of message is sent when government is overrun by parallel powers that occupy *favelas* as if they were foreign territory? Why was civil society unable to exert due pressure on elected officials on these issues? These questions cannot be wholly satisfied by explanations centered on theories of police resistance or economic constraints. In the following chapter, a different perspective is presented.

Notes

1. In addition to state associations, in June 2001 the Permanent National Forum of Police Forces (Fórum Nacional Permanente dos Policiais) was formed, encompassing police associations across Brazil, plus associations of penitentiary officers.

2. While the PM Officers Club filed suit with the Rio State Supreme Court (Tribunal de Justiça do Rio), ADEPOL filed its with the Brazilian Supreme Court (Supremo Tribunal Federal).

3. Police officers also routinely ran for political office in states other than Rio. A police officer who had been involved in the PM strike in Minas Gerais State in 1997, PM Corporal Júlio (of the PL, or Liberal Party), was elected to federal Congress the following year with the most votes of any candidate. Similarly, the second most voted candidate to the São Paulo State Legislature was a PM captain, Conte Lopes of the PPB (Brazilian Progressive Party).

4. As a reserve force of the army, the PM is governed by the same rules that prohibit strikes by members of the armed forces. The PCs, on the other hand, have the same right to strike as other public servants, although they can carry firearms while striking. In mid-2001 the legislature began deliberations on whether this right should be overturned or otherwise restricted. Congressional debate continued nearly five years later, at the time of writing.

5. In terms of sheer geographical dimensions, Brazil is larger than the contiguous United States.

6. For more on the economic miracle, see Eakin (1997). Specifically on Brazil's efforts to diversify from reliance on petroleum, see Street (1982).

7. In June 1994, just before the launch of the new currency, Cardoso had lagged behind Luiz Inácio "Lula" da Silva (Lula) with only 16 percent in the polls relative to Lula's 40 percent.

8. During these years, Brazil increased its GDP by 8.4 times, while Japan and South Korea expanded their GDP by 13.1 and 20 times, respectively. Figured on the basis of historical GDP data compiled in Maddison (2003).

9. Calculated on the basis of figures presented in Maddison (2003).

10. "FT 500: Top 100 Latin American companies," *Financial Times,* May 11, 2001.

11. According to the head of the Ministry of Foreign Affairs' Financial Office in New York, Brazil has the tenth largest industrial complex in the world; it is the twelfth largest automaker and has the fourth largest aerospace industry—the Embraer aeronautics company exports jets and turbo propellers to the United States, France, Italy, Switzerland, Holland, and China, among others. The company is so successful that Canada attempted to block its export to protect its own company, Bombardier; after a five-year dispute in the World Trade Organization, Brazil's trade negotiators finally won the case in 2001. In addition, Brazil has an internationally recognized scientific capacity, being a pioneer both in the mapping of genomes of agricultural pests and in the manufacture of inexpensive AIDS-fighting drugs. See "Facts, Figures, and Factors That Make Brazil a Strong Market Opporunity," *Brasilians,* November 2001.

12. See for example Montoro (1998) for the case of Brazilian privatization of steel in the early 1990s and Manzetti (1999: ch. 4) on the experience of the 1990s more generally, with particular reference to the Brazilian case in comparison to those of Argentina and Peru.

13. Joseph Stiglitz, "Tres Hurras por Brasil," *El País,* August 15, 2002.

14. Drivers who do venture out at night routinely ignore traffic lights for fear of being assaulted.

15. In 1996, Rio received only about half a million foreign tourists and one million from other parts of Brazil, compared to London's 25 million visitors and New York's 31 million (who spent more than US$13 billion). See World Bank (1999: sec. 38).

CHAPTER 11

The Brazilian
Political Game

If the failure by successive federal and Rio administrations to accomplish systematic police reform cannot be entirely attributed to police opposition or to economic issues, where did responsibility lie? I argue in this chapter that the vagaries of the police reform process are inextricably linked to the lingering patrimonial and clientelist patterns that shape the political game in Brazil, as they do in Argentina. In Brazil, higher levels of social exclusion and poverty, coupled with deficient institutional accountability, have further contributed to pervasive official unresponsiveness to the needs and interests of the majority population. Even though in both countries the transfer of political power has been effected within democratic structures since the end of military rule, embedding democratic values, principles, and practices has proven far more elusive. As far as the police role is concerned, not too much has changed since President Washington Luis (1926–1930) famously intoned, "The social question is a police matter."

Political Culture and Accountability

Politicians feel little compulsion to respond to the interests of their constituencies. . . . The state is still lording over the population as if anything they do for you is a favor, rather than their responsibility.
    —A representative of a prominent Rio-based NGO[1]

As previously discussed, Brazil is characterized by some of the highest rates of inequality and social exclusion in the world. Stark inequities are present not only in terms of income and land tenure but also in gender, racial, and educational realms,[2] as well as between urban and rural dwellers and northern and southern states. As one scholar put it, on the whole Brazilian society has been "characterized by a sharp, social duality, an enduring social framework in which the majority are systematically excluded from the majority of political and economic benefits generated by the system" (Roett 1999: 27).

As argued by various scholars (e.g., Kant de Lima 1997; Silva 1998), this duality is encoded in a legal system that sets the tone for class discrimination at all levels of the criminal justice system. For example, the Code of Criminal Procedures guarantees "special prisons" for convicted persons holding a university degree, so they can be housed separately from "common prisoners." Members of Congress are guaranteed immunity from prosecution for common crimes committed during their term of office.[3] In light of such anachronisms, it is not surprising that public opinion surveys consistently show dismally low rates of confidence in the legal system. In one poll, only 2.5 percent of respondents believed that a poor person and a rich one would receive equal treatment if they committed the same crime (CPDOC-FGV/ ISER 1997: 49). In a rare admission, even a judge on the Brazilian Superior Court of Justice stated, "In a democracy the law is applied to all. In this country, only to some."[4]

Particularistic Use of Public Office

Underpinning the skewed structure of social and economic relations are vast clientelistic structures, a network of relationships wherein individuals of different status are tied to one another based on "unequal but reciprocal exchange of particularistic benefits and protection for obedience and support" (Weyland 1996: 33). To feed these clientelistic networks, public officials and politicians routinely divert state resources for patronage and special favors, trading public services, contracts, licenses, and appointments in exchange for political support by local power brokers.

In the 1990s, the media exposed many of these often corrupt arrangements, detailing cases of unabashed personal enrichment by public officials in addition to traditional political patronage. Much rarer, however, were successful prosecutions. Renowned anthropologist Roberto da Matta has argued that corruption in Brazil is hard to prosecute because "it is never an individual act. It always involves groups of people bound by one fundamental rule of association: an exchange of favors. This collective corruption is founded on traditional morality, well-established friendships and the opportunities at hand. It allows crimes to be practiced with impunity and is characterized by an intolerable arrogance" (1993).

The case of Fernando Collor de Mello, whose presidential campaign promised to "clean house" and rid the country of corruption in the civil service, is illustrative. As noted in Chapter 9, Collor decreed the freezing of four-fifths of all savings accounts for eighteen months immediately upon assuming office in 1990, a draconian measure that left many working families

unable to meet their obligations. As the president was appealing to the panicked population to stay calm, the media went public with news that not
only was his wife spending US$20,000 a month on clothes and jewelry but
her registered charity was funneling donations to phantom companies run
by her relatives. Within a short period, Collor's closest associate was also
accused of influence-peddling schemes designed to fund the presidential
couple's lavish lifestyle, including a US$2.5 million landscaping job for the
family estate (Weyland 1993).

President Collor initially dismissed all charges as the "ranting of a
deranged schizophrenic," pointing a finger at his own younger brother, who
was promptly disinherited by the aging family matriarch. While under different circumstances the Brazilian population might have found this real-
life soap opera highly engrossing, the president's freezing of savings accounts
had caused severe deprivation; amid ever more scandalous accusations, the
Senate finally ordered an investigation. When efforts to buy the vote of several key congresspersons with state funds came to light, hundreds of thousands of protesters took to the streets. Facing imminent impeachment, President Collor was allowed to resign in December 1993. The siphoned funds,
however, were not returned, and the Supreme Court acquitted the former
president of criminal charges two years later.

While arguably the most damaging example of blatant official corruption in the 1990s, the Collor case was by no means unique. President Cardoso, a renowned sociologist with a reputation for integrity, was publicly
accused by a former minister of "allowing others to steal"—including
members of Congress, judges, ministers, and other government officials.
During his second term, the discovery of a web of fraud and influence-peddling schemes implicated the president's former chief of staff and ultimately brought down three senators and a senior judge.

The saga can be traced back to 1999, when a federal congressional inquiry on corruption unearthed that Senator Luiz Estevão and federal judge
Nicolau dos Santos Neto had appropriated US$170 million (73 percent of
the total budget) from the construction of a labor court building in São
Paulo. In a move unprecedented in its 174-year history, the Senate expelled
one of its own, while Judge Nicolau became a fugitive for seven months.
After the judge was finally apprehended, convicted, and imprisoned, his
lawyers argued that he had become "depressed"; the presiding judge then
released him to return to his own lavish home under house arrest—in the
process turning Judge Nicolau into a national symbol of impunity.[5]

Within a year, two more senators were forced to resign in spin-off
cases: a former Senate president and leader of Bahia's powerful political
dynasty, Antônio Carlos Magalhães, and the long-term rival who had succeeded him as Senate president, Jader Barbalho. Over his lengthy political
career, Magalhães had amassed enormous power, which allowed him to

gain access to the Senate's computer voting system to see how his colleagues had voted in the Senator Estevão case—secret information that he expected to use as a blackmail tool to discredit his successor. Within months of Magalhães's resignation, Barbalho was also facing graft charges dating back to his tenures as governor of Pará State and minister for agrarian reform in the 1980s. Among other irregularities, the Senate president was accused of embezzling US$4 million from the state development bank and of diverting millions more from the Amazon Development Agency (SUDAM) to his wife's phantom frog-raising company.

That both Senate presidents had been key players in President Cardoso's governing coalition and the main proponents of federal congressional investigations into corruption in the judiciary and banking sectors made their downfall all the more scandalous. Their vexation was, however, short lived: Bahia State overwhelmingly reelected Magalhães as senator in October 2002, while Pará State elected Barbalho to the Chamber of Deputies, giving him a record number of votes. His son, meanwhile, was also elected overwhelmingly to serve in the Pará State Legislature. The return of both Magalhães and Barbalho to Congress reestablished their parliamentary immunity from criminal prosecution.

Vertical Accountability

In Brazil, as elsewhere, clientelistic patterns breed not only venality but dependency, since most poor and marginalized people find that claiming their rights does not come easily when they are on the receiving end of trickle-down handouts. Moreover, the convolutions of the Brazilian electoral process have posed daunting obstacles to transparency. It was only in 1985 that illiterates gained the right to vote; until then, the ban had effectively ruled out political participation by millions of poor citizens. Three years later, the 1988 constitution lowered the voting age to sixteen, making the vote compulsory for citizens between eighteen and seventy, and optional for sixteen- and seventeen-year-olds.[6] These changes, however significant, did not fundamentally deepen participatory democracy, as the process remained fraught with voter manipulation by special interests.

Fleeting political parties. Rather than serving as instruments to represent diversity and otherwise enable the electorate to better monitor elected officials, Brazilian political parties have been largely characterized by weak ideological bases, disorganization, and indiscipline. The ephemeral nature of Brazilian parties in the 1990s was in fact among the most extreme in Latin America. Unlike other South American countries such as Chile, Argentina, Colombia, and Uruguay, none of Brazil's major pre-1964 parties survived the military dictatorship. The military dissolved existing parties in October

1965, creating instead an official progovernment party and an official opposition party. By allowing Congress to continue functioning while simultaneously curtailing its legislative powers and tightly controlling elections,[7] as Scott Mainwaring and others have noted, "the military government unwittingly stimulated the proliferation of clientelistic politicians with limited legislative abilities and concerns" (Mainwaring 1995: 368).

The electoral rules drawn following the return to civilian rule had a limited impact in redressing this situation. At both federal and state levels, Brazil has a low party threshold coupled with a proportional representation system (PR).[8] This means that parties can gain seats in the Lower Chamber of Congress and state assemblies with even minimal percentages of the national or state vote respectively, particularly as smaller parties are allowed to pool their share of votes (Mainwaring 1997: 69). Moreover, Brazil is one of only two countries in the world (Finland is the other) that combine PR with an open-list system. In Brazil, the share of seats won by each party is distributed among whichever candidates have personally received the most votes within the party rather than according to their party rank (Kinzo 1993: 143). This configuration dramatically weakens party discipline and coherence, since candidates must compete not only with external rivals but also with candidates from their own party. Therein lies the problem: since to defeat same-party rivals a shared party platform cannot be invoked, candidates must rely on personalistic or patronage-based appeals. The open-list system, moreover, wrests from the party one of the main tools for punishing voting indiscipline—the capacity to place such disloyal persons in a low-ranking position in the party list in subsequent elections (Geddes and Neto 1992: 649).

Party indiscipline in Brazil is further aggravated by the fact that there are no sanctions against those who change parties. This is such a common occurrence, in fact, that in the 1994–1998 Congress, 230 out of 513 members of the Chamber of Deputies changed parties, some of them up to four times. Within just three weeks of being sworn in, forty-seven members of Congress had switched allegiances.[9] In many cases, it was not ideology but handsome payoffs that led to the switch.

Neither presidential nor gubernatorial elections are linked to the proportion of votes received by the party in legislative elections, as often occurs in PR systems, many of which are parliamentary systems governed by prime ministers. Rather, executive elections operate independently of legislative elections and are determined by a two-round absolute majority system (Mainwaring 1997: 69). Given the right circumstances, the presidency is therefore attainable even by a candidate from an insignificant or hastily constructed party. For example, Collor de Mello became president despite the fact that his brand-new party had gained less than 8 percent of seats in congressional elections.[10] Also worth noting is that interim president

Franco was not affiliated with any party, and President Cardoso did not name his party, the Brazilian Social Democracy Party (PSDB),[11] even once in his 300-page 1994 election manifesto (Power 2000: 29).

The electoral rules in Brazil have encouraged such a proliferation of parties that in 1990, for example, nineteen were represented in the Chamber of Deputies. The largest party won only 21.5 percent of congressional seats; the largest three combined accounted for only 47.5 percent of seats. In the 1999 Lower Chamber there were eighteen parties holding seats,[12] again with the largest party holding only roughly 21.25 percent of all seats. Given that states serve as single electoral districts, moreover, and any party can run 1.5 times the number of seats in each state, the choice of candidates for congressional office among all the different parties is enormous. In São Paulo State, the country's largest voting district, for example, in the 1994 legislative elections the competition for seventy legislative seats was waged among 532 candidates (Samuels 2001: 30). Because of the plethora of parties and because many disappear from one election to the next, even committed voters find it difficult to keep track of the policy record of any given party, let alone the voting record of an individual legislator, particularly if she or he has switched affiliation. Within this atmosphere of perpetually shifting allegiances, holding legislators accountable becomes a slippery task.

The high cost of campaigns increase the odds for undue influence from all sides, since, with the exception of media airtime, candidates receive only limited financial assistance from their party. While it is difficult to determine exactly what is spent on Brazilian campaigns, it is likely that it far exceeds what is spent in the United States, even though the PR system should theoretically be less onerous since candidates need to target only small proportions of the population. One study estimated that total expenditures for all 1994 Brazilian elections stood at between US$3.5 and 4.5 billion, in contrast to the $3 billion spent in the 1996 US elections. Lavish sums are spent on flyers, pamphlets, parties, rodeos, barbecues, and the distribution of food, clothing, and building materials to drum up personal support, particularly within impoverished communities (Samuels 2001: 33).

Civil society. If Brazil's political party system is mired in fragmentation and particularistic practices, are other participatory organizations emerging from civil society capable of transcending these traits to promote a joint national project to strengthen vertical accountability? In a society of such immense socioeconomic disparities, can real convergence be found in the interests of such diverse groups as business groups, the media, community associations, and NGOs?

Business sector and media. The role and power of Brazilian economic elites and the media have been extensively studied. Although they are as prone to power struggles as other segments of society, the economic elites have rallied around one primary goal: to maintain social stability and pursue economic growth. If by virtue of their economic dominance elites were already perceived as being antagonistic to majority interests, in the 1990s their enthusiastic support for trickle-down forms of economic development pitted them repeatedly against advocates of social progressivism. During that period, in spite of the fact that Brazilian business lobbies and federations are subject to more formal regulations than similar groups in other Latin American countries,[13] their vast influence allowed them to freely circumvent restrictions and advance their interests. Government ministries, particularly the ministries linked directly to the economy, are often staffed with prominent businesspersons, and prominent industrialists have close informal ties with and easy access to the political establishment (Schneider 1997: 97). During the 1990s, in particular, business poured money into the coffers of centrist and right-wing candidates, as corporations could make direct contributions to political campaigns with no clear limits on contributions, while labor unions were prohibited from making such contributions (Samuels 2001: 35).

In a country where literacy rates in many regions remain low,[14] television in particular has proved an enormously influential tool to shape social opinion.[15] During the Sarney government (1985–1990), a survey found that the overwhelming majority of respondents thought television networks had "much more" influence on the government than all other actors, including the national legislature, external creditors, labor unions, armed forces, the church, business associations, and multinational firms (Schneider 1997: 104). It is not coincidental that one study found that more than half of legislators in some states owned a radio station, television station, or both. One such media mogul, the aforementioned Antônio Carlos Magalhães, former Senate president, served as minister of communications during the whole of the Sarney presidency (1985–1990), without divesting himself of his television stations and other media holdings (Power and Roberts 2000: 258).

For decades Brazilian television was the virtual domain of one network, the Rede Globo. The network, owned and managed by the Marinho family of Rio de Janeiro, received its first television station license in 1957 and began transmission in 1965. In the ensuing years, Globo would prove instrumental in promoting the military regime's goal of "national integration," a program that entailed extensive road and highway building, colonization of distant territories, subsidies for investment in the telecommunications industry, and special credits to consumers to purchase television sets.[16] With the launching of the *Jornal Nacional* newsbroadcast in September 1969, both the military and the Globo network were assured of a virtual news monopoly throughout Brazil. Through his endorsement of the military regime, the founding patriarch of the Globo network constructed "a [media] supremacy of gigantic proportions" (Miguel 2000: 70).

Although the media can play a crucial role in promoting democratic governance by enabling wide-ranging debate, strengthening participation in public life, and acting as a watchdog, the Globo network primarily exercised its civic muscle in favor of its own class interests. As several studies have shown, news coverage, particularly during campaign times, was routinely edited and manipulated to showcase allies and associates and deride others (e.g., Herz 1987; Lima and Ramos 1988; Mello 1994). Even the content of soap operas, which last an average of nine months and have a huge cultural influence, has been found to be subtly laced with political content designed to lend support to particular candidates or to galvanize social opinion. At the national level, Globo's support was pivotal in ensuring the triumph of Collor de Mello. Despite the fact that Collor was a virtual unknown nationally, his family ties[17] and the fact he was running against two left-wing candidates (Luiz Inácio "Lula" da Silva and Leonel Brizola, former Rio State governor)[18] guaranteed him Globo's support—although the scandal accompanying President Collor's resignation ultimately weakened Globo's credibility. In later years, when liberalization of the telecommunications market brought competition from other networks, Globo shifted gears and, in a feat of cunning pragmatism, repositioned itself as a socially progressive and unbiased corporation.

Unions and the middle class. Although the influence of the Brazilian elites and the media on national life in the 1990s has been widely acknowledged, the question whether civil society exerted much real clout on the government opens up a grayer area. There had been considerable optimism in this regard following the period of political *abertura* initiated in 1977. One reason was the strength of union militancy and alliances formed with the middle class to agitate for direct presidential elections. In 1979, in particular, although strikes were expressly forbidden, more than 3 million workers in fifteen states shut down schools, universities, hospitals, and automobile plants, causing important economic losses that accelerated the decline of the military regime (Alves 1985: 198). A year later, the Workers' Party (PT) was formed.[19]

In early 1984, Diretas Já, a massive campaign to demand immediate direct elections for president, was launched in major cities, attracting over a million participants. Although direct elections would not take place until five years later, the campaign energized civil society and raised hopes that concerted political action could indeed influence the government. Although rising economic turmoil during the debt crisis of the mid-1980s weakened political activism, the federal government's opening of the constitutional drafting process to civil society in 1987 was an important factor in diverting rising frustration.

During a two-year period, Congress, doubling as a constituent assembly, received nearly 12,000 constitutional proposals from civic and labor organizations. It took 100 volumes to file the proceedings since "no interest group was too insignificant to weigh in and no demand too marginal to include" (Prillaman 2000: 89). The result was a 193-page, 315-article constitution—the country's eighth since independence in 1822. The document contained sweeping social, economic, and political guarantees, as well as new labor regulations granting workers a minimum wage, a forty-hour work week, a limit of six hours for continuous shifts, the right to strike, severance pay, and 120-day maternity leave (arts. 7–11). Despite multiple divisions,[20] organized labor was able to come together throughout the constitutional drafting process to obtain a significant expansion of workers' rights, at least on paper, over the opposition of big business.

The 1988 constitution contained myriad clauses to end racism, promote regional equality, eradicate poverty, advance Afro-Brazilian culture, and promote leisure and sports activities. The timetable and modality for implementing these guarantees was left, however, to ordinary legislation and to state governments (Rosenn 1990: 778–779). By the time it became apparent that many of these provisions and guarantees were being ignored, many of the civic coalitions active during the constitutional drafting process had already demobilized.

By the 1990s, when President Cardoso expanded the neoliberal reforms initiated by Collor, trade unions' capacity to serve as a voice for change had worn thin. High unemployment and the rise of the informal sector greatly eroded the unions' main base: by 1997, the informal sector had risen to 50.6 percent of the Brazilian labor force, while union membership as a proportion of the population had declined to 14 percent, from 23 percent in 1979 (ILO 2002: 238). In 1989, there were 4,000 strikes, the second highest rate in the world; by 1998 the number was reduced to 320.[21]

Neighborhood associations and the Catholic Church. As Chapter 7 noted, the economic miracle of the 1970s attracted a large number of impoverished peasants to Brazil's urban areas, triggering a rapid multiplication of *favelas.* Although neighborhood associations had initially arisen in the 1950s as centers for sports activities, the middle class started using them as a means to channel their concerns to the authorities on the expansion of *favelas* in their midst and as forums for political resistance (Boschi 1987: 63–75). In Rio, however, the expansion of associations in middle-class neighborhoods was far outmatched by the rapid growth of *favela* associations. Between 1969 and 1981, while 40 new associations sprang up in affluent neighborhoods, 206 were created in marginalized areas (Boschi 1987: 68). In 1978, two umbrella groups were formed: the Federation of Neighborhood Associations of the State of Rio de Janeiro (FAMERJ), representing the interests of affluent communities, and the Federation of Favela Associations of the State of Rio de Janeiro (FAFERJ), representing the interests of *favela* residents.

New urban social movements were given special impetus by the progressive stance of the Catholic Church in the 1960s; by the mid-1970s, many bishops were openly challenging the military regime. Unlike its counterpart in Argentina, the Brazilian Catholic Church took an activist social role, voicing support for a radical preferential option for the dispossessed and consistently denouncing human rights violations against peasants and workers. The church also used the organizational structures of ecclesiastical base communities (CEBs), small groups previously dedicated to the discussion of religious issues, to step up education programs among the urban and rural poor. It was a bishop active in the Catholic Church's Pastoral Land Commission (CPT), José Gomes, who helped found the Movement of Landless Rural Workers (MST), a national squatter movement of peasants, church leaders, and lawyers that advocates for agrarian reform and organizes land invasions throughout Brazil's interior.

Largely under the leadership of the Catholic Church, the poor in Rio had been using neighborhood associations to lobby against their forcible removal from *favelas* to distant housing projects, to advocate for more public services, and to legalize property titles. Faced with an increasingly vocal grassroots movement, the military government opted for corporatist control rather than open confrontation. In November 1969, they authorized the creation of *favela* associations but reserved the prerogative to intervene in their organization, activities, and leadership (Gay 1994: 20). Civic groups continued to grow, with an almost limitless range of activities.

By the 1990s Rio had multiple human rights organizations; education and technology groups; citizenship groups; health and family-oriented groups; sports and recreational associations; groups seeking to stimulate artistic potential; groups promoting racial, cultural, and linguistic pride; religious, charitable, ecological, and gender groups. Many of these entities were able to tap into foreign fascination with Brazil's cultural and racial diversity, garnering substantial funding from European and North American governments as well as from NGOs, the World Bank system, and international religious entities, in addition to more modest local government contributions. Still, during the 1990s the impact of most civil society organizations in promoting stronger vertical accountability was less substantial or sustained than their sheer numbers would indicate. What specific factors hampered their effectiveness in Rio de Janeiro?

Despite the gains made by the Catholic Church in the 1970s, sustained collaboration toward a common political project has remained an uphill struggle for *favela* residents. Brazilian anthropologist da Matta has argued that "the poor perceive elections as a mere mechanism to enrich dishonest and inoperative politicians and . . . see the formal institutions connected with the voting and the electoral processes as a sort of confirmation of the perverse power of some groups." Conscious of the abysmal quality of most public services available to them, the poor "are left with a feeling of being nobodies," particularly in terms of their ability to "question, demand from, or complain about public institutions" (1995: 52, 55).

Most *favela* residents live precarious lives: they do not own their land or pay taxes, and many lack even basic documentation, such as birth certificates.[22] By and large, they have extremely low educational levels or are functionally illiterate; they suffer disproportionately from a wide array of diseases, including malnutrition, and from alcohol and drug addictions and domestic violence. Those who work typically do so in the informal sector, enjoying none of the rights granted by labor legislation and earning far less than Brazil's US$46 monthly minimum wage. The poor remain, in short, in Oscar Lewis's 1963 description, "only partially integrated into national institutions . . . marginal people even when they live in the heart of a great city."[23]

Many of Rio's *favelas* recreate outside patterns: those who live at the foot of a hill enjoy a higher status within the community than those who squat higher up on the slopes; migrants from the affluent southeastern region of Brazil look down on migrants from the impoverished northeast. There are also deep cleavages between a traditionally Catholic population and converts to evangelical Protestantism,[24] a religious movement that vastly increased its influence in Rio de Janeiro, particularly among the poor, in the 1980s. There are also residual carryovers from rural life and customs. In the drought-ridden interior of the northeastern states, landowners and political bosses[25] have traditionally controlled social and political relations; they own the police, the media, and access to jobs and public services. Those migrants enterprising enough to escape the semifeudal order have carried with them a deeply conservative and fatalistic ethos.

The election of leftist Governor Leonel Brizola in 1982 during the period of military *abertura* unwittingly contributed to slowing down the development of the *favela* associations: when Brizola abandoned the policy of forcibly uprooting *favelas* and moving them to outlying areas, he reduced one of the main threats that had previously galvanized residents. When he invited leaders from some of the more prominent associations to serve in his administration, he also divested these communities of some of their brightest and most energetic minds. While a few associations succeeded against the odds at becoming active in the late 1970s and early 1980s, the vast majority of *favela* residents remained passive spectators, free-riding on the efforts of a few (Boschi 1987: 49, 146).

In the 1990s, associational life was further inhibited when drug traffickers took control of Rio's *favelas*, not only because their agendas were far removed from grassroots concerns but because their violent tactics restricted free movement. Increasingly, candidates for public office arrived to pay their respects, most often with neighborhood associations as proxies, as without the endorsement or permission of the "parallel powers" they dared not campaign or even distribute leaflets.[26] These arrangements created new clientelistic patterns, with extremely pernicious implications (Leeds 1996: 76). In the words of one former Rio judge, "Wherever drug traffickers are, only those who make a deal with them can go up into the *favelas*."[27] Even NGOs found it difficult to avoid drug traffickers. According to one NGO representative involved in a large legal advisory project in several *favelas,* their presence was not allowed unless the dominant drug trafficking gangs gave tacit approval—an approval that was also negotiated by using the neighborhood associations as proxies.[28] Overall, engendering greater activism among local residents, even when projects were directly targeted to them, proved very difficult.

For their part, the majority of middle-class neighborhood associations retreated into localized issues, driven by the "favelization"[29] of their neighborhoods and rising crime. Their efforts revolved around demands for more police presence; removal of beggars, prostitutes, vagrants, and homeless families from their streets; and control over roving vendors who cluttered boulevards and beaches in endless procession. As the overall quality of life continued to deteriorate, the Viva Rio coalition and other NGOs endeavored to bring people together by staging marches, demonstrations, candlelight vigils, and weapons destruction ceremonies, some carried out under the auspices of the United Nations. But while the symbolic appeal of peace and unity marches was tailor-made for media coverage, an editorial by the chief of Rio's Association of Detectives, published in one of Brazil's most prominent news dailies, took a hardened view of Rio's troubles:

> It would be wonderful if the criminals would put down their arms and hand them over to be burned in a public square. It would be even better if they could stop killing, stealing, kidnapping, and wounding for a while. . . . But none of this, sadly, has come to pass, nor will it. Armed to the teeth, the gangsters will continue spreading terror through the city and tormenting the population. They will keep drawing boundaries, imposing their demands, and denying citizens their constitutional right to come and go. . . . The March on Sunday and all previous ones like it were nice images for the media and good public relations for some, but it didn't affect the criminals in the slightest. . . . In reality, marchers should have taken a radically different approach: they should have gone dressed in black [rather than white] in mourning for the deaths of so many innocents, and demanded retaliation against criminals. . . . There is only one cure for the thousands of traffickers and armed robbers who have imposed a climate of fear in Rio de Janeiro: strong and unequivocal repression by a police freed to exercise the right to legally kill in defense of society. The criminals will only respect that kind of response, and without it, society will keep losing the war.[30]

Horizontal Accountability

The fractured nature of Brazilian civil society and the undisciplined political parties, long accustomed to patrimonial politics, pose serious constraints to the success of bottom-up pressure tactics to ensure more responsive governance and the implementation of overdue reforms. As has been the case in Argentina, the pernicious shortcomings of vertical accountability are themselves aggravated by a malfunctioning system of checks and balances across different branches of government.

The legislature and the encroaching executive. The 1988 constitution endeavored to break with the highly centralized style of rule adopted by the military regime by strengthening the legislature and the judiciary, and by increasing the authority and power of state and municipal governments. The tradition of ruling by fiat was not, however, easily effaced: through a clause in article 62, the president still retained a wide degree of latitude in lawmaking through the enactment of *medidas provisórias*. These "provisional measures" had many parallels to the decrees issued by the military regime, even though in principle they were to be adopted only in cases of "relevance and urgency" and could be abrogated after thirty days unless ratified by Congress (Rosenn 1990: 784). In practice, however, the emergency provision of article 62 was widely ignored, giving rise to an unfettered multiplication of decrees. Whenever the legislature failed to ratify them within thirty days, decrees were simply reissued, often with minor modifications, lest they expire. Thus, in a period of approximately thirteen years, five presidential administrations issued a grand total of 6,110 decrees. President Sarney issued 147 between 1988 and 1990; President Collor (1990–1992), 159; President Franco (1992–1994), 505. In his first term (1995–1998), President Cardoso issued an astonishing 2,609; in the first third of his second term alone (January 1, 1999–September 2001), he issued 2,690.[31]

Decrees have been justified in the name of "governability" or keeping the country running. In fact, owing to the multitude of political parties, frequent party switching, and the complex proportional representation system, presidents have usually governed with a stable voting bloc of barely 20 percent—not close to what is needed to push the executive agenda forward. Still, executive decrees represent an obvious truncation of the democratic process.

Heavy reliance on decrees, moreover, was not the only symptom of a malfunctioning balance of power across government throughout the 1990s. Other tools, such as bribery, patronage, and selective use of appointments to ensure the passing of presidential agendas were just as common. Whenever an institutional reform required a constitutional amendment—a procedure that requires two consecutive approvals by each chamber with a three-fifths majority each time—presidents usually avoided this cumbersome attempt to curtail presidential power by using a little *jeito* (informal way of doing things). For example, before the end of his first mandate, President Cardoso was alleged to have acquiesced to a plan by his minister of communications that entailed bribing key congresspersons to ensure the passing of a constitutional amendment to allow Cardoso (and future Brazilian presidents) to run for reelection. Another means to bypass procedure is that, in a reversal of normal patterns, Brazilian presidents initiate the majority of bills. One study showed that between 1989 and 1994, 79 percent of the 1,259 laws passed were initiated by the president, 14 percent by the legislature, and 7 percent by the judiciary (Mainwaring 1997: 65).

The Brazilian executive also enjoys significant latitude over budgetary and spending matters. While it is Congress's prerogative to approve the president's budget guidelines, the multiyear budget plan, and the annual budget itself, Congress does not have power over programs and projects not included in the president's budget (Dillinger and Webb 1999: 11). The president can issue line-item vetos, cutting out any undesired nonconstitutionally mandated expenditure from the budget before signing it. While the majority of federal transfers to the states occur through a standardized mechanism of revenue sharing set by the constitution, the president has access to key discretionary funds, which can be dangled in front of recalcitrant states or individuals to sway political outcomes. The president can also withhold or redirect subsidized federal loans and guarantees of international loans away from states or individuals in order to induce cooperation and bestow ministerial appointments in exchange for support.[32]

The judiciary. Given the truncated nature of presidential-legislative checks and balances, the strength of the judiciary's commitment to upholding the rule of law and promoting responsible government becomes all the more important. The Brazilian judiciary, during and after the military era, showed a considerably higher degree of assertiveness than its Argentine counterpart (Osiel 1995: 533–540). The judiciary, for instance, ruled in favor of freeing illegally detained students, declared unconstitutional certain portions of the National Security Law enacted by the military, and overturned other military decisions, particularly during the period of political *abertura* in the late 1970s.

The drafters of the 1988 constitution went to considerable lengths to ensure that the judiciary's autonomy was dramatically increased: judges were granted life tenure, guaranteed salaries, and near total control over administrative affairs. While Supreme Court justices were subject to impeachment and removal by the Senate, lower court judges were subject to removal only by higher courts. The Supreme Court was given the power to forward its annual budget directly to Congress, bypassing the executive, and lower levels of the courts enjoy a similar privilege (Prillaman 2000: 81–82). With this relative degree of freedom from financial tribulations, the Brazilian judiciary was able to assert itself to a considerable degree. It overruled or modified numerous decrees issued by Presidents Collor, Franco, and Cardoso, annulled the reelection of a powerful Senate president because of campaign finance irregularities, blocked privatization attempts and pension reform efforts, and even mandated wage increases (Power 1998: 209). Constant changes to the Brazilian tax system—the federal income tax, for instance, had been subjected to an average of fifteen changes a year—led the judiciary to rule against the government on numerous occasions. In 1993 alone it was estimated that the federal government lost US$3 billion in tax revenues owing to judicial rulings (Souza 1998: 7).

Despite the relative independence of the Brazilian judiciary in some spheres, the institution has never quite accomplished the strength, integrity, and autonomy envisioned when new institutions, largely based on US models, were set up following the end of the monarchy in 1889. According to comparative legal scholar William Prillaman, in 1997 the eleven Supreme Court justices were earning more than the president—US$10,800 monthly; further, federal judges enjoyed sixty days of annual paid vacation, a car and driver, a gasoline allowance, a free luxury apartment, and extensive funds for staffers (2000: 86). Such perks, coupled with repeated charges of illicit enrichment and nepotism, led Prillaman to assert that the Brazilian judiciary was "devoid of all accountability . . . rife with nepotism and corruption, indifferent to public and congressional calls for transparency, and capable of resisting any measures that would improve its efficiency and scale back the generous and unjustifiable perquisites the courts had granted themselves" (2000: 76–77).

Extensive judicial backlog deterred the judiciary's capacity to serve as a credible monitor of other government institutions. Although the 1988 constitution created a new federal court of appeals, the Superior Court of Justice. to free the Supreme Court to concentrate only on constitutional matters, in 1997 the Supreme Court had a backlog of over 30,000 cases (Prillaman 2000: 76).[33] The absence of a codified system establishing legal precedent caused the court to rule thousands of times on similar issues, often inconsistently, and allowed lower courts to disregard higher-court rulings. Another hindering factor was that the constitution's all-encompassing nature meant that even trivial cases were brought before the Supreme Court. As one former Supreme Court president lamented in 1997, its judges were so swamped by minutiae and small claims cases that the "Supreme Court was close to becoming inoperable."[34] It was not until December 2004 that a constitutional amendment established the principle of binding precedent.[35]

A fourth branch of government? In a country as large and diverse as Brazil, it would be almost inevitable that individual states would engage in varied forms of political bargaining to secure their place in the sun. Some states are in fact so remote and unknown that they have established consulates in large Brazilian cities.[36] On the other hand, the influence of some state governors on national politics has led some scholars to refer to them as a kind of "fourth branch" of government, capable of acting as a powerful restraining force and counterweight on the president (Samuels and Abrucio 2000). It was precisely to neutralize the power of local and regional leaders that Vargas's Estado Novo (1937–1945) (and the 1965–1988 military regime) centralized decisionmaking and budget allocations and installed loyal supporters as governors and mayors.

This control began to crack during the *abertura* period, when local political elites agitated alongside organized civil society and other protesters for a return to democracy, leading to the first direct gubernatorial elections in 1982. The process was completed with the enactment of the 1988 constitution, which devolved such a significant amount of tax-and-spend powers to state and local governments that among developing countries Brazil is considered the most fiscally decentralized (Shah 1991; Souza 1998).

Argentina's brand of federalism gives the federal government a central role; this is largely a function of the fact that Buenos Aires, the seat of government, holds a disproportionate share of economic power. Only one province has the economic clout or the demographics needed to pose a significant challenge to the central government: Buenos Aires Province. In Brazil, on the other hand, there are several powerful economic hubs with significant local markets. State governors, moreover, often guide the political position of their state's legislators in Brasilia, the country's capital, so a president's relationship with a given governor affects executive capacity to secure support in Congress. Among Brazilian states, São Paulo is so economically powerful that it accounts for more than one-third of the country's GDP; when it is grouped with three other southeastern states—Minas Gerais, Espirito Santo, and Rio de Janeiro—this share goes up to nearly 60 percent of GDP.[37] Through their discretionary use of resources and provision of public services, jobs, and many other forms of patronage, state governors can mobilize large political followings and exert significant influence over federal legislators. In 1993, for example, President Collor's increasing political isolation forced him to court his former opponent in the 1989 presidential elections, Rio governor Leonel Brizola. In exchange for Brizola's pledge to influence the vote of Rio's forty-six-member congressional delegation in his favor, Collor federalized the Rio subway system's US$2.5 billion debt and granted another US$100 million in federal funds to build the Linha Vermelha highway.

The power of state governors was highlighted in 1999 when Minas Gerais governor Itamar Franco[38] refused to accept President Cardoso's plans for economic austerity: he unilaterally declared a ninety-day moratorium on his state's US$15 billion debt to the federal government. Fears that the other state governors might follow suit caused a massive capital flight abroad and precipitated the devaluation of the real. During the 2001 energy crisis, Governor Franco defied the federal government again when he announced that he would not force consumers in Minas Gerais to meet energy-rationing targets set by the Cardoso administration.

While the economic might of the southeastern states enhances their influence, the overrepresentation of even small states and parties in Congress ensures that any president will have to bargain with them as well.[39] In 1996, for example, President Cardoso was believed to have released federal funds to build a highway in Rondônia State to obtain eight key votes for a social security reform amendment.[40] In the same year, the state of Espirito Santo, whose public sector payroll alone exceeded state revenues, led a movement among six small states to bargain for the rollover of state debts at favorable interest rates. Taking advantage of President Cardoso's need for votes to secure the passing of his reelection amendment, the campaign spread to nine more states and culminated in the eventual federalization of a substantial portion of the debt of twenty states. The debt was to be repaid at subsidized rates for a period of thirty years—an arrangement that cost the federal government US$5.45 billion and would eventually increase by several billion more. In exchange, the states were to commit themselves to reducing payrolls, undergo fiscal restructuring, and privatize state banks implicated in illegal lending to state governments and political cronies. While some states undertook measures to follow through, eleven states, including Espirito Santo, did not.[41]

These examples show that, indeed, state governors hold vast influence not just locally but federally. But it should also be noted that their powers serve primarily as a stumbling block to presidential unilateralism and as a means of garnering patronage rather than as a source of presidential or local accountability. Since gubernatorial authority is largely unchecked by either the local judiciary or civil society, the weak horizontal accountability observed at the federal level is reproduced in even more extreme fashion at the state level. While hard data are lacking, use of the executive decree by governors is routine; state legislatures, by and large, "have no strong or innovative legislative tradition, being heavily subservient to the governors" (Selcher 1998: 27). The state budget is commonly used to boost the governor's political agenda, as are funds from government contracts, state development banks, and influence-peddling schemes.

As a result, corruption thrives at the state level on a grand scale. In 1993, for example, a highway expansion project linking São Paulo and Belo Horizonte, financed by federal funds and the Inter-American Development Bank, doubled the real cost of the project to US$540 million. A 1996 Senate investigation of nine governors and mayors uncovered fraud amounting to US$1 billion in federal bonds, which had been used to finance state payroll deficits and political campaigns and to fatten accounts in Paraguayan and offshore banks. The brazen corruption of state politicians has even inspired popular slang expressions, as in the case of the verb *malufar* (to steal), coined from the name of Paulo Maluf, a former governor of São Paulo State. Although Maluf was accused of skimming US$740 million out of the construction budget of a road tunnel and was later found to hold personal accounts exceeding US$200 million in Jersey Islands banks off the coast of England,[42] his prosecution was stalled for years. In 2001, at least six out of twenty-six state governors were facing congressional and judicial inquiries into corruption scandals.

Favelas and other neighborhoods that fail to vote for a given governor or mayor risk losing out on social programs and other benefits; similarly, state police forces and public prosecutors can be used to create difficulties for political opponents through untimely criminal investigations and other forms of intimidation. Although the media frequently report on these abuses, the intricate web of deceit and misinformation that surrounds most public funding and public decisionmaking frustrates many efforts to increase transparency in public life. As the well-known Brazilian dictum puts it, "To our friends, everything; to our enemies, the law."

Political Competition

In the 1990s, then, both vertical and horizontal checks and balances functioned so haltingly that even when a genuine effort was made to increase accountability, an undercurrent of "business as usual" continued to predominate. In Rio de Janeiro, where institutional restraint was largely a nominal issue, public office at both the municipal and state levels usually served as a mere springboard to higher grounds. In general, public officials spent an enormous amount of time maneuvering for position and preempting possible advances by potential rivals. As was the case in Argentina, these characteristics of political contests limited the available time and resources in which to debate public policy, acquire technical capacity, and promote reform.

In the case of public security, which was a central issue in every campaign in Rio during the 1990s,[43] the issue was relentlessly simplified and exploited by politicians and the media. With insecurity and public expectations constantly rising, it was promises of quick fixes that won or lost elections.

Public Office as Springboard, Public Security as Missile

In Rio de Janeiro in the 1990s, there were three things that worked like clockwork in the political sphere: first, as soon as a mayor or governor got elected, he or she would begin planning for higher office; second, immediately following that candidacy announcement, political opponents would begin a campaign of destruction; third, the public security situation would be used as the main weapon against these candidates.

In 1993, when Governor Leonel Brizola of the PDT resigned his office nine months early to run for president, his opponents (including the media) latched on to the public security issue to discredit not only his presidential bid but any protégé's chances for election. The media depicted Rio as a city out of control, assaulted by youth gangs, terrorized by drug traffickers, riddled with corrupt police who massacred street children. Vice Governor Nilo Batista, who was occupying the gubernatorial seat on an interim basis, denounced the media for intentionally "deforming, dramatizing, ignoring, and omitting facts."[44]

Rio's mayor, Marcello Alencar, joined the chorus of Brizola haters, blasting his permissiveness on crime issues and becoming what one newspaper referred to as Brizola's "biggest political enemy"[45]—despite the fact that he owed his 1989 mayoral triumph to Brizola's support. Toward the end of his mayoral term, Alencar made a timely switch to the PSDB—the party of Cardoso—and launched his own campaign for governor. Alencar's main opponents in the 1994 elections were Anthony Garotinho, mayor of the small town of Campos and member of Brizola's party (PDT), and a retired army general and former head of the disbanded National Intelligence Service, Newton Cruz of the PSD.[46] When General Cruz lost in the first round of the gubernatorial race, Alencar obtained his endorsement in exchange for a promise that, if elected, he would bring an army general to head public security—an arrangement that tipped the balance in his favor. After assuming office, Alencar bypassed Cruz and instead appointed another hard-line general as secretary of public security.

Shortly afterward, Cesar Maia (PMDB),[47] who had been elected mayor of Rio with Alencar's support in 1992, went from ally to rival, having decided that he would pursue the governorship in 1998. A public war of words ensued between the new governor and the new mayor, who disagreed over virtually every issue, including education, public works, and responsibility for the handling of natural emergencies. Mayor Maia's most potent invective was reserved for Governor Alencar's security policies; echoing an argument that had been used by opponents to discredit Brizola years earlier, he alleged that because of excessive violence, industry was deserting Rio and causing unemployment. Reminiscent of events in Buenos Aires, Mayor Maia created a "shadow cabinet" of public security despite the lack of a formal role for the municipal government in such matters. Governor Alencar responded by ridiculing Maia's shadow cabinet and saying that the mayor "is capable of researching everything, even the number of fleas that come out following rain."[48]

Undeterred, Maia charged that Governor Alencar had misused a loan the city had granted him by purchasing outdated armaments for the PM, a force that he said belonged to the "stone age" and was "worse than cops in Colombia, Venezuela and Mexico." As for Governor Alencar's hard-line secretary of public security, General Nilton Cerqueira did not "understand anything about public security"[49]; his perspective was that of "an army general from the time of the war against Paraguay [fought in the 1800s]. . . . He talks only of how many criminals were defeated, armaments captured. It is like a war chronicle. I want to hear and see how criminals were convicted through scientific investigations." Mayor Maia also recommended that the bearded chief of the PC, Hélio Luz, be sent packing to a "hippie colony" and claimed that thanks to Governor Alencar's public security policies, "in Rio we live in a tropical Bosnia."[50]

Mayor Luiz Paulo Conde (1997–2000), a Maia protegé, picked up where his mentor left off. Though his Liberal Front Party (PFL)[51] was part of Governor Alencar's coalition, Conde opposed him on almost every issue, including the legalization of cockfighting.[52] His most damning accusation was that Governor Alencar was jeopardizing the implementation of Favela Bairro, an urban renewal program financed by the Inter-American Bank, by allowing a parallel state to fester in the *favelas*. Governor Alencar's reelection prospects were seriously damaged by these attacks, as well as by various high-profile crimes in the city, including a bank robbery carried out inside the very seat of government, Guanabara Palace, only a few months before the election. As had invariably occurred before, the unresolved public security crisis created a backlash against the incumbent; with his poll ratings plummeting, Governor Alencar dropped out of the race.[53] The gubernatorial campaign was then hotly contested by former mayor Cesar Maia (who had switched parties to the PFL) and Anthony Garotinho (in a second election attempt with the PDT).

Despite having served as Brizola's finance minister back in the 1980s, when the two shared party affiliation, Maia took aim at his former mentor just as Alencar had done, telling voters that if they elected his rival Garotinho (a Brizola protegé), a Brizola-like chaos would ensue. Notwithstanding Maia's alarmist rhetoric, Garotinho won the gubernatorial election. A committed evangelical Christian, he had scored points by pledging a "government of peace," calling on noted sociologist Luis Eduardo Soares to find a "third way" to bridge the security policies of previous governments. At times playing the role of corruption crusader and father figure to the poor and at times playing the crime hard-liner, Garotinho had a chameleonic personality that sent his popularity ratings soaring.[54] When police opposition to Soares intensified, and with his gaze firmly planted on the 2002 presidential elections, Garotinho fired police reformer Soares on live television.

During this time, trouble was also brewing between Garotinho and his vice governor, Benedita da Silva. A populist raised in the Chapeu Mangueira *favela* behind one of Rio's most affluent neighborhoods, da Silva was the first black woman ever to serve in the federal legislature; she was also a major figure in the PT and a Lula supporter.[55] Although she had been instrumental in helping Garotinho win the race for governor, her rising political prominence was posing such a threat that when da Silva decided to challenge Mayor Conde in the 2000 municipal elections, Garotinho publicly scorned his vice governor.

Mayor Conde was himself battling two rivals in these elections: his former friend and patron Maia and the perennial Brizola. After seeing his gubernatorial aspirations thwarted, Maia had set his sights on regaining his former mayoral seat (for which purpose he changed parties yet again, for the third time in eight years, aligning himself with the Brazilian Labor Party, or PTB).[56] Just as he had refused to endorse the mayoral candidacy of his own vice governor, da Silva, Garotinho now also turned against Brizola, his political mentor and fellow PDT party member, opting instead to support Conde. The issue of public security was once more at the core of the mayoral campaign.

When Maia emerged victorious, Governor Garotinho was expelled from Brizola's PDT and remained without party affiliation for several months. His already tense relationship with Vice Governor da Silva finally collapsed after the governor accused her of absconding with some US$218,000 donated by private enterprise to subsidize restaurants for the poor.[57] In addition, his relations with Mayor Maia were so acrimonious that their mutual attacks made daily front-page news. Their longstanding rivalry was aggravated when Maia admitted he harbored hopes of becoming governor and then president in 2006. As soon as Maia assumed the mayor's office, previous existing accords and collaboration between the state and municipal administrations, on issues such as traffic control, urbanization policy, and sanitation, were suspended.

The community policing program in Pavão-Pavãozinho was a particular bone of contention. As seen in Chapter 9, this program had attracted such high-level international attention and media coverage that both the state and municipal governments were eager to claim credit for it. New urbanization and social programs in the *favela* were announced at a feverish pace by Mayor Maia, who claimed the Inter-American Development Bank would provide financing and technical assistance. When Governor Garotinho opened his own bidding process to develop Pavão-Pavãozinho, effectively excluding the municipal government, the mayor retaliated by accusing the "Pentecostal Populist," as he took to calling the governor, of turning the *favela* into a safe haven for drug traffickers.[58] Their conflict soon extended to other, elite areas of the city. When the state announced plans for a cleanup of the polluted beach of affluent Leblon, the municipal government denied it the license needed to commence work. In turn, when the city launched plans to build a tunnel in the eastern part of Rio, the state government blocked the initiative, demanding financial compensation for building a tunnel on state-owned land.

On April 5, 2002, Governor Garotinho left office nine months prematurely to campaign for president, having announced his candidacy almost a

year earlier.[59] He also switched parties, choosing to run for the Brazilian
Socialist Party (PSB).[60] His arch-rival da Silva (his beleaguered vice governor) filled the seat, promptly bringing back Garotinho's nemesis Soares to
advise her on security matters and to share her ticket in her own gubernatorial campaign. Competing against her was Rosinha Matheus de Oliveira,
Garotinho's wife.

In a turn of events reminiscent of the Brizola and Alencar administrations, Interim Governor da Silva was soon dogged by serious security scandals that derailed her gubernatorial campaign. First, unknown assailants
launched a brazen daytime attack against City Hall with automatic weapons
and missiles, causing substantial damage. Later, following a bloody revolt
at Bangu prison, the Comando Vermelho gang defiantly flew its flag from
the rooftop after gaining control of the prison. Ridiculed by the media, da
Silva fought back by claiming that the smear campaign against her was
really aimed at her left-wing party, Lula's PT, which was leading in the
polls before the October 2002 presidential elections.

Conclusion

When viewed within the context of the Brazilian political game, the seemingly erratic marches and countermarches of Rio's police reform process
follow a certain logic. In a profoundly unequal society, the depoliticization
of the police and their transformation into a professional and disciplined
force might have risked significantly altering the stratified social order.
Altering the status quo would have required colossal political will, courage,
time, and strong pressure from organized civil society.

As this chapter highlights, in the 1990s civil society lacked the necessary cohesion to mobilize mechanisms of vertical accountability, not just in
Rio but also in Brazil as a whole. The multitude of nonprogrammatic parties running a small army of candidates and the routine switching of allegiances from one party to the other posed further obstacles to the development of monitoring systems and representational politics. Not only were
most institutions sucked into clientelistic politics and elite capture, but
steep divisions along (and even within) class lines frequently subverted the
potential strength of civic society to serve as democratic watchdogs.

In large cities such as Rio, these weaknesses were compounded by the
power and violence of the drug trade, whose influence on public life reversed many of the gains accomplished by civil activism in the aftermath of
military rule. The urban poor had few avenues to exercise civic and social
citizenship; most were exhausted by the sheer effort required to survive.
Efforts to pressure the state on their behalf, be it to obtain basic public services or to attain relief from drug gangs, were usually acknowledged only

at election time. By the 1990s, decades-long efforts to exile the poor to distant outlying areas had failed, and *favelas* were again dominating the Rio landscape; with crime and creeping "favelization" on the rise, and the police impotent to contain the crisis, the middle class had nowhere to turn. While the elites were not immune to crime, their vast resources allowed them a large degree of insulation as they hired private security guards, lived in gated communities with satellite tracking systems, and traveled with bodyguards in armored cars. As one police officer interviewed put it, "The elites don't smell the stench of poverty."[61]

Although presidents showed no hesitation to issue a profligate number of decrees to accomplish their economic goals, they put no comparable impetus behind security sector reform, an issue of crucial national importance. The wildly pluralistic nature of the legislative branch, its members' paper-thin allegiances, and co-optation by the executive increased the odds that Congress could serve as an effective counterweight to the executive or as generator of meaningful laws on the issue of police reform. The twenty-six state governors (plus the governor of the Federal District of Brasilia) and their respective legislative blocs concentrated their efforts on two fronts: they either secured particularistic gains, such as federal funds for public works projects and bailouts of state-owned banks, or set up obstructionist roadblocks to increase their bargaining power.

Courts were inefficient and overloaded, crisscrossed by a current of corruption that further discredited the judicial system as a whole. Although the Supreme Court's legitimacy was not threatened by the extensive presidential packing experienced by its Argentine counterpart, it was nevertheless similarly burdened by the monstrous volume of trivial and repetitive cases brought before it—a fact that diluted the court's power to exercise restraining force on the other two branches of government.

While local politics usually offer more potential to bridge the disconnect between government and the citizenry, Brazilian states all too often reproduced even more sharply the same tendencies observed at the federal level. The preeminent concern of many governors appeared to be their climb to higher political office, failing which they immediately plotted a return to their former status. To fund their exorbitantly expensive campaigns and grease fragile political coalitions, public officials at both the state and federal levels engaged in corrupt practices that would not have been tolerated had a strong and independent judiciary been in place.

If elected officials often got away with stealing millions, what was to deter a police officer earning a pittance from income supplementing through whatever means were available? In a country where the legal framework allows straying members of the "educated classes" to be treated with leniency or outright impunity, what kind of message filters down to those who have few options? Granted, legislative and judicial controls over the police were weak, yet they were not much stronger for overseeing public life in general. If the repetitive plundering of public coffers was any indication, few institutions in Brazil were policing themselves as the police were supposed to do.

In Rio de Janeiro specifically, there were several worthy programs launched to mitigate the tensions between the police and the poor. Most had good intentions but limited reach—not only because of the vast numbers of urban poor but also because municipal and state governments were too preoccupied with fending off encroachment by the other to work cooperatively. By the end of a governor's term, the disarray in the public security situation usually produced a backlash, leading to the election of any candidate promising the opposite approach. With each reversal, the chances that a sustainable public security policy would be established, or uniform professional standards for policing would develop, were substantially reduced.

In the 1980s and 1990s, the Rede Globo, a powerful and conservative media conglomerate, was a decisive factor in discrediting the policies of any politician whose ambitions it did not support. But if the elites were aware that growing fissures were threatening the survival of traditional structures, they did not yet show it. In the relative insulation of their heavily guarded cocoons, some among them could insist, "There is no hunger in Brazil. . . . Anyone in this country can eat a little rice, a small banana."[62] On September 30, 2002, however, not a single *carioca* could continue to ignore reality. On this ignominious date, which became known as Black Monday, the entire city obeyed a command by drug traffickers to shut down, finally united in fear. Banks, schools, offices, commerce, and public transportation closed their doors, and except for heavily armed gang members on patrol, Rio was like a ghost town.

Less than a month after Black Monday, Brazilians across the social spectrum expressed their fatigue with old models at the polls. But if Luiz Inácio "Lula" da Silva's triumph in the presidential elections offered fresh promise, in Rio de Janeiro there was a sense of déjà vu. As had happened to Governors Brizola and Alencar, Interim Governor Benedita da Silva was so thoroughly destabilized by the security situation—including the attack on City Hall, the decapitation of an investigative reporter by drug traffickers, and the events of Black Monday—that her chances for election vanished in thin air. It was Rosinha Matheus de Oliveira, the wife of former governor Garotinho, who was elected governor of Rio State. One of her first official acts was to appoint her husband as public security secretary.

These events notwithstanding, Brazil continued to project a much more cohesive international image than Argentina. In contrast to an Argentine political establishment that appeared grossly dysfunctional, the Brazilian federal government skillfully managed to convey a seriousness of purpose and commitment to reform that kept foreign investment flowing. This is in part derived from the extreme pragmatism that lies at the core of the Brazilian political game. At its best, this pragmatism generates hope that even seemingly irreconcilable opposites can come together in the interest of national unity—as demonstrated by the business elites' sudden embrace of Lula da Silva in the second round of the 2002 presidential elections. At its worst, it reeks of ûnscrupulous theatrics—as in the incessant turnarounds examined in the context of police reform in Rio.

Notes

1. Author interview, June 26, 2001.

2. Differences in educational opportunities and peformance are one of the most significant sources of income inequality in Brazil. The authors of one joint IDB and World Bank study found that whereas the child of a wealthy family usually completes university education, there is only a 15 percent chance that a student in the lowest three income deciles (roughly equivalent to the proportion of the population under the poverty line, where Afro-Brazilians are significantly overrepresented) will complete his or her primary education; the chances of completing secondary education drop further to 4 percent. In racial terms: only one in four students with nine or more years of educational attainment is nonwhite, even though Brazilians of mixed African ancestry constitute close to half of the population. See IDB and World Bank (1999: esp. p. 13).

3. Brazilian Code of Criminal Procedure, title 9, art. 295, esp. sec. 7, and constitution of Brazil, title 4, ch. 1, sec. 5, art. 53 specify that "members of Congress may not be arrested, except in flagrante delicto of a crime not entitled to bail, nor may they be criminally sued, without prior authorization from the respective Chamber of Congress" (para. 1). "In the event of flagrante delicto of a crime not entitled to bail, the case record has to be sent within twenty-four hours to the respective Chamber of Congress, which, by secret ballot of a majority of its members, shall resolve on the arrest and authorize or not the determination of criminal liability" (para. 3).

4. Edson Vidigal in "A Teoria Que Embala um Sonho," *Jornal do Brasil,* July 5, 2001.

5. "A pena que dói," *O Globo,* July 4, 2001.

6. In 1945 only 16 percent of the entire population had the right to vote, whereas by 1995 over 60 percent had this right, making for an electorate of over 100 million voters. See Power and Roberts (2000: 239).

7. With the exception of a ten-month period from 1968 to 1969, the military regime allowed Congress to function; elections were maintained for federal and state senators, congresspersons, and certain local positions. albeit with significant restrictions. All main executive positions, however, such as the presidency and vice presidency, governorships, and mayoral positions in state capitals, were effectively appointed by the military regime. See Mainwaring (1995: 364).

8. In a PR system, candidates to the legislature or parliament are elected according to the proportion of votes received by the party. Once a determination is made on how large the share of seats of each party will be, representatives are typically chosen from the party list, which in most countries is a fixed closed list based on rank order. In this system, if candidates receive 20 percent of the vote, that party receives

20 percent of the seats, with candidates being drawn from the preelection list. Those at the bottom are thus not as likely to be elected unless the party receives a large share of the seats.

9. Another study found similar trends in the 1986–1990 and 1990–1994 Congress. Thirty percent changed party affiliation, some up to seven times. See Desposato (1997). The left-wing Workers' Party (PT) shows one of the lowest incidences of party switching. In contrast to less ideological catchall parties, the PT set in place various sanctions to ensure that members vote the party line. For more on the origins and distinctiveness of the PT, see Nylen (2000).

10. Unstable alliances were subsequently made with other parties, accounting for 39.6 percent of seats. See Mainwaring (1997: 70–73).

11. The Party of Brazilian Social Democracy (Partido da Social Democracia Brasileira, PSDB) is a centrist party with social democratic roots created by a dissident group of the PMDB. The party was founded by Fernando Henrique Cardoso and was formally approved by the TSE on August 24, 1989.

12. This number rose to twenty-one as of the October 2002 elections. However, the number of officially recognized parties is far higher. In 2002, the Federal Superior Electoral Tribunal (TSE) had approved thirty different parties.

13. Many of the corporatist restrictions on business and labor that were laid down during Vargas's Estado Novo in the late 1930s remain in force. By law, business could set up one syndicate per sector in each municipality. Each sectoral syndicate had to belong to a state federation, which formed part in turn of the National Confederation of Industry (CNI). Because each syndicate, regardless of its size, has equal vote in the CNI, small and often backward firms hold disproportionate influence in the organization. This system was designed to "dilute the voice of the most important and powerful firms"; the result has been to discourage them from using the CNI. Instead they lobby the government individually. See Kingstone (1998: 78). For more on the CNI, the São Paulo FIESP, the Rio FIRJAN, and business associations more generally, see Schneider (1997).

14. Official Brazilian literacy rates, like other official statistics, are much debated. Given that people are classified as illiterate only if they cannot sign their name, 1998 estimates placed illiteracy at 13.8 percent among all those over fifteen and at 20.8 percent among blacks specifically. Yet as the same official source estimates that, on average, Brazilians over the age of twenty-five have completed only 5.6 years of schooling (4.3 in the case of blacks), it is questionable whether most are able to read or do basic math. Argentine statistics on illiteracy are significantly lower, although they are just as likely to suffer from distortions, as indicated by UN Development Programme figures for 1998, which place illiteracy at only 3.3 percent. See IPEA (2002: tables 2.1 and 2.4) and UNDP (2000: 157).

15. Television is by far the preferred news source among the population. In 1995, 74 percent of Brazilian households had at least one television, more than the number of refrigerator owners, despite the fact that Brazil is a tropical country. While in Argentina daily circulation of newspapers stands at 143 per 1,000 inhabitants, and in Venezuela at 205, in Brazil it is only 55. See Power and Roberts (2000: 257).

16. For more on the Rede Globo, see Miguel (2000: 70) and Straubhaar, Olsen, and Nunes (1993: 121).

17. Collor's father had been one of Roberto Marinho's original partners, and the Collor family still owned Globo affiliates in his home state of Alagoas (through which they had promoted his successful campaign for state governor).

18. As previously noted, he was an avowed enemy of the Rede Globo, which had waged a constant destabilization campaign against his government in Rio.

19. The Workers' Party (PT) is President "Lula" da Silva's party. It is a heterogeneous party linked to various urban and rural workers' movements and was formally approved by the TSE on February 11, 1982.

20. Pro-PT unions subsequently formed a leftist extralegal umbrella group in 1983, the All Workers' Association or Central Unica de Trabalhadores (CUT), which eventually increased its membership to become the most powerful labor umbrella association in Brazil (Almeida 1987). CUT did not remain representative of all workers for long, however. In 1986, opponents advocating a procapitalist position formed a new association, the General Labor Confederation, or Confederação Geral dos Trabalhadores (CGT), soon to be eclipsed by another breakaway faction known as the Union Force, Força Sindical (FS). For more on these divisions, see Mainwaring (1999).

21. "Brazil Unions Wary of Pulling the Trigger as Members' Job Security Fears Grow," *Financial Times,* May 11, 1999.

22. By official estimates, in 1996 30 percent of the entire Brazilian population lacked a birth certificate and thus legal identity. See Pereira (2000: 221).

23. In the introduction to his seminal book *The Children of Sanchez* (1963), Oscar Lewis defined a "culture of poverty" among urban Mexicans. He drew attention to the fact that "poverty in modern nations is not only a state of economic deprivation, of disorganization, or of the absence of something. . . . The culture of poverty has its own modalities and distinctive social and psychological consequences for its members. It is a dynamic factor which affects participation in the larger national culture and becomes a subculture of its own."

24. One priest in the Catholic Church Favela Parish suggested in an author interview on July 17, 2001, that US financial support for these evangelical groups had dramatically increased in order to countermand the left-wing posture of the Catholic Church.

25. Landowners and political bosses, who sometimes are one and the same, are known in backward regions as *colonels.* For more on this, see the classic works of Leal (1978) and Faoro (1979).

26. One newsweekly estimated that for the October 2002 electoral campaign, drug traffickers were charging US$1,200 in some *favelas* to distribute pamphlets. See "Tribunal Eleitoral Paralelo," *Isto É,* September 18, 2002.

27. Ibid.

28. Author interview, June 26, 2001.

29. In Brazil, the neologism *favelização* is used to refer to the spreading in society at large of the disorder that characterizes *favelas.*

30. Wladimir Real, chief of the Association of Chief Detectives (ADEPOL), in "A Paz Não Comove Bandidos," *O Globo,* May 15, 2002.

31. Twenty-two of Sarney's decrees were reissued provisional measures; 70 of Collor's decrees were reissues; 363 of Franco's decrees were reissues; 2,449 of the decrees issued by Cardoso in his first term were reissues; in Cardoso's second term 2,587 were reissues. Congress subsequently passed a constitutional amendment on September 11, 2001, to increase control over presidential provisional measures. Those pertaining to certain subjects such as citizenship rights, political rights, the organization of the judicial branch, the Attorney General's Office, or penal, civil, or procedural codes were forbidden, as was reissuing of a provisional measure unless it was approved into law by Congress after 120 days. For full specifics, see Constitutional Amendment 32. While this amendment halted reissues of provisional measures, President Cardoso nevertheless issued 102 new ones between September 2001 and January 2003. Similarly, President Lula issued 124 in his first twenty-four

months in office. All above statistics on decrees from Sub-chefia para Assuntos Jurídicos, Presidência da República, and Secretaria de Assuntos Parlamentares, Secretaria Geral da Presidência da República (2002).

32. In 1996, for example, to secure votes from the mayor's party legislators for the social security reform amendment, President Cardoso was widely believed to have absorbed the US$3.3 billion debt of the city of São Paulo. Later, the accusation was made that to avoid the establishment of an investigative commission into corruption in government, President Cardoso had ordered the selective liberation of funds from the Caixa Econômica Federal to key swing legislators. For more on patronage and use of appointments in Brazilian politics more generally, see Ames (1995).

33. Across various levels of the judiciary, on issues of taxation alone, it was estimated that 350,000 legal cases against the Federal Treasury were pending. See Souza (1998: 7).

34. Interest rates, fishing, pollution, minimum wage levels, retirement benefits for civil servants, military service, divorce—as one popular newsweekly put it, "Everything in Brazil Is a Constitutional Matter." See "Exaustos Meritíssimos," Veja, March 26, 1997.

35. For full specifics, see Constitutional Amendment 45, passed December 8, 2004.

36. I in fact had occasion to visit the Consulate of the Amazonian state of Amapá in São Paulo.

37. In 1998, São Paulo accounted for 37 percent of GDP, Minas Gerais for 9.8 percent, Espirito Santo for 1.5 percent, and Rio de Janeiro State for 11 percent, for a total of 59.4 percent of Brazil's GDP of US$645 billion. See Tribunal de Contas (1999: 13).

38. During Franco's tenure as interim president (following Collor's resignation) he had appointed Fernando Henrique Cardoso as his finance minister, thus setting Cardoso on the path to the presidency.

39. Congress is highly malapportioned. Each state is entitled to three senators and to a minimum of eight representatives and a maximum of seventy. Thus, despite having only 42 percent of the population, the more underdeveloped center-west, north, and northeastern regions have 74 percent of Senate seats and roughly 50 percent of Lower Chamber seats. São Paulo, a state with 21 percent of the country's population, has only 14 percent of seats in the Lower Chamber and less than 4 percent of Senate seats. This overrepresentation of weaker states was originally introduced in 1932 to decrease the historic control of Minas Gerais and São Paulo over the federation. It was also a means of ensuring that the need to redress regional inequalities would figure high on the national political agenda. For more on this, see Dillinger and Webb (1999) and Mainwaring (1999).

40. "Governo Investe Tudo para Mudar Votos no Congresso," Folha de São Paulo, March 22, 1996.

41. See "A Rebelião dos Estados," Folha de São Paulo, October 11, 1996; "Buaiz Troca Estatais por R$300m," Folha de São Paulo, October 26, 1996; and "Subsídio do Governo Federal a 24 Estados Deve Atingir R$8bi," Folha de São Paulo, April 6, 1998.

42. "Heavyweights Humbled," Economist, October 6, 2001.

43. As discussed in relation to Argentina, public security has lent itself to becoming a major campaign issue because rising crime rates are a priority issue among all classes, because of the ease with which it can be simplified, and because its sensationalistic nature makes it appealing to the media. It also makes for a good

missile to discredit the opposition.

44. "Nilo Apóia Ação das Forças Armadas no Rio," *Jornal do Brasil,* August 16, 1994.

45. "Brizola Desaparece do Segundo Turno no Rio," *Folha de São Paulo,* November 14, 1994.

46. The Social Democratic Party (PSD) is a center-left party modeled on Scandinavian social democratic parties. It was formally approved by the TSE on March 16, 1990.

47. The Party of the Brazilian Democratic Movement (PMDB) is a catchall centrist party formerly called MDB (Movimento Democrático Brasileiro)—the party that was created by the military regime to serve as the official opposition party in 1966. It was formally recognized by the TSE on June 30, 1981.

48. "Marcello Parte para o Revide," *Jornal do Brasil,* February 28, 1996.

49. Nevertheless, a few years later, General Cerqueira found himself in Maia's employ.

50. See "César Diz Que Rio Virou Bosnia Tropical," *Jornal do Brasil,* December 6, 1996, and "Cesar Maia Promete Emprego e Segurança Se Eleito em 1998," *Jornal do Brasil,* December 31, 1996.

51. The Liberal Front Party (PFL) is a conservative party created by dissidents from the PDS (Democratic Social Party), which was the official partisan party of the military regime. It is the party of Bahia political magnate Antônio Carlos Magalhães and was formally recognized by the TSE on October 11, 1986.

52. Alencar's state legislature legalized cockfighting in Rio State in March 1998; Conde promptly banned it within the city, sparking controversy over his legal right to do so.

53. Alencar endorsed instead his vice governor, Luiz Paulo Corrêa da Rocha, from his same party, the PSDB.

54. When he left office, his approval ratings were roughly 88 percent

55. She was elected to the Chamber of Deputies in 1986 and as senator in 1994.

56. After he won the election, Maia changed back to the PFL yet again.

57. "Garotinho Deixa o Governo de Rio e Faz da Campanha a Presidência um Show de Populismo," *Veja,* April 3, 2002.

58. "César e Garotinho Voltam a Brigar," *O Globo,* July 10, 2001.

59. Once Garotinho announced his presidential ambitions, he claimed that President Cardoso's administration was seeking to discredit him by instructing the Office of the Public Prosecutor (Ministerio Público) to investigate fraud and bribery charges dating back to 1995. These were not, by the way, the same corruption charges that Maia had dug up to discredit the governor years before.

60. The Brazilian Socialist Party (PSB) is a center-left party linked to various union movements. It was formally approved by the TSE on July 1, 1988.

61. Author interview with a high-ranking police officer with more than thirty years' experience, June 25, 2001.

62. "Não Ha Fome no Brasil," *Jornal do Brasil,* July 19, 2001.

PART 3
CONCLUSION

CHAPTER 12

Democratic Policing: A Distant Reality?

Failed Expectations

Democracy, even after two decades, has brought only a semblance of democratic policing to Argentina and Brazil. Despite the profusion of reform initiatives undertaken in both countries, the police entered the new millennium still a shadowy organization with limited capacity to render protection, reassurance, and redress to a citizenry beleaguered by violence and crime. Admittedly, even in long-established democracies some of the conflicts inherent to policing and police reform have proven difficult to reconcile, and thus it would be unrealistic to expect that Argentina and Brazil could have resolved them thoroughly. Nevertheless, in a democratic polity governments are expected to yield the state's coercive apparatus to democratic control; in the face of glaring deficiencies, they must be able to raise the political will and resources needed to set in place workable mechanisms for sustainable change. If the state cannot exert effective control over its designated legal enforcers, its capacity to uphold laws and policies, protect its population from the arbitrary actions of others, and shape the norms and procedures within its borders is substantially diminished. Yet even as threats rose, successive governments in Brazil and Argentina continued to manipulate the public security situation and the police for their own political purposes and to respond to every crisis with improvised and superficial reforms.

There can be little doubt that perennial economic instability and police resistance to change constrained the development of more legalistic, service-oriented, and trustworthy police forces—goals that were encased in the language of almost all reform initiatives. Still, I have argued that these factors could not by themselves wholly account for the wavering commitment and lack of rigor that characterized official responses to an issue that not only threatened the state's own laws and ability to govern but indeed the very fabric of society. Only when viewed through the perspective of the

Argentine and Brazilian political game do these marches and counter-marches seem to manifest a certain perverse logic.

Shaped by cultural toleration for corruption in public office, low accountability, impunity, and destructive competition, the political game in Argentina and Brazil is consumed by an overriding interest in self-preservation and predicated on an insular form of governance that primarily benefits particularistic interests. In countries where mechanisms of vertical and horizontal accountability function only haltingly, there is an enormous window of opportunity for all players to exploit an already weakened concept of public good. In the 1990s, the increasingly diffuse philosophical underpinnings of political parties enabled candidates to make brazen policy reversals once elected. In Brazil, where political parties were already weaker and more numerous than those in Argentina, problems of backpedaling and fragmentation became especially acute, since candidates also routinely engaged in serial switching of party labels, both before and after elections.

With the ballot box falling short of its main purpose—to promote responsive political representation—it was largely left to civil society to find alternative avenues for influencing and monitoring public policy. But although the postmilitary era witnessed a groundswell of civic associations in both Argentina and Brazil, these organizations were more successful at highlighting systemic failures than at working cooperatively to shape policy outcomes and enhance transparency. Lacking an established tradition of independent action and deeply divided by socioeconomic status and other fissures, such channels of popular participation as unions, NGOs, and community associations tended to dissolve into extreme factionalism, leaving themselves vulnerable to co-optation by clientelistic interests. An additional factor restricting associational life was fear. In Rio de Janeiro, for instance, the hold of the drug trade over impoverished communities not only hampered the provision of public services but also created a climate of intimidation inimical to political participation and the development of stronger citizenship rights.

In Argentina, a reform of the Penal Code carried out during Perón's first presidency established that "to offend in any way the dignity of a public official" was a crime punishable by prison. Since then the spirit, if not the letter, of this law has remained alive and well. Although from the 1990s onward a multitude of anticorruption offices, ombudsmen, and special commissions were set up trumpeting "transparency" in government, the commitment and controls necessary to enforce it have been sorely wanting. As in much of Latin America, imbalance among the three branches of government remains very much in evidence. The Argentine legislature serves as a vehicle for patronage and for passing laws at the behest of the executive—frequently without debate or regard for their enforceability. The judiciary system, charged with safeguarding equality before the law and guaranteeing citizen rights, has been equally prone to executive manipulation and corruption, all the way to the highest legal institution in the land, the Supreme Court. In a system where presidents attempt to influence impeachment procedures for justices appointed by their predecessors, such maneuvers seem a political ploy to pack the court anew, rather than an attempt to cleanse the institution.

In the 1990s, the prevalence of selective accountability allowed Argentine and Brazilian elected officials considerable latitude to pursue their personal agendas. Such factors as low educational indices among socially excluded groups and a generalized predisposition toward charismatic figures heightened the tendency of political contests to be dominated by cults of personality and symbolic destruction of rivals. Most candidates faced constant destabilization attempts by rivals from within and outside their parties; fanned by scandal-digging media, expensive and protracted political campaigns often degenerated into mud-slinging fests of theatrical proportions. As a corollary, the careful process needed to build basic consensus prior to devising and implementing comprehensive state policies was easily eroded; it was more politically expedient for officials to launch measures purposely designed to create a minimum of ripples.

The thorny issue of police reform taxed political will still further: politicians attempting to open clearer channels of accountability risked opening a can of worms, since dismantling networks of corruption might easily unleash the ire not only of police hierarchies but of the powerful vested interests across government that thrived in obscurity. Maintaining the status quo has another advantage for political and police hierarchies: an inefficient, poorly paid, and demoralized police corps can more easily be co-opted by bribery, cajoled into illegal acts, and manipulated into silence. In Argentina, these unwritten pacts turned the issue of public security into a missile, fired at will to obtain political advantage, by the Radical and Peronist parties against one another, by the municipal government against federal authorities, by the governor of Buenos Aires Province against the president, by presidents to discredit predecessors and successors, and by the Argentine Federal Police against any politician who threatened its power. At the same time, officials were acutely aware of the need to maintain an *appearance* of responsiveness to public demands. Striving to project an image of concern, they promised a doubling of police presence on the street; to convey sophistication, they imported policing schemes from the United States and Europe without regard to crucial local variables. But with a political class thoroughly tainted by corruption, the motives behind any promised reforms became immediately suspect.

In Brazil's urban areas, where public security has been a galvanizing issue for far longer than it has been in Argentina, the reform process throughout the 1990s was equally politicized and inconstant. As the chapters on Rio de Janeiro illustrate, state governors, who are constitutionally responsible for operational control over the police, blithely discarded security policies and officials at the first sign of a dip in popularity. Always eager to run for higher office, they switched their ideological banner as swiftly as their party affiliation; whenever the public security situation deteriorated further, they rushed to call on the federal government to send in the army, claiming that the states could not be expected to solve Brazil's problems. The federal government, in turn, was all too eager to acquiesce, since a military display of decisiveness was an effective temporary cover for its inconstancy in supporting national police reform. The police were thus caught in an almost schizophrenic cycle, alternatively expected to crack heads, to respect human rights, to raid *favelas,* to refrain from using force. As the most visible face of law enforcement, the police were also a convenient scapegoat that could be blamed for almost everything that went wrong.

With support from state and federal authorities subordinated to political expediency, the police forged ahead in the 1990s as best they could in a losing fight against violent crime and drug trafficking. It is hardly surprising that the police were distrustful of all reform initiatives, since incumbent governors not only dissociated themselves from prior policies but also dismissed their own appointed "reformers" as soon as they appeared to be a political liability. Hoping to thwart each other's ambitions, governors and mayors often sabotaged each other's programs by initiating jurisdictional disputes. While public frustration grew, their political bickering was a bonanza for criminal elements, who sealed pacts with any and all sides to extract concessions for themselves. Under these circumstances, could the police have had much confidence that any reformer would act in the public interest, even if he or she survived in office for more than a few months? With impunity, backtracking, and betrayal of the rules of the game, to expect the police to have played their cards straight would be to pretend that they were not embedded in the context in which they operated.

Faithful to the praxis of expediency, Argentine and Brazilian governments set up alternative mechanisms or created new institutions rather than fix existing ones. With each pledge to increase resources to the police, to purchase more vehicles and equipment, to put more officers on the street, or to purge police ranks, they provided an illusion of reform that helped to temporarily assuage a frightened population. Ultimately, however, these palliatives served only to fire up public expectations for rapid resolution of the problem, making the subsequent disenchantment all the greater. In both Argentina and Brazil, the pressing need to reform the police and institutionalize effective state oversight has been consistently at odds with the old patterns of patronage, clientelism, impunity, and rule by fiat that continue to thrive decades after the transition from military rule—and even after the historic election of "reformer" presidents in 2003. Néstor Kirchner in Argentina and Luiz Inácio "Lula" da Silva in Brazil inaugurated a period of renewed hope for political and social change. In spite of their high approval ratings, however, neither president has demonstrated the political will to reverse the insidious patterns analyzed in this book. As concerns public security and police reform specifically, the situation, alas, has only continued to deteriorate.

Echoes of the 1990s

At the peak of the political and social crisis that followed President de la Rúa's resignation in December 2001, Eduardo Duhalde was installed as interim president of Argentina by congressional decree—the fifth president of the republic in a two-month period. With polls indicating widespread popular disgust with the political establishment, Duhalde, a powerful old-guard Peronist politician who had lost the 1999 presidential elections to de la Rúa, edged carefully into office. Announcing he would vacate the presidential seat seven months ahead of schedule, he postponed most pressing economic and political decisions, devoting instead most of his interim presidency to a futile attempt to quell internal dissension within his party. Since the Peronists could not unite behind a single presidential candidate, three different ones entered the fray under the same party banner. On April 27, 2003, the obscure governor of a remote Patagonian province and Duhalde protegé, Néstor Kirchner, was elected to the Argentine presidency with less than 20 percent of the popular vote.

Kirchner assumed office on May 25, 2003, without any political base of his own. Immediately expressing strong commitment to human rights in order to establish his autonomy over old-style politics (specifically his patron Duhalde), he set the stage for future actions in his inaugural speech, proclaiming, "There can be no sustainable change if we permit impunity to continue. We give our guarantee that we will fight corruption and impunity implacably in order to strengthen and cleanse our institutions." In reference to public security, he asserted, "Among the fundamental and irreplaceable roles of the state are its ability to exert a monopoly over the legitimate use of force and the fight against any form of criminal impunity, so that we can construct citizen security and justice in a democratic society that respects human rights."[1] Kirchner followed up quickly on his promises. Within his first six weeks in office, he launched a purge of the armed forces, the Supreme Court, and the national intelligence agency. Although the chief of police kept his job, 80 percent of the PFA senior commanders, most of whom were under suspicion of corruption, were dismissed.

Just five months later, however, the chief of police was embroiled in a scandal of his own, whose implications reached the highest levels of government: a prominent newsdaily accused the chief in October 2003 of masterminding an elaborate phantom contracting plan that netted him and his family more than US$700,000 in public funds. Within days, hounded by rumors that he had known about these allegations for months, President Kirchner ordered the chief's recall from Spain, where he had been attending a meeting of Interpol, and fired him. To forestall further political damage, the president subsequently ordered an internal investigation, which uncovered the fact that that the chief of police had in fact collected US$5.5 million in false contracts over the nearly eighteen months of his tenure, which began when he was appointed by one-week president Adolfo Rodríguez Saá and continued when he was ratified as chief by Duhalde and then by Kirchner.

In the ensuing months, a wave of kidnappings and murders, combined with a resurgence in social and political unrest, brought about another frantic cycle of police purges, blame trading, promises of modernization, legislative tinkering with criminal penalties, and accusations of police collusion with both criminals and protesters. In mid-2004, after the Blumberg case described in Chapter 1, a group of local captains of industry charged that crime and lawlessness were scaring investors away and impeding Argentina's economic development. The business group demanded that the government act with "competence, coherence and forcefulness" against common criminals and various groups of jobless protesters, known as *piqueteros,* who had been shutting off highways, disrupting traffic, and forcibly occupying national and foreign businesses for several months.[2]

Despite the fact that the most militant wing of the *piquetero* movement had taken over more than 1,000 businesses, as well as two police precincts, in a twelve-month period, the police were under a presidential order to follow a strict "no-repression" policy. Perhaps fearing that dissenting factions within his own Peronist Party might attempt to recreate the December 2001 chaos that led to President de la Rúa's resignation, Kirchner publicly declared that he would not be induced into sending in "the trigger-happy police to repress social protests."[3] With the police under executive order to remain passive, the protest movement grew bolder. In early July 2004, a motley group of street vendors, prostitutes, transvestites, and *piqueteros* invaded the Buenos Aires Legislature to prevent debate on yet another revision of the Code for Urban Public Behavior (examined in Chapter 4 of this book) that they deemed inimical to their interests. In a rampage that lasted over three hours and was filmed live by television crews, protesters destroyed furniture, computers, documents, and even electrical appliances in the legislative building, watched passively by the police. It was only after protesters attempted to set the building on fire that some arrests were made.

After the live broadcasts, President Kirchner was targeted by a tidal wave of criticism, both internally and from the foreign media, for failing to enforce the state's own laws and bringing the country once more to the brink of anarchy. Under threat of further protests by various groups, the chief of police requested special authorization for a group of handpicked officers to carry routine firearms in self-defense. The president rejected this plea, upon which the chief of police resigned after only nine months on the job. Amid continuing uproar over the public security situation, a few weeks later President Kirchner dismissed the secretary of security and the minister of justice and security—the architects of his showcase security megaplan. With the top echelon of the president's security team effectively dismantled, the government was forced to admit that the megaplan, launched only three months earlier in response to the Blumberg kidnapping and murder, had been "deactivated."

If patterns in Argentina in the new millennium are reminiscent of those in the 1990s, they also show significant parallels to those of neighboring Brazil. In October 2002, when Luis Inácio "Lula" da Silva of the Workers' Party was elected on his fourth try as Brazil's first working-class president, exultant crowds, intellectuals, and commentators around the globe proclaimed the triumph of popular democracy. A year later, constraints posed by the monumental debt, demands made by international creditors, and pressure from local business elites to avoid the debacle of neighboring Argentina had forced President Lula to adopt a program of economic austerity. Because campaign promises to concentrate on social issues had been one of the pillars of Lula's popularity, drastic cuts in social spending sent the president's approval ratings down by thirty points. In 2004, after Lula fought Congress to lower proposed increases in the minimum wage and involved himself in trying to stem the acceleration of agrarian reform, the former head of the Workers' Party became the target of labor and landless peasant protests.

On the issue of police reform, Lula's policies underwent similar reversals. Asserting that "without security for all, no one will be secure in Brazil," during his 2002 presidential campaign candidate Lula had introduced a 100-page blueprint for reform of the security sector.[4] In his January 2003 inaugural speech, he pledged again his personal resolve to place his government at "the service of a more vigorous and efficient public security policy."[5] But while the president launched a plan to eradicate hunger in Brazil immediately after assuming office, later appearing before the UN General Assembly to propose a global tax to feed the world's hungry, he did not exercise comparable leadership on issues relating to crime and police reform. At a political rally a few months after returning from New York, federal police officers who had gone on strike in March 2004 to (unsuccessfully) demand an 83 percent salary increase met President Lula with banners proclaiming, "We are hungry too."

President Lula had initially entrusted the responsibility of police reform policies to Luiz Eduardo Soares, his national public security secretary. Soares, whose prior tenure in a similar position in Rio de Janeiro is examined in

Chapter 9, had drafted the blueprint for national police reform and crime reduction that was featured in Lula's presidential campaign. One of his most prominent proposals was the creation of a showcase federal project targeting the renewal of the *favela* known as City of God, which had become a notorious symbol of urban crime after the blockbuster international success of the film of the same name. Railing against improvisation, proclaiming his independence from the ruling party, calling for reform of the penal code and for unification of the police forces, Soares soon ran afoul of traditional political patterns, just as had happened in Rio de Janeiro in 2000. After he announced that states that did not elaborate detailed multiyear plans to reform their police forces would have federal funds withdrawn, Soares found himself isolated and vilified. He resigned after only ten months in office.

Spurred on by the diminishing returns of appearing indifferent to the public security issue, President Lula successfully advocated for the approval of a law banning civilians from carrying firearms, which was buttressed by special measures against illegal gun ownership.[6] In January 2004, however, Lula's government was stung by a scathing report by a UN Special Rapporteur on Extrajudicial Executions denouncing the persistence throughout Brazil of extrajudicial executions and the "[appalling] situation of the population living in the *favelas*, where innocent citizens are trapped in a cycle of violence fostered by heavily armed drug gangs or indiscriminate repressive police operations" (2004: 12). In Rio, a few months later, 100 heavily armored drug traffickers invaded what is believed to be Latin America's largest *favela*, Rocinha, in an effort to gain control of the key drug-selling points. The Rio State governor ordered the police to launch a counterattack, and the ensuing battle between the police and rival drug gangs lasted one full week. Among the many casualties was Rocinha's twenty-six-year-old drug boss, for whose funeral hundreds of residents turned out in an outpouring of grief—a televised event that prompted national indignation over the parallel statelike powers of drug traffickers in Brazil. In the aftermath of these events, the government of Rio State floated the idea of constructing a ten-foot-thick wall to encase Rio's largest *favelas*—a concrete hedge to buttress the divide between rich and poor.

The crime epidemic that prompted politicians to envisage such desperate measures was not confined to Rio de Janeiro. Throughout Brazil, a series of bloody prison revolts (including the televised decapitation of a hostage during a prison revolt in the Amazonian state of Rondônia) and police strikes eventually forced President Lula to order federal troops to take control of the deteriorating public security situation in several states. By mid-2005, however, these issues were placed once again on the back burner. With several of President Lula's closest aides and top officials of his Workers' Party accused of widespread corruption involving irregular campaign financing, extortion, money laundering, and congressional vote buying, the president's proclamations in support of ethical government were increasingly perceived as desperate attempts to regain credibility. As three separate inquiries advanced toward direct implication of Lula in the scandal and cover-up, the hopes of millions of Brazilians for honest government and lasting change in the political game were once again dashed.

Resonance in the Region

If this is the situation in South America's two giants, what can reasonably be expected of the rest of the region? While in the 1980s the restoration of democracy gave rise to considerable optimism, in 2004 a UN report found that a startling majority of Latin Americans would prefer to live under an authoritarian regime if it could solve their economic problems (UNDP 2004a). The guarantee of quick military action, in fact, is one promise that Latin American presidents usually manage to keep: troops are not only being sent to troubled countries like Haiti to maintain peace but also being called out of their barracks to keep public order in unsafe cities.

Amid continuing poverty, corruption, and lack of opportunity, crime has rapidly become one of the few growth areas in Latin America, with organized criminal groups, in particular, emboldened by the rampant "marketization" of national life, wherein even political decisions can be bought if the price is right. Savvy politicians, aware of the appeal of First World solutions, rush to import police strategies and foreign expertise that are rarely contextualized to local conditions. Almost identical paradigms inspired by New York's Zero Tolerance initiative have been introduced in cities as diverse as Tegucigalpa, Mexico City, and Buenos Aires, while costly geosatellite referencing systems and closed-circuit television are offered as failsafe means to monitor crime aboard buses and on the streets throughout the region. In mid-2004, microchip tracking devices implanted in the arm were introduced to deter kidnappings among the rich and prominent, with Mexico's attorney general one of the first takers.

The insertion of such high-technology initiatives as crime-fighting tools, particularly in countries that can ill afford them, all too often precedes the establishment of more basic elements to improve policing: efficient statistical systems, adequate education, common professional standards, enhanced training, and standardized systems of monitoring and evaluation. More fundamentally, the potential for success of any technological or methodological innovation is correlated to the integrity and accountability not only of the criminal justice system but of government overall. Unless widespread lack of accountability and respect for norms are addressed, it will be difficult to overturn the predatory nature of policing or sustain reform in any sector.

The causes of the chaotic public security situation in Latin America have been long in the making, while the potential for relief is inextricably linked to the collective will to strengthen the quality of democracy. The self-serving political game examined in this book through the lens of the Argentine and Brazilian cases is a disease metastasized throughout the region, hindering not only reform but also the fulfillment of these countries' great potential. At a minimum, zero tolerance policies must be applied to any and all elected public officials who flagrantly abuse public trust and state coffers. The alternative is that Latin American countries, already weighted down by a long history of authoritarianism, will grow permanently accustomed to the façade and language of democracy rather than to its obligations.

In the new millennium, the stakes are even higher. If Cold War–era national security doctrines no longer justify covert training of the armed forces and the police in espionage and torture, the global spread of international terrorism and the vast corrupting power of the drug trade provide a contemporary context for further corrosion of state legitimacy and sovereignty. By continually defaulting on their fundamental responsibilities, many Latin American countries have become vulnerable to coup attempts and other democratic interruptions. Between 2000 and 2005, popular fury prematurely drove out of office six Latin American presidents—Jamil Mahuad in Ecuador, Alberto Fujimori in Peru, Fernando de la Rúa in Argentina, Gonzalo Sánchez de Losada in Bolivia, Lucio Gutiérrez in Ecuador, and Carlos Mesa in Bolivia—and others continue to struggle against pressures to resign. In 2004, a quarter of a million people took to the streets of Buenos Aires, Guatemala City, and Mexico City to demand government action against rampant crime and corruption, while in indigenous villages of Peru and Bolivia mobs took matters in their own hands and lynched their mayors for corruption.

This is not a pretty picture. Still, these events were not isolated phenomena of spontaneous combustion but rather the uncorking of a long-simmering rage against an obdurate political game that has produced a profound disconnection between governments and their people. Unless the Latin American tradition of policing only the lowest rungs of state and society is turned on its head, time may run out for actual democratic consolidation in the region.

Notes

1. Discurso del Señor Presidente de la Nación, Doctor Néstor Kirchner, ante la Honorable Asamblea Legislativa, May 25, 2003.
2. "Según el Empresariado, la Ola Delictiva Afecta la Economía," *La Nación,* June 17, 2004.

3. "Kirchner: 'No Vamos a Reprimir con Esta Policía de Gatillo Fácil,'" *Clarín,* June 27, 2004.

4. See p. 1 of Luiz Inácio Lula da Silva, "Projeto Segurança Pública para o ·Brasil: Síntese do Projeto," São Paulo, Instituto Cidadania, February 27, 2002.

5. See p. 13 of Discurso do Presidente da República, Luiz Inácio Lula da Silva, na Sessão Solene de Posse, no Congresso Nacional, Brasília, DF, January 1, 2003.

6. The Statute of Disarmament passed in December 2003. See Lei 10.826 (Estatuto do Desarmamento), Congresso Nacional, December 22, 2003.

Methodological
Appendix

When I set out to do this study of policing and politics in two of Latin America's largest metropolises, I knew that carrying out sensitive research in societies with an ingrained tradition of private "public" information and secretive governance would require extensive preliminary preparation and care. Although problems of access and trust are not unique to police research, the "difficulty is particularly severe in studying policing because of the highly charged nature of its secrets. . . . Police researchers are investigating subjects whose job it is to investigate the deviance of others" (Reiner 2000a: 218–219). When one undertakes sensitive research, problems that "arise from the social, political, and economic environment within which the research takes place," together with issues of "personal security," are a "prominent feature of the research design and fieldwork, having to be continually borne in mind by the researcher at all stages of the research rather than just contemplated as a vague possibility or a theoretical truism once fieldwork is completed" (Brewer 1993).

In determining what research tools and methods to employ, I decided in favor of in-depth interviews over participant observation because my interests were broader in scope than those I believed microlevel ethnography could address, and also because the open-ended (albeit purposefully guided) in-depth interview is considered one of the most useful methods for exploring sensitive subjects (Lee 1993). More than rigidly constructed questionnaires or precoded structured interview formats, in-depth interviews provide the distinct advantage of allowing for the emergence of opinions, attitudes, and events not previously contemplated by the researcher. At the same time, in-depth interviews provide a good opportunity to gain access to sites and data that might be otherwise difficult to obtain.

As regards statistical data, one of the most important needs was the capacity to compare and triangulate official statistics with information obtained from other sources due to the fact that statistical data in Argentina and Brazil are often unobtainable or unreliable. In attempting to portray a positive image of their country abroad, both countries have frequently politicized, submerged, and distorted their statistics. Successive Argentine governments, for example, have posted literacy rates that exceed those of many developed countries. Both Argentina and Brazil have attempted to "disappear" social blights from sight by ordering the wholesale removal of shantytowns prior to a papal visit or the arrival of foreign delegations. In Brazil, where decentralization is higher, I came across significant discrepancies when comparing social and financial data provided by the federal government, states, and municipalities on identical issues. In Argentina, on the other hand, statistics (albeit of the unreliable variety) are plentiful only in the city of Buenos Aires, owing to its status as the federal capital. As for the collection and systematic analysis of criminal justice statistics specifically, this is still a nascent science in both Argentina and Brazil, owing not so much to technological barriers as to reluctance to relinquish control of potentially damaging data. Given all this, I was reluctant to rely too heavily on quantitative analysis in this study, preferring to use statistics as benchmarks to provide perspective and range.

Undertaking the Research

In postmilitary regimes such as Argentina and Brazil, discussion of security issues stirs up considerable wariness in the population at large and even more so among police officers, who are normally suspicious of outsiders under any circumstance. First in Buenos Aires and later in Rio, I purposely avoided close identification with a local institutional base for fear of being pigeonholed into a particular category or political affiliation. Initially, I sought out those sectors traditionally associated with the right, since prior experiences had shown that human rights activists and others would likely be more eager to speak with outsiders, particularly an academic from abroad who presumably would be likely to share their views. The ice was broken after I interviewed key former military officers, whose recommendations were instrumental in gaining access to many high-ranking police officials. As for hopes of achieving access *downward*—the "gatekeeper" strategy is common in many research studies of the police in many developed countries—this could not be relied upon, particularly in Buenos Aires, since most high officials were not at all eager for me to interview their subordinates. To reach the lower echelons, as well as officials in previous administrations, I decided to pursue informal channels—childhood friends of interviewees, associates, advisers, and counterparts. Other times I attended selected events, such as book launches, seminars, and cocktail parties, to avail myself of opportunities for direct human contact with reluctant individuals.

While conducting interviews in Buenos Aires, I would immediately be asked why I spoke "Argentinean" Spanish so fluidly. After explaining that my mother is from Argentina, I was interrogated on why she left Argentina, in what year, her reasons for doing so, and so on. I was also asked repeatedly about my own political affiliation and opinions; several police officials suggested that I might be coming at the behest of the British government and speculated on the reasons that Britain would be interested in my study. In both Buenos Aires and Rio, interview subjects would routinely ask the names of people I had already met with, what they had told me, what my conclusions were, or what hypothesis I was trying to prove. A significant number of interviewees expressed concern that our conversations might be bugged; this suspicion led some to request that interviews be conducted in public places, where they would invariably choose to sit near air-conditioning machines or other noisy equipment. This level of paranoia, though manifest in both cities, appeared more intense in Buenos Aires, which made the task of containing my opinions, masking any apprehension, and maintaining composure at all times quite essential. On various on-site visits, I was the only female among scores of armed men; in Rio I would be driven back home in the backseat of a police car, with one or two police officers pointing cocked machine guns out the car windows.

I guaranteed anonymity to all interviewees, as I had concluded that providing the option of attribution in such a milieu would not encourage maximum frankness. The police in particular responded positively to my expressed interest to air their seldom-heard voices and perspective. Since I took great care not to frame questions in accusatory terms or argue, the opportunity to be fairly listened to rather than attacked proved cathartic for many interview subjects, who sometimes spoke for several hours and eventually expounded on many thorny subjects. The decision not to tape-record interviews in Buenos Aires and Rio, owing in large part to the counsel of a prominent Argentine academic with many decades of experience, proved wise. Instead, I asked permission from those interviewed to take notes, confident that the shorthand I had developed during innumerable hours of university lectures would allow me to write down nearly everything that was said. Several police officers in Buenos Aires were sufficiently impressed with my note-taking skills to ask if I was a professional shorthand typist, especially marveling at my ability to write while maintaining substantial eye contact. One former chief of police asked if he could read my notes, and grabbed the book from my hands before I could respond. Another former chief of police agreed to meet only after I assured his secretary that I would not be taping the interview; when I later arrived at his office, he complained of frequent misquotes and misrepresentations and asked if he could tape our conversation. After his tape ran out, however, he felt sufficiently comfortable to carry on for another hour.

Following my interviews, I would typically go to a cafe nearby to clarify any obscurities in my handwriting and write down basic impressions; evenings were mostly devoted to transcribing the full interview into the computer. On average, one day a week was set aside for working the phone and for visits to libraries and newspaper archives. During the main period of my field research in Buenos Aires (winter-spring 2000), government offices frequently lacked working photocopiers or extra paper; at times I was asked if I minded paying for photocopies. During the period I lived in Rio (fall-winter 2001), rooms would suddenly turn pitch black during interviews and on-site visits, due to energy-rationing measures that were in force throughout the city and much of the country for the better part of 2001. At the Rio State Assembly, I concluded one interview with the aid of a large flashlight.

Although the time allotted for in locus work in Rio and the preparations I undertook were similar to those for Buenos Aires, it was soon apparent following my arrival that the city had its own challenges. For one, a far larger number of international scholars and researchers were present there, so demands for official time were higher; for another, *cariocas* are notoriously hard to pin down, so vague promises to meet would require an endless number of follow-up calls. Even after an appointment was finally confirmed, individuals would dither nonchalantly before committing themselves to assist in any significant way. Because on average *cariocas* are less politicized and opinionated than *porteños*, in the early stages broadening my base of contacts beyond one small circle of specialists proved rather daunting. Halfway through my stay, though, the floodgates opened, and a snowballing effect opened up the possibility of more interviews that I had time for.

Organizing the Research

After returning from the field, I spent nearly seven months analyzing my interviews by theme, concept, and category. I sorted through the mass of documentation I had brought back and wrote a rough draft of the Argentine case, so that its particularities would not later blend in my mind with the Brazilian case. Shortly after I returned from Rio, I repeated the process. In total, I conducted 165 interviews, encompassing a diverse range of sectors and individuals in federal, state, and municipal government and civil society. My subjects included police officers, military officers, legislators, NGO representatives, directors of trade associations, owners of private security companies, prostitutes, members of the clergy and unions, community organizers and residents, intellectuals, academics, judges, lawyers, and economists. All interviews in Argentina and Brazil were conducted, respectively, in Spanish and Portuguese; although on average they lasted for one and a half hours, some took up to six hours. Interviews were supplemented by field visits to police training and educational institutions, social outreach programs, and shantytowns, where I could observe firsthand some of the contradictions between official statements and objective reality. In this manner, I obtained not only extremely varied perspectives on normative and political issues but direct understanding of the conditions under which my interview subjects lived and worked.

I concurrently consulted government and police documents, relevant legislation, public opinion information polls, socioeconomic data, secondary materials and studies, public sector budgets, and historical sources. The archives of the leading newspapers in both Buenos Aires and Rio and the libraries of academic institutions and government ministries were also important sources of information. In addition, prior to my fieldwork I had conducted interviews with officials from the World Bank, the Inter-American Development Bank, the Ford Foundation, the Organization of American States, and the International Narcotics and Law Enforcement Agency in the US Department of State. Upon returning from the field, I carried out additional interviews with UK police officials with international training experience.

Throughout all stages of my research, I triangulated discerned views, information, and attitudes against many diverse statistical, legal, and journalistic secondary sources so as to achieve a holistic picture of the context in which public insecurity grew, the police operated, and policies were formulated and undertaken. Having chosen the case study format precisely because of its ability to incorporate a "full variety of evidence," including interviews, documents, news clippings, and direct observation, I determined to give a broad "historical range of historical, attitudinal, and observational issues" due place (Yin 1984). While no study is free from interviewer effects, subjective judgment, or human error, I have endeavored to provide a historically and culturally grounded study, avoiding the traps of being so "general as to be insufficiently informative" and so "conditional as not to be general" (Hawthorn 1991).

Acronyms and Abbreviations

AAA	Argentine Anticommunist Alliance (Alianza Argentina Anticomunista)
ADEPOL	Association of Chief Detectives (Associação dos Delegados de Policía do Brasil)
AGN	General Auditor of the Nation (Auditoría General de la Nación)
BNH	National Housing Bank (Banco Nacional de Habitação)
BRL	Brazilian real
CCDC	Center for the Defense of Citizenship (Centro Comunitário de Defensa da Cidadania)
CEB	ecclesiastical base community (comunidades eclesias de base)
CELS	Center for Legal and Social Studies (Centro de Estudios Legales y Sociales)
CGT	General Confederation of Workers (Confederación General de Trabajadores [Argentina]; Confederação Geral dos Trabalhadores [Brazil])
CNI	National Confederation of Industry (Confederação Nacional da Indústria)
COFAVI	Committee of Relatives of Innocent Victims of Social Violence (Comisión de Familiares de Víctimas Indefensas de la Violencia Social)
CORREPI	National Coordinator Against Police and Institutional Repression (Coordinadora contra la Represión Policial e Institucional)
CPT	Pastoral Land Commission (Commissão Pastoral da Terra)
CTA	Congress of Argentine Workers (Congreso de Trabajadores Argentinos)
CUT	All Workers' Association (Central Unica de Trabalhadores)

DAS	Antikidnapping Division of the Civil Police (Divisão Anti-Seqüestros)
ECA	Statute of the Child and Adolescent (Estatuto da Criança e do Adolescente)
FAFERJ	Federation of Favela Associations of the State of Rio de Janeiro (Federação das Associações de Favelas do Estado do Rio de Janeiro)
FAMERJ	Federation of Neighborhood Associations of the State of Rio de Janeiro (Federação das Associações de Moradores do Estado do Rio de Janeiro)
FIESP	Industry Federation of São Paulo State (Federação das Industrias do Estado de São Paulo)
FIRJAN	Federation of Industry Owners of Rio de Janeiro State (Federação das Industrias do Estado de Rio de Janeiro)
FREPASO	National Solidarity Front (Frente País Solidario)
FS	Union Force (Força Sindical)
GDP	gross domestic product
GNP	gross national product
GPAE	Special Areas Policing Squad (Grupamento de Policiamento em Áreas Especiais)
HRW	Human Rights Watch
IACHR	Inter-American Commission on Human Rights
IADB	Inter-American Development Bank
IBGE	Brazilian Institute for Geography and Statistics (Instituto Brasileiro de Geografia e Estadística)
IFI	international financing institution
IML	Forensic Medical Institute (Instituto Médico Legal)
ISER	Institute for Studies on Religion (Instituto de Estudos da Religião)
ISI	import substitution industrialization
ISP	Institute of Public Security (Instituto de Segurança Pública)
MDB	Brazilian Democratic Movement (Movimento Democrático Brasileiro)
MST	Movement of Landless Rural Workers (Movimento dos Trabalhadores Rurais Sem Terra)
MTA	Movement of Argentine Workers (Movimiento de Trabajadores Argentinos)
NGO	nongovernmental organization
PC	Civil Police (Polícia Civil)
PDS	Democratic Social Party (Partido Democrático Social)
PDT	Democratic Labor Party (Partido Democrático Trabalhista)
PFA	Argentine Federal Police (Policía Federal Argentina)
PFL	Party of the Liberal Front (Partido da Frente Liberal)

PL	Liberal Party (Partido Liberal)
PM	Military Police (Policía Militar)
PMDB	Party of the Brazilian Democratic Movement (Partido do Movimento Democrático Brasileiro)
PPB	Brazilian Progressive Party (Partido Progressista Brasileiro)
PR	proportional representation
PRI	Institutional Revolutionary Party (Partido Revolucionario Institucional)
PSB	Brazilian Socialist Party (Partido Socialista Brasileiro)
PSD	Social Democratic Party (Partido Social Democrático)
PSDB	Brazilian Social Democracy Party (Partido da Social Democracia Brasileira)
PT	Workers' Party (Partido dos Trabalhadores)
PTB	Brazilian Labor Party (Partido Trabalhista Brasileiro)
ROTA	Patrol Squad Tobias de Aguiar (Rondas Ostensivas Tobias de Aguiar)
SIDE	Secretariat of State Intelligence (Secretaría de Inteligencia del Estado)
SIGEN	Federal Comptroller's Office (Sindicatura General de la Nación)
SUDAM	Amazon Development Agency (Superintendência do Desenvolvimento da Amazônia)
TSE	Superior Electoral Tribunal (Tribunal Superior Electoral)
UERJ	State University of Rio de Janeiro (Universidade do Estado do Rio de Janeiro)
UFF	Fluminense Federal University (Universidade Federal Fluminense)
UN	United Nations
UNESCO	United Nations Educational, Social, and Cultural Organization
UNICRI	United Nations Interregional Crime and Justice Institute

Bibliography

Abramovich, Eduardo. 1998. "Documento Sobre el Código Contravencional." Gobierno de la Ciudad de Buenos Aires, Gabinete de Suárez Lastra, n.p.

Acuña, Carlos H., and Smulovitz, Catalina. 1995. "Militares en la Transición Argentina: del Gobierno a la Subordinación Constitucional." In C. H. Acuña, I. G. Bombol, E. Jelin, and O. Landi (Eds.), *Juicio, Castigos, y Memorias: Derechos Humanos y Justicia en la Política Argentina.* Buenos Aires: Ediciones Nueva Visión.

Aguinis, Marcos. 1989. *Un País de Novela.* Buenos Aires: Editorial Planeta.

Almeida, Maria Hermínia Tavares de. 1987. "Novo Sindicalismo and Politics in Brazil." In J. D. Wirth, E. d. O. Nunes, and T. E. Bugenschild (Eds.), *State and Society in Brazil.* Boulder and London: Westview Press.

Almond, Gabriel A., and Verba, Sidney. 1963. *The Civic Culture.* Princeton: Princeton University Press.

Alves, Maria Helena Moreira. 1985. *State and Opposition in Military Rule.* Austin: University of Texas Press.

Ames, Barry N. D. 1995. "Electoral Rules, Constituent Pressures, and Pork Barrel: Bases of Voting in the Brazilian Congress." *Journal of Politics* 57: 324–343.

Amnesty International. 2003. *Rio de Janeiro 2003: Candelária and Vigário Geral 10 Years On.* London: Amnesty International.

Amorim, Carlos. 1993. *Comando Vermelho: A História Secreta do Crime Organizado.* Rio de Janeiro: Record.

Baer, Werner. 1990. "Brazil's Rocky Economic Road to Democracy." In L. S. Graham and R. H. Wilson (Eds.), *The Political Economy of Brazil: Public Policies of an Era in Transition.* Austin: University of Texas Press.

Baer, Werner, and Paiva, Claudio. 1998. "Brazil's Drifting Economy: Stagnation and Inflation During 1987–1996." In P. D. Oxhorn and G. Ducatenzeiler (Eds.), *What Kind of Democracy? What Kind of Market? Latin America in the Age of Neo-liberalism.* University Park: Penn State University Press.

Barcellos, Caco. 1992. *Rota 66: A História da Policia Que Mata.* São Paulo: Globo.

Barclay, Gordon C., and Tavares, Cynthia. 2002. *Home Office Statistical Bulletin: International Comparisons of Criminal Justice Statistics.* London: Home Office.

Barros, Ricardo Paes de, Henriques, Ricardo, and Mendonça, Rosane. 2000. "A Estabilidade Inaceitável: Desigualdade e Pobreza no Brasil." In R. Henriques (Ed.), *Desigualdade e Pobreza no Brasil.* Rio de Janeiro: IPEA.

Bates, Robert H. 1981. *Markets and States in Tropical Africa: The Political Basis of Agricultural Policies.* Berkeley: University of California Press.

Bayley, David H. 1975. "The Police and Political Development in Europe." In C. Tilly (Ed.), *The Formation of National States in Europe.* Princeton, NJ: Princeton University Press.

———. 1994. *Police for the Future.* New York: Oxford University Press.

———. 1995a. "A Foreign Policy for Democratic Policing." *Policing and Society* 5: 79–93.

———. 1995b. "Getting Serious About Police Brutality." In P. Stenning (Ed.), *Accountability for Criminal Justice: Selected Essays.* Toronto: University of Toronto Press.

———. 1996. "The Contemporary Practices of Policing: A Comparative View." In *Civilian Police and Multinational Peacekeeping: A Role for Democratic Policing.* Washington, DC: National Institute of Justice, Police Executive Research Forum, Center for Strategic and International Studies.

Bayley, David, and Shearing, Clifford. 1996. "The Future of Policing." *Law and Society Review* 30, no. 3: 585–606.

Becker, Gary. 1986. "Crime and Punishment: An Economic Approach." *Journal of Political Economy.*

Beetham, David. 1991. *The Legitimation of Power.* London: Macmillan Education.

Benjamin, Cid. 1998. *Hélio Luz: Um Xerife da Esquerda.* Rio de Janeiro: Relume Dumará.

Bhagwati, Jagdish N. 1982. "Directly Unproductive, Profit-Seeking (DUP) Activities." *Journal of Political Economy* 90: 988–1002.

Bittner, Egon. 1970. *The Functions of the Police in Modern Society: A Review of Background Factors, Current Practices, and Possible Role Models.* Rockville, MD: National Institute of Mental Health Center for Studies of Crime and Delinquency.

Bonelli, Regis, and Malan, Pedro S. 1987. "Industrialization, Economic Growth, and Balance Payments: Brazil, 1970–1984." In J. D. Wirth, E. d. O. Nunes, and T. E. Bugenschild (Eds.), *State and Society in Brazil.* Boulder and London: Westview Press.

Boschi, Renato Raul. 1987. *A Arte da Associação.* São Paulo: Editora Revista dos Tribunais.

Bretas, Marcos Luiz. 1997. *Ordem na Cidade: O Exercíco Cotidiano da Autoridade Policial no Rio de Janeiro, 1907–1930.* Rio de Janeiro: Rocco.

Brewer, John D. 1993. "Sensitivity as a Problem in Field Research: A Study of Routine Policing in Northern Ireland." In R. M. Lee and C. M. Renzetti (Eds.), *Researching Sensitive Topics.* Newbury Park, CA: Sage.

Brodeur, Jean-Paul. 1999. "Comments on Chevigny." In J. E. Méndez, G. O'Donnell, and S. P. Pinheiro (Eds.), *The (Un)Rule of Law and the Underprivileged in Latin America.* Notre Dame: University of Notre Dame Press.

Bureau of Justice Statistics. 1997. *Justice Data On-Line: Law Enforcement Agency Profile for New York City Police Department.* Washington, DC: US Department of Justice.

Burzaco, Eugenio. 2001. *Rehenes de la Violencia.* Buenos Aires: Atlántida.

Caldeira, Teresa P. R. 2000. *City of Walls: Crime, Segregation, and Citizenship in São Paulo.* Berkeley: University of California Press.

Cancelli, Elizabeth. 1993. *O Mundo da Violência: A Polícia da Era Vargas.* Brasília: Universidade de Brasília.

Cano, Ignacio. 1997. *The Use of Lethal Force by Police in Rio de Janeiro.* Rio de Janeiro: Instituto de Estudos da Religião (ISER).

Cano, Ignacio, and Santos, Nilton. 2001. *Violência Letal, Renda, e Desigualdade Social no Brasil.* Rio de Janeiro: 7 Letras.

Carneiro, Leandro Piquet. 1999. *Determinantes do Crime na América Latina: Rio de Janeiro e São Paulo, Relatório de Pesquisa.* World Bank Discussion Paper. Washington, DC: World Bank.

CELS (Centro de Estudios Legales y Sociales). 1999. *Muertes en Enfrentamientos.* Buenos Aires: CELS.

———. 2000. *Derechos Humanos en Argentina: Informe Anual 2000.* Buenos Aires: Eudeba, Universidad de Buenos Aires.

CELS (Centro de Estudios Legales y Sociales) and HRW (Human Rights Watch). 1998. *La Inseguridad Policial: Violencia de las Fuerzas de Seguridad en la Argentina.* Buenos Aires: Editorial Universitaria de Buenos Aires.

Cerqueira, Carlos Magno Nazareth. 1994. "The Military Police of Rio de Janeiro." Manuscript, International Police Executive Symposium, Geneva.

———. 2001. *O Futuro de uma Ilusão: O Sonho de uma Nova Polícia.* Rio de Janeiro: Freitas Bastos.

Cerqueira, Nilton Albuquerque. 1996. *Violência e Segurança.* São Paulo: Federacão das Industrias do Estado de São Paulo (FIESP).

Chan, Janet B. L. 1997. *Changing Police Culture: Policing in a Multicultural Society.* New York: Cambridge University Press.

Chevigny, Paul G. 1991. "Police Deadly Force as Social Control: Jamaica, Brazil, and Argentina." In Martha K. Huggins (Ed.), *Vigilantism and the State in Modern Latin America: Essays on Extralegal Violence.* New York: Praeger.

———. 1995. *Edge of the Knife: Police Violence in the Americas.* New York: New Press.

Chillier, Gastón. 1998a. *La Denuncia de un Ex-Policía: Análisis de las Consecuencias de las Prácticas de la Policía Federal.* Buenos Aires: CELS, Programa Violencia Institucional, Seguridad Ciudadana, y Derechos Humanos.

———. 1998b. "La Sanción de un Código de Convivencia Urbana." Paper presented at the conference "Las Reformas Policiales en Argentina," sponsored by CELS, Buenos Aires, December 1–2.

Choongh, Satnam. 1998. "Policing the Dross. A Social Disciplinary Model of Policing." *British Journal of Criminology* 38: 623–634.

CIDE (Centro de Informações e Dados do Governo do Estado de Rio de Janeiro). 2001. *Anuário Estatístico do Estado de Rio de Janeiro 2000/1999.* Rio de Janeiro: CIDE.

Coelho, Edmundo Campos. 1987. *A Oficina do Diabo: Crise e Conflitos no Sistema Penitenciário do Rio de Janeiro.* Rio de Janeiro: Espaço e Tempo e Instituto Universitário de Pesquisas do Rio de Janeiro (IUPERJ).

CONADEP (Comisión Nacional sobre la Desaparición de Personas). 1984. *Nunca Más.* Buenos Aires: Eudeba.

Consejo Federal de Seguridad. 2000. "Bases de Consenso del Plan Federal de Seguridad." Manuscript, Buenos Aires.

CPDOC-FGV/ISER (Centro de Pesquisa e Documentaçao de História Contemporânea do Brasil, Fundação Getulio Vargas, Instituto de Estudos da Religião). 1997. *Lei, Justiça, e Cidadania: Sinopse dos Resultados da Pesquisa.* Rio de Janeiro: CPDOC-FGV/ISER.

Dahl, Robert A. 1971. *Polyarchy: Participation and Opposition.* New Haven, CT: Yale University Press.

———. 1989. *Democracy and Its Critics.* New Haven, CT: Yale University Press.

Dammert, Lucia. 2000. *Violencia Criminal y Seguridad Pública; La Situación en la Argentina.* Santiago de Chile: Comisión Económica para América Latina y el Caribe (CEPAL), United Nations.

Defensoría CBA (Defensoría del Pueblo de la Ciudad de Buenos Aires). 2000. *Informe Anual 1999*. Buenos Aires: Defensoría CBA.

Desposato, Scott. 1997. "Party Switching and Democratization in Brazil." Paper presented at the Latin American Studies Association (LASA) annual conference, Guadalajara, Mexico, April 17–19.

Diaz-Alejandro, Carlos Federico. 1970. *Essays on the Economic History of the Argentine Republic*. New Haven, CT: Yale University Press.

Dillinger, William, and Webb, Steven. 1999. *Fiscal Management in Federal Democracies: Argentina and Brazil*. Policy Research Working Paper 2121. Washington, DC: World Bank.

Dirección de Gastos Sociales Consolidados. 2000. *Caracterización y Evolución del Gasto Público Social*. Buenos Aires: Secretaría de Política Económica, Ministerio de Economía.

DNPC (Dirección Nacional de Política Criminal). 1999. *Sistema Nacional de Información Criminal, Informe Anual de Estadísticas Policiales: Años 1990–99*. Buenos Aires: DNPC.

———. 2000. *Informe: Hacia un Diagnóstico Sobre la Seguridad Urbana en la Ciudad de Buenos Aires—Análisis de las Estadísticas Policiales 2000*. Buenos Aires: Dirección Nacional de Política Criminal. Available at http://sntweb.jus.gov.ar/polcrim/polcrim.htm.

———. 2002. *Sistema Nacional de Información Criminal, Informe Anual de Estadísticas Policiales: 2002*. Buenos Aires: DNPC.

Dowdney, Luke. 2003. *Crianças do Tráfico: Um Estudo de Caso de Crianças em Violência Armada Organizada no Rio de Janeiro*. Rio de Janeiro: 7 Letras.

Eakin, Marshall C. 1997. *Brazil: The Once and Future Country*. London: Macmillan.

Economist Intelligence Unit Data Services. 2004. *Economist Intelligence Unit Country Data*. London: EIU.

Faoro, Raymundo. 1979. *Os Donos do Poder: Formação Patronato Político Brasileiro*. Porto Alegre: Globo.

FBI (Federal Bureau of Intelligence). 1995. *Uniform Crime Report*. Washington, DC: FBI.

———. 1998. *Uniform Crime Report*. Washington, DC: FBI.

Fernandes, Edesio. 1995. *Law and Urban Change in Brazil*. Aldershot, UK: Avebury.

Filliol, Tomás Roberto. 1961. *Social Factors in Economic Development: The Argentine Case*. Cambridge, MA: MIT University Press.

Fishlow, Albert. 1986. "Latin American Adjustment to the Oil Shocks of 1973 and 1979." In J. H. a. S. Morley (Ed.), *Latin American Political Economy: Financial Crisis and Political Change*. Boulder: Westview Press.

Freedom House. 2004. "Colombia." In Freedom House (Ed.), *Freedom in the World, 2003*. Washington, DC: Freedom House.

Frieden, Jeffry. 1991. *Debt, Development, and Democracy: Modern Political Economy and Latin America, 1965–1985*. Princeton, NJ: Princeton University Press.

Frühling, Hugo. 1998. "Judicial Reform and Democratization in Latin America." In Felipe Agüero and Jeffrey Stark (Eds.), *Fault Lines of Democracy in Post-transition Latin America*. Miami: North-South Center Press.

Fukuyama, Francis. 1999. "The Great Disruption." *Atlantic Monthly*, May, 55–80.

Garotinho, Anthony, Soares, Luiz Eduardo, Soares, Barbara M., Sento-Sé, João Trajano, Musumeci, Leonarda, and Ramos, Silvia. 1998. *Violência e Criminalidade no Estado do Rio de Janeiro: Diagnóstico e Propostas para uma Política Democrática de Segurança Pública*. Rio de Janeiro: Editora Hama.

Gay, Robert. 1994. *Popular Organization and Democracy in Rio de Janeiro: A Tale of Two Favelas*. Philadelphia: Temple University Press.

Geddes, Barbara, and Neto, Arturo Ribeiro. 1992. "Institutional Sources of Corruption in Brazil." *Third World Quarterly* 13: 641–661.

Geuss, Raymond. 2001. *History and Illusion in Politics*. New York: Cambridge University Press.

Goldsmith, Andrew. 1990. "Taking Police Culture Seriously: Police Discretion and the Limits of the Law." *Policing and Society* 1: 91–114.

Goldstein, Herman. 1977. *Policing a Free Society*. Cambridge: Ballinger Publishing Company.

Governo do Estado do Rio de Janeiro. 2000. *Política Pública para a Segurança, Justiça, e Cidadania*. Rio de Janeiro: Governo do Estado do Rio de Janeiro.

Grindle, Merilee S., and Thomas, John W. 1991. *Public Choices and Policy Change*. Baltimore: Johns Hopkins University Press.

Hagopian, Frances. 1996. *Traditional Politics and Regime Change in Brazil*. New York: Cambridge University Press.

Hamill, Hugh M. 1992. *Caudillos: Dictators in Spanish America*. Norman: University of Oklahoma Press.

Hawthorn, Geoffrey. 1991. *Plausible Worlds*. Cambridge: Cambridge University Press.

Hernández, José. 1982. *Martín Fierro: El Gaucho Martín Fierro y La Vuelta de Martín Fierro*. Madrid: Sociedad General Española de Librería.

Herz, Daniel. 1987. *A História Secreda da Rede Globo*. Porto Alegre: Tchê.

Herzer, Hilda María. 1996. *Ciudad de Buenos Aires: Gobierno y Descentralización*. Buenos Aires: Colección CEA-CBC (Centro de Estudios Avanzados and Ciclo Básico Común), Universidad de Buenos Aires.

Hobbes, Thomas. 1651. *Leviathan*. Reprint. Cambridge: Cambridge University Press.

Holloway, Thomas. 1993. *Policing Rio de Janeiro*. Stanford, CA: Stanford University Press.

Huggins, Martha K. 1997. "From Bureaucratic Consolidation to Structural Devolution: Police Death Squads in Brazil." *Policing and Society* 7: 207–234.

———. 1998. *Political Policing: The United States and Latin America*. Durham, NC: Duke University Press.

Human Rights Watch. 1993. *Urban Police Violence in Brazil: Torture and Police Killings in São Paulo and Rio de Janeiro After Five Years*. New York: Human Rights Watch.

———. 1994. *Final Justice: Police and Death Squad Homicides of Adolescents in Brazil*. New York: Human Rights Watch.

———. 1996. *Brazil: Fighting Violence with Violence: Human Rights Abuse and Criminality in Rio de Janeiro*. New York: Human Rights Watch.

———. 1997. *Police Brutality in Urban Brazil*. New York: Human Rights Watch.

Hunter, Wendy. 1996. *State and Soldier in Latin America: Redefining the Military's Role in Argentina, Brazil, and Chile*. Washington, DC: US Institute for Peace.

Huntington, Samuel P. 1968. *Political Order in Changing Societies*. New Haven, CT: Yale University Press.

IACHR (Inter-American Commission on Human Rights). 1997. *Country Report: Brazil, 1997*. Washington, DC: IAHCR.

IBGE (Instituto Brasileiro de Geografia e Estatística). 2000. *Censo 2000*. Brasilia: IBGE.

———. 2002. *Perfil dos Municípios Brasileiros: Gestão Pública*. Brasilia: IBGE.

IDB (Inter-American Development Bank) and World Bank. 1999. *Secondary Education in Brazil: Time to Move Forward*. IDB Report BR-014 and World Bank Report 19409-BR. Washington, DC: World Bank and IDB.

ILO (International Labour Office). 2002. *Key Indicators of the Labour Market, 2001–2002*. Geneva: ILO.

INDEC (Instituto Nacional de Estadísticas y Censos). 2002. *Encuesta Permanente de Hogares: Hogares y Personas Bajo Líneas de Pobreza y de Indigencia, Octubre 2002*. Buenos Aires: INDEC.

———. 2003. *Encuesta Permanente de Hogares: Evolución de la Indigencia, la Pobreza, y la Desocupación en el GBA Desde 1988 en Adelante*. Buenos Aires: INDEC.

Instituto Gallup Argentina. 1984–2000. *Muestra Nacional: Confianza en las Instituciones*. Buenos Aires: Instituto Gallup Argentina.

———. 1994. *Estudio de Opinión Acerca de la Administración de Justicia*. Buenos Aires: CEJURA (Centro de Estudios Judiciales de la República Argentina).

Interpol. 2004. *International Crime Statistics*. Paris: Interpol.

IPEA (Instituto de Pesquisa Econômica Aplicada). 2002. *Desigualdade Racial: Indicadores Socioeconômicos—Brasil, 1991–2002*. Brasilia: IPEA.

Jones, Trever, and Newburn, Tim. 1997. *Policing After the Act: Police Governance After the Police and Magistrates' Courts Act 1994*. London: Policy Studies Institute.

Jones, Trever, Newburn, Tim, and Smith, D. J. 1996. "Policing and the Idea of Democracy." *British Journal of Criminology* 36: 182–198.

Kahn, Tulio. 2002. *Conjuntura Criminal: Estatísticas, Homicídio Doloso nas Capitais e no Distrito Federal (1999–2001)*. www.conjunturacriminal.com.br.

Kalmanowiecki, Laura. 2000. "Origins and Applications of Political Policing in Argentina." *Latin American Perspectives* 27, no. 2 (March 2000): 36–56.

Kant de Lima, Roberto. 1995. *A Polícia da Cidade do Rio de Janeiro: Seus Dilemas e Paradoxos*. Rio de Janeiro: Forense.

———. 1997. "Polícia e Exclusão na Cultura Judiciária." *Tempo Social* 9: 169–183.

Kearney, Christine. 2001. "The Poverty of Neo-liberalism in Brazil: Economic Culture and Policy Choice." Paper presented at Latin American Studies Association (LASA) conference, Washington, DC, September 6.

Kelling, George L. 1985. "Order Maintenance, the Quality of Urban Life, and Police: A Line of Argument." In W. A. Geller (Ed.), *Police Leadership in America*. New York: Praeger.

Kingstone, Peter R. 1998. "Corporatism, Neo-liberalism, and the Failed Revolt of Big Business: Lessons from the Case of IEDI." *Journal of Interamerican Studies and World Affairs* 40: 73–95.

Kinzo, Maria D'Alva G. 1993. "Consolidation of Democracy, Governability, and Political Parties in Brazil." In M. D. A. G. Kinzo (Ed.), *Brazil: The Challenges of the 1990s*. London: Institute of Latin American Studies and British Academy Press.

Klitgaard, Robert. 1988. *Controlling Corruption*. Berkeley: University of California Press.

Krueger, Anne O. 1990. "Government Failures in Development." *Journal of Economic Perspectives* 4: 9–23.

Lagos, Marta. 1997. "Latin America's Smiling Mask." *Journal of Democracy* 8, no. 3: 125–138.

Leal, Victor Nunes. 1978. *Coronelismo, Enxada, e Voto*. São Paulo: Alfa-Omega.

Lee, Raymond M. 1993. *Doing Research on Sensitive Topics*. London: Sage.

Leeds, Elizabeth. 1996. "Cocaine and Parallel Polities in the Brazilian Urban Periphery: Constraints on Local Level Democratization." *Latin American Research Review* 31: 47–83.

Lemgruber, Julita. 2002. "Controle da Criminalidade: Mitos e Fatos." In Nilson Vieira Oliveira (Ed.), *Insegurança Pública: Reflexões Sobre a Criminimalidade e a Violência Urbana.* São Paulo: Nova Alexandria.

Lewis, Oscar. 1963. *The Children of Sánchez.* New York: Vintage Books.

Lima, Venicio A. de, and Ramos, Murilo. 1988. "A Televisão no Brasil: Desinformação e Democracia." In D. Fleischer (Ed.), *Da Destenção à Abertura: As Eleições de 1982.* Brasilia: Editora da Universidade de Brasilia.

Lima, William da Silva. 1991. *Quatrocentos Contra Um: Uma História do Comando Vermelho.* Rio de Janeiro: ISER (Instituto de Estudos da Religião) and Vozes.

Llach, Juan José, and Cerro, Fernando. 1998. "The Third Stage of Argentine Economic Growth." In Joseph Tulchin and A. Garland (Eds.), *Argentina: The Challenges of Modernization.* Wilmington, DE: Scholarly Resources.

Loader, Ian. 1994. "Democracy, Justice, and the Limits of Policing: Rethinking Police Accountability." *Social and Legal Studies* 3: 521–544.

Lorences, Valentín H. 1997. *Poder de Policía: Edictos Policiales—Justicia Contravencional y de Faltas.* Buenos Aires: Editorial Universidad.

Loveman, Brian, and Davies, Thomas M. (Eds.). 1978. *The Politics of Antipolitics: The Military in Latin America.* Lincoln: University of Nebraska Press.

Maddison, Angus. 2003. *The World Econonomy: Historical Statistics.* Paris: Organisation for Economic Co-operation and Development's Development Centre Studies.

Mafud, Julio. 1984. *Psicología de la Viveza Criolla.* Buenos Aires: Editorial Distal.

Maguire, Mike. 2002. "Crime Statistics: The 'Data Explosion' and Its Implications." In Mike Maguire, R. Morgan, and Robert Reiner (Eds.), *Oxford Handbook of Criminology.* Oxford: Oxford University Press.

Mainwaring, Scott. 1995. "Brazil: Weak Parties, Feckless Democracy." In Scott Mainwaring and Timothy R. Scully (Eds.), *Building Democratic Institutions: Party Systems in Latin America.* Stanford, CA: University of Stanford Press.

———. 1997. "Multipartism, Robust Federalism, and Presidentialism in Brazil." In Scott Mainwaring and M. S. Shugart (Eds.), *Presidentialism and Democracy in Latin America.* Cambridge: Cambridge University Press.

———. 1999. *Rethinking Party Systems in the Third Wave of Democratization: The Case of Brazil.* Stanford: Stanford University Press.

Mainwaring, Scott, and Scully, Timothy R (Eds.). 1995. *Building Democratic Institutions: Party Systems in Latin America.* Stanford, CA: Stanford University Press.

Mandela, Nelson. 1994. *Long Walk to Freedom: The Autobiography of Nelson Mandela.* Boston: Little, Brown.

Manzetti, Luigi. 1999. *Privatization South American Style.* Oxford: Oxford University Press.

Manzetti, Luigi, and Blake, Charles. 1996. "Market Reforms and Corruption in Latin America." *Review of International Political Economy* 3, no. 4: 662–697.

Marenin, Otwin. 1982. "Parking Tickets and Class Repression: The Concept of Policing in Critical Theories of Criminal Justice." *Contemporary Crises* 6: 241–266.

———. 1996. "Policing Change, Changing Police: Some Thematic Questions." In Otwin Marenin (Ed.), *Policing Change, Changing Police: International Perspectives.* New York: Garland.

———. 1998. "The Goal of Democracy in International Police Assistance Programs." *Policing: An International Journal of Police Strategies and Management* 21: 159–177.

Matta, Roberto da. 1993. "Is Brazil Hopelessly Corrupt?" *New York Times*, December 13, 1993.
————. 1995. *On the Brazilian Urban Poor: An Anthropological Report.* Working Paper 10, Democracy and Social Policy Series. Notre Dame, IN: Kellogg Institute, University of Notre Dame.
McFarlane, Anthony. 1996. "Political Corruption and Reform in Bourbon Spanish America." In W. Little and E. Posada-Carbo (Eds.), *Political Corruption in Latin America and Europe.* New York: St. Martin's Press.
McGann, Thomas. 1966. *Argentina: The Divided Land.* Princeton, NJ: Van Nostrand.
McSherry, Patrice J. 1997. *Incomplete Transition: Military Power and Democracy in Argentina.* Basingstoke, UK: Macmillan.
Mello, Geraldo Anhaia. 1994. *Muito Além do Cidadão Kane.* São Paulo: Scritta.
Miguel, Luis Felipe. 2000. "The Globo Television Network and the Election of 1998." *Latin American Perspectives* 27: 65–84.
MinJus and MinInt (Ministerio de Justicia y Derechos Humanos de la Nación y Ministerio del Interior de la Nación). 2000. *Plan Nacional de Prevención del Delito.* Buenos Aires: MinJus and MinInt.
Molas, Richard Rodríguez. 1985. *Historia de la Tortura y el Orden Represivo en la Argentina.* Buenos Aires: Eudeba.
Montesinos, Verónica, and Markoff, John. 2001. "From the Power of Economic Ideas to the Power of Economists." In M. A. Centeno and F. López-Alves (Eds.), *The Other Mirror: Grand Theory Through the Lens of Latin America.* Princeton, NJ: Princeton University Press.
Montoro, Alfred P. 1998. "State Interests and the New Industrial Policy in Brazil: The Privatization of Steel, 1990–1994." *Journal of Interamerican Studies and World Affairs* 40: 27–62.
MS/SE/Datasus (Ministério da Saúde, Secretarias Estaduais de Saúde, Data do Sistema Único de Saúde). 2002. *Informações Demográficas e Socioeconômicas.* Available at www.datasus.gov.br.
Muniz, Jaqueline. 2001. "A Crise de Identidade das Polícia Militares Brasileiras: Dilemas e Paradoxos da Formação Educacional." *Security and Defense Review* 1: 177–198.
Murillo, Maria Victoria. 2001. *Labor Unions, Partisan Coalitions, and Market Reforms in Latin America.* Cambridge: Cambridge University Press.
NECVU/UFRJ (Núcleo de Estudos da Cidadania, Conflito e Violência Urbana, Universidade Federal de Rio de Janeiro). 1984–2000. *Polícia Civil, Principais Occorências, Registros, Regiões RJ, Números Absolutos e Taxas por 100,000 Habitantes.* Rio de Janeiro: NECVU/UFRJ.
————. 2001. *Polícia Civil, Principais Occorências, Registros, Regiões RJ, Números Absolutos e Taxas por 100,000 Habitantes.* Rio de Janeiro: NECVU/UFRJ.
Nino, Carlos. 1995. *Un País al Margen de la Ley.* Buenos Aires: Emece.
NYC (New York City). 2001. *Municipal Services, 1994–2001: Mayor Rudolph Giuliani's Management Report, Fiscal 2001 Supplement.* New York: City of New York.
Nylen, William R. 2000. "The Making of a Loyal Opposition: The Workers' Party (PT) and the Consolidation of Democracy in Brazil." In Peter R. Kingstone and Timothy J. Power (Eds.), *Democratic Brazil: Actors, Institutions, and Processes.* Pittsburgh: University of Pittsburgh Press.
O'Donnell, Guillermo. 1994. "Delegative Democracy." *Journal of Democracy* 5: 55–69.
————. 1998. "Horizontal Accountability in New Democracies." *Journal of Democracy* 9: 112–126.

————. 1999. "Polyarchies and the (Un)Rule of Law in Latin America: A Partial Conclusion." In J. E. Méndez, Guillermo O'Donnell, and S. P. Pinheiro (Eds.), *The (Un)Rule of Law and the Underprivileged in Latin America.* Notre Dame, IN: University of Notre Dame Press.

Oliveira, Alicia, and Tiscornia, Sofía. 1997. "Estructura y Prácticas de las Policías en la Argentina: Las Redes de Ilegalidad." In Centro de Estudios Legales y Sociales (Ed.), *Control Democrático de los Organismos de Seguridad Interior en la República Argentina.* Buenos Aires: CELS.

Olson, Mancur. 1965. *The Logic of Collective Action.* Cambridge: Harvard University Press.

Ortega y Gasset, José. 1929. "La Pampa . . . Promesas." In R. d. Occidente (Ed.), *Obras Completas de José Ortega y Gasset,* vol. 2, *El Espectador.* Madrid: Ediciones Castilla.

Osiel, Mark J. 1995. "Dialogue with Dictators: Judicial Resistance in Argentina and Brazil." *Law and Social Inquiry* 20: 533–540.

Ouvidoria RJ (Ouvidoria da Polícia do Estado do Rio de Janeiro, Rio de Janeiro Ombudsman's Office). 1999. *Tablea de Denúncias.* Rio de Janeiro: Ouvidoria RJ.

Ouvidoria SP (Ouvidoria da Polícia do Estado de São Paulo, São Paulo Ombudsman's Office). 1999. *Relatório Anual de Prestação de Contas, 1999.* São Paulo: Ouvidoria SP.

Page, Joseph. 1983. *Perón: Una Biografía.* Buenos Aires: Javier Vergara.

Panizza, Francisco, and Barahona de Brito, Alexandra. 1998. "The Politics of Human Rights in Democratic Brazil: 'A Lei Não Pega.'" *Democratization* 5, no. 4 (1998): 20–51.

Pastor, Manuel, and Wise, Carol. 1997. "Stabilization and Its Discontents: Argentina's Economic Restructuring in the 1990s." *World Development* 27: 477–503.

Pelacchi, Adrián. 2000. *Tratado Sobre la Seguridad Pública.* Buenos Aires: Editorial Policial.

Pereira, Anthony W. 2000. "An Ugly Democracy? State Violence and the Rule of Law in Postauthoritarian Brazil." In Peter R. Kingstone and Timothy J. Power (Eds.), *Democratic Brazil: Actors, Institutions, and Processes.* Pittsburgh: University of Pittsburgh Press.

PFA (Policía Federal Argentina). 1999. *Ideas Centrales del Tercer Milenio.* Buenos Aires: Editorial Policial.

Philip, George. 2003. *Democracy in Latin America: Surviving Conflict and Crisis?* London: Polity Press.

Pinheiro, Paulo Sérgio. 1991. "Police and Political Crisis: The Case of the Military Police." In Martha K. Huggins (Ed.), *Vigilantism and the State in Modern Latin America: Essays on Extralegal Violence.* New York: Praeger.

————. 1999. *Primeiro Relatório Nacional Sobre os Direitos Humanos no Brasil: Realizações e Desafios.* São Paulo: Universidade de São Paulo, Núcleo de Estudo da Violência.

Power, Timothy J. 1998. "The Pen Is Mightier than the Congress: Presidential Decree Power in Brazil." In J. M. Carey and M. S. Shugart (Eds.), *Executive Decree Authority.* Cambridge: Cambridge University Press.

————. 2000. "Political Institutions in Democratic Brazil: Politics as a Permanent Constitutional Convention." In Peter R. Kingstone and Timothy J. Power (Eds.), *Democratic Brazil: Actors, Institutions, and Processes.* Pittsburgh: University of Pittsburgh Press.

Power, Timothy J., and Roberts, J. Timmons. 2000. "A New Brazil? The Changing Socio-demographic Context of Brazilian Democracy." In Peter R. Kingstone and Timothy J. Power (Eds.), *Democratic Brazil: Actors, Institutions, and Processes.* Pittsburgh: University of Pittsburgh Press.

Prillaman, William C. 2000. *The Judiciary and Democratic Decay in Latin America: Declining Confidence in the Rule of Law.* Westport, CT: Praeger.

Programa de Seguridad Ciudadana. 1999a. *Inseguridad Urbana Creciente, Informe 1.* Buenos Aires: Gobierno de la Ciudad de Buenos Aires.

————. 1999b. *Perfil de los Consejos de Prevención del Delito y la Violencia.* Buenos Aires: Gobierno de la Ciudad de Buenos Aires.

Programa Integral de Reforma Judicial. 2000. "Componentes Preliminares del Programa." Ministerio de Justicia y Derechos Humanos, Argentina.

PROVEA (Programa Venezolano de Educación-Acción en Derechos Humanos). 2003. *Informe Anual de la Situación de los Derechos Humanos en Venezuela, 2002–2003: Derecho a la Seguridad Ciudadana.* Caracas: PROVEA.

Ramsdell, Lea. 1990. "National Housing Policy and the Favela in Brazil." In L. S. Graham and R. H. Wilson (Eds.), *The Political Economy of Brazil: Public Policies of an Era in Transition.* Austin: University of Texas Press.

Reiner, Robert. 1991. *Chief Constables.* Oxford: Oxford University Press.

————. 2000a. "Police Research." In R. D. King and E. Wincup (Eds.), *Doing Research on Crime and Justice.* Oxford: Oxford University Press.

————. 2000b. *The Politics of the Police.* Oxford: Oxford University Press.

Reiss, Albert J., Jr. 1971. *The Police and the Public.* New Haven, CT: Yale University Press.

Reiss, Albert J., Jr., and Bordua, Avid J. 1967. "Environment and Organization: A Perspective on the Police." In *The Police: Six Sociological Essays.* New York: John Wiley and Sons.

Resende, Juliana. 1995. *Operação Rio.* Rio de Janeiro: Página Aberta.

RNR (Registro Nacional de Reincidencia, Ministerio de Justicia y Derechos Humanos). *Estadistica de Sentencias Condenatorias: Duración del Proceso,* 1996. Available online at www.jus.gov.ar.

Rock, David. 1986. *Argentina, 1516–1987: From Spanish Colonization to the Falklands War.* London: I. B. Tauris.

————. 1987. *Argentina, 1516–1987: From Spanish Colonization to the Falklands War and Alfonsín.* London: I. B. Tauris.

Rodríguez, Adolfo Enrique, and Zappietro, Eugenio Juan. 1999. *Historia de la Policía Federal Argentina en las Puertas del Tercer Milenio: Génesis, Desarrollo, Desde 1580 Hasta la Actualidad.* Buenos Aires: Editorial Policial.

Rodríguez Molas, Ricardo. 1985. *Historia de la Tortura y el Orden Represivo en la Argentina.* Buenos Aires: Eudeba.

Roett, Riordan. 1999. *Politics in a Patrimonial Society.* Westport, CT: Praeger.

Rosenn, Keith S. 1990. "Brazil's New Constitution: An Exercise in Transient Constitutionalism for a Transitional Society." *American Journal of Comparative Law* 38: 773–802.

Samuels, David. 2001. "Money, Elections, and Democracy in Brazil." *Latin American Politics and Society* 43: 27–48.

Samuels, David, and Abrucio, Fernando Luiz. 2000. "Federalism and Democratic Transitions: The 'New' Politics of the Governors in Brazil." *Publius: The Journal of Federalism* 30: 43–61.

Sarney, José. 1986. "Brazil: A President's Story." *Foreign Affairs* 65: 101–117.

Scheetz, Thomas. 1995. "A Peace Dividend in South America? Defense Conversion in Argentina and Chile." In Nils P. Gleditsch, O. Bjerkholt, Å. Cappelen, R. P.

Smith, and J. P. Dunne (Eds.), *The Peace Dividend*. Contributions to Economic Analysis. Amsterdam: Elsevier Science.

Schneider, Ben Ross. 1997. "Organized Business Politics in Democratic Brazil." *Journal of Interamerican Studies and World Affairs* 39: 95–127.

Schneider, Ronald M. 1996. *Brazil: Culture and Politics in a New Industrial Powerhouse*. Boulder: Westview Press.

Secretaría de Hacienda. 1993–2000. *Ley de Presupuesto Nacional*. Buenos Aires: Ministerio de Economía.

Selcher, Wayne A. 1998. "The Politics of Decentralized Federalism, National Diversification, and Regionalism in Brazil." *Journal of Interamerican Studies and World Affairs* 40: 25–50.

Shah, Anwar. 1991. *The New Fiscal Federalism in Brazil*. World Bank Discussion Paper 124. Washington, DC: World Bank.

Shearing, Clifford. 1992. "The Relation Between Public and Private Policing." In Michael Tonry and Norval Morris (Eds.), *Modern Policing*. Chicago: University of Chicago Press.

Sheptycki, J. W. E. 1996. "Law Enforcement, Justice, and Democracy in the Transnational Arena: Reflections on the War on Drugs." *International Journal of the Sociology of Law* 24: 61-75.

Sherman, Lawrence W. 1992. "Attacking Crime: Police and Crime Control." In Michael Tonry and Norval Morris (Eds.), *Modern Policing: Crime and Justice, a Review of Research*. Chicago: University of Chicago Press.

Silva, Jorge, da. 1998. "Para uma Reforma da Segurança Pública: Direitos Humanos e Ideologia dos Algozes-Vítimas." Paper presented at the international conference "Policía y Sociedad Democrática," sponsored by the CED (Centro de Estudios del Desarrollo) and the Ford Foundation, Santiago, August 18–19.

Silver, Alan. 1967. "The Demand for Order in Civil Society: A Review of Some Themes in the History of Urban Crime, Police, and Riot." In D. J. Bordua (Ed.), *The Police: Six Sociological Essays*. New York: Wiley and Sons.

Skolnick, Jerome H. 1994. *Justice Without Trial: Law Enforcement in a Democratic Society*. New York: Macmillan.

Skolnick, Jerome H., and Bayley, David H. 1988. *Community Policing: Issues and Practices Around the World*. Washington, DC: National Institute of Justice.

Smith, Peter. 1998. "The Rise and Fall of the Developmental State in Latin America." In Menno Vellinga (Ed.), *The Changing Role of the State in Latin America*. Boulder: Westview Press.

Soares, Luiz Eduardo. 1999. "O Que Estamos Fazendo na Segurança Pública do Rio." *NO* magazine, www.no.com.br.

———. 2000. *Meu Casaco de General: Quinhentos Dias no Front da Segurança Pública do Rio de Janeiro*. São Paulo: Companhia das Letras.

———. 2001. "Polícia e Bandido: Retratando a Realidade." Paper presented at Bienal do Livro 2001, Rio Centro, Rio de Janeiro, May 18.

Soares, Luiz Eduardo, Sento-Sé, João Trajano, Rodrigues, José Augusto de Souza, and Carneiro, Leandro Piquet. 1996. "Criminalidade Urbana e Violência: O Rio de Janeiro no Contexto Internacional." In Luiz Eduardo Soares (Ed.), *Violência e Política no Rio de Janeiro*. Rio de Janeiro: Relume Dumará, ISER (Instituto de Estudos da Religião).

Souza, Celina. 1998. "Regional Interest Intermediation in Brazil and Its Impact on Public Policies." Paper presented at the LASA annual conference, Chicago, September 24–26.

Stares, Paul B. 1996. *Global Habit: The Drug Problem in a Borderless World.* Washington, DC: Brookings Institution.

Stepan, Alfred. 1973. "The New Professionalism of Internal Warfare and Military Role Expansion." In Alfred Stepan (Ed.), *Authoritarian Brazil: Origins, Policies, and Future.* New Haven, CT: Yale University Press.

———. 1971. *The Military in Politics: Changing Patterns in Brazil.* Princeton: Princeton University Press.

Straubhaar, Joseph, Olsen, Organ, and Nunes, Maria Cavaliari. 1993. "The Brazilian Case: Influencing the Voter." In T. E. Skidmore (Ed.), *Television, Politics, and the Transition to Democracy in Latin America.* Washington, DC: Woodrow Wilson Center Press.

Street, James H. 1982. "Coping with Energy Shocks in Latin America: Three Responses." *Latin American Research Review* 17: 128–147.

Teixeira, Ib. 1994. "Por Que o Rio Treme de Medo." *Conjuntura Economica* 48, no. 8: 194–195.

Theobald, Robin. 1990. *Corruption, Development, and Underdevelopment.* Durham, NC: Duke University Press.

Toronto Police Service. 1999. *Toronto Police Service 1999 Statistical Report.* Toronto: Toronto Police Service.

Transparency International. 2004. *Corruption Perception Index.* Berlin: Transparency International.

Tribunal de Contas do Estado de Rio de Janeiro. 1986–1999. "Execução Orcamentária do Estado do Rio de Janeiro, 1986–1999." Electronic spreadsheet, Tribunal de Contas, Gabinete do Conselheiro Sergio F. Quintella, Rio de Janeiro.

———. 1999. *Finanças Públicas do Estado e Dos Municípios do Rio de Janeiro.* Rio de Janeiro: Tribunal de Contas, Gabinete do Conselheiro Sergio F. Quintella.

Tyler, Tom. 1990. *Why People Obey the Law.* New Haven, CT: Yale University Press.

UN Special Rapporteur on Extrajudicial Executions. 2004. *Report of the Special Rapporteur on Extrajudicial, Summary or Arbitrary Executions, Asma Jahangir, on Her Mission to Brazil (16 September–8 October 2003).* Geneva: United Nations, Commission on Human Rights. Economic and Social Council.

UNCHR (United Nations Commission on Human Rights). 2001. *Civil and Political Rights, Including the Questions of Torture and Detention: Report of the Special Rapporteur, Nigel Rodley's Visit to Brazil.* Geneva: UN Commission on Human Rights, Economic and Social Council.

UNDP (United Nations Development Programme). 2000. *Human Development Report 2000.* New York: UNDP and Oxford University Press.

———. 2001. *Human Development Report 2001.* New York: UNDP.

———. 2004a. *La Democracia en América Latina.* Lima: UNDP.

———. 2004b. *La Democracia en América Latina: Compendio Estadístico.* Lima: UNDP.

———. 2004c. *La Democracia en América Latina: Ideas y Aportes.* Lima: UNDP.

Ungar, Mark. 2002. *Elusive Reform: Democracy and the Rule of Law in Latin America.* Boulder: Lynne Rienner Publishers.

UNICRI (United Nations Interregional Crime and Justice Research Institute). 1998. *Victims of Crime in the Developing World.* Rome: UNICRI.

United Nations. 1976. *Demographic Yearbook 1975.* New York: United Nations.

———. 1991. *Demographic Yearbook 1989.* New York: United Nations.

———. 2004. *Seventh United Nations Survey of Crime Trends and Operations of Criminal Justice Systems, Covering the Period 1998–2000.* Vienna: UN Office on Drugs and Crime, Division for Policy Analysis and Public Affairs.

UNM (Unión para la Nueva Mayoría). 1997. *Sondeos de Opinión Sobre la Problematica de la Seguridad.* Buenos Aires: Editorial Centro de Estudios UNM.
———. 1998. *La Seguridad Pública.* Buenos Aires: Editorial Centro de Estudios UNM.
———. 2003. *Sensible Disminución de los Cortes de Rutas en Enero.* Buenos Aires: Centro de Estudios UNM.
UNODOC (United Nations Office on Drugs and Crime). 2000. *Global Illicit Drug Trends.* Vienna: UNODOC.
US Committee for Refugees. 2003. *World Refugee Survey 2003.* Washington, DC: US Committee for Refugees.
US Department of State. 1996. *Country Reports on Human Rights Practices for 1995: Brazil.* Washington, DC: US State Department, Bureau of Democracy, Human Rights, and Labor.
———. 1999. *Country Reports on Human Rights Practices for 1998: Brazil.* Washington, DC: US State Department, Bureau of Democracy, Human Rights, and Labor.
———. 2000. *Country Reports on Human Rights Practices for 1999: Brazil.* Washington, DC: US State Department, Bureau of Democracy, Human Rights, and Labor.
———. 2002. *Country Reports on Human Rights Practices for 2001: Brazil.* Washington, DC: US State Department, Bureau of Democracy, Human Rights, and Labor.
Vecinos Solidarios. 1999. "Plan Alerta: Su Seguridad Es la Nuestra." Manuscript, Vecinos Solidarios, Buenos Aires.
Véliz, Claudio. 1980. *The Centralist Tradition of Latin America.* Princeton, NJ: Princeton University Press.
Vellinga, Menno. 1998. "The Changing Role of the State in Latin America." In Menno Vellinga (Ed.), *The Changing Role of the State in Latin America.* Boulder: Westview Press.
Ventura, Zuenir. 1994. *Cidade Partida.* São Paulo: Companhia das Letras.
Verbitsky, Horacio. 1991. *Robo para la Corona.* Buenos Aires: Planeta.
von Hirsch, Andrew, Bottoms, Anthony E., Burney, Elizabeth, and Wikström, P.-O. 1999. *Criminal Deterrence and Sentence Severity: An Analysis of Recent Research.* Oxford: Hart.
Waisman, Carlos. 1987. *The Reversal of Development in Argentina: Postwar Counterrevolutionary Policies and Their Structural Consequences.* Princeton, NJ: Princeton University Press.
Wall, David. 1998. *The Chief Constables of England and Wales: The Socio-legal History of a Criminal Justice Elite.* Aldershot, UK: Avebury.
Ward, Heather H. 1998. "Country Overviews: Argentina, Focus on Buenos Aires." Paper presented at the "Workshop on Police in Democratic Societies: Advancing Public Safety and Accountability," sponsored by the Vera Institute of Justice and Ford Foundation, Harriman, NY, March 23–24.
Weber, Max. 1958. "Politics as Vocation." In H. H. Gerth and C. W. Mills (Eds.), *From Max Weber: Essays in Sociology.* New York: Oxford University Press.
Weil, Feliz J. 1944. *The Argentine Riddle.* New York: John Day.
Weyland, Kurt. 1993. "The Rise and Fall of President Collor and Its Impact on Brazilian Democracy." *Journal of Interamerican Studies and World Affairs* 35: 1–37.
———. 1996. *Democracy Without Equity.* Pittsburgh: University of Pittsburgh Press.
———. 1998. "The Politics of Corruption in Latin America." *Journal of Democracy* 19: 108–120.

————. 2002. *The Politics of Market Reform in Fragile Democracies*. Princeton, NJ: Princeton University Press.

Williamson, John. 1993. "Democracy and the 'Washington Consensus.'" *World Development* 21: 1329–1336.

World Bank. 1983. *World Bank Development Report*. Washington, DC: World Bank.

————. 1999. *Rio de Janeiro: A City Study*. Washington, DC: World Bank.

————. 2000. *Argentina: Country Assistance Strategy, 2000 Progress Report (Memorandum of the President of the International Bank for Reconstruction and Development to the Executive Directors on a Country Assistance Strategy of the World Bank Group for the Argentine Republic)*. Washington, DC: World Bank.

————. 2002. *Brazil: Country Assistance Strategy, 2002 Progress Report (Memorandum of the President of the International Bank for Reconstruction and Development and the International Finance Corporation to the Executive Directors on a Country Assistance Strategy Progress Report for the Federative Republic of Brazil)*. Washington, DC: World Bank.

————. 2004. *Inequality in Latin America and the Caribbean: Breaking with History?* Washington, DC: World Bank.

Wynia, Gary W. 1992. *Argentina: Illusions and Realities*. New York: Holmes and Meier.

Yin, Robert K. 1984. *Case Study Research: Design and Methods*. London: Sage.

Zaluar, Alba. 1996. "Qualidade de Dados: Políticas Públicas Eficazes e Democracia, I, Sessões Temáticas, Violência e Criminalidade do Encontro Nacional de Produtores e Usuários de Informações Sociais, Econômicas, e Territoriais." Manuscript, Rio de Janeiro.

Index

Action Plan for the Economic and Social Development of the State of Rio de Janeiro, 129

Alencar, Marcello, 177–178; public security policies of, 132–136

Alfonsín, Raúl, 9, 37, 85

Álvarez, Chacho, 85

Argentina: anarchist movement in, 31; as delegative democracy, 82–83; history of internal conflict in, 29–31; individualist and extremist culture of, 80–81; military expenditures (1980–1989) in, 38*fig;* military rule in, 18–19, 31–32; *piquetero* movement in, 196; poverty and inequality in, 20, 71; terrorist attacks in, 49

Argentine Catholic Church, nongovernmental organizations and, 82

Argentine civil society: factiousness and protagonism in, 81–82, 88; nongovernmental organizations in, 81–82; and sustainable public policy, 73; and vertical accountability, 79–82

Argentine crime, 49–50, 57; factors in, 21*fig;* failures to report, 24, 25*fig;* and high-level cover-ups, 27–28; historical context of, 17–19; and homicide rates, 9; media coverage of, 23–24; political, history of, 29–30; rise in, 20–21, 22; and violent street crime, 9

Argentine criminal justice system: and crime-solving rate, 26–27; and

misdemeanors/secondary issues, 55–57; probation system in, 27

Argentine economy, 19; crime's impact on, 196; deterioration of, 20, 70–71; international financing institutions and, 71–72; privatization and, 19–20; and public service budgets, 72; as reform issue, 70–71, 73; and risk investment, 71

Argentine Federal Police (PFA), 31–45; abuse by, 58; accountability of, 40–41; advancement in, 32; arbitrary detainment and interrogation by, 34–36; budgets, 37–39, 43, 51; corruption in, 2, 35, 41–42, 52; creation of, 31; "crime boycotts" of, 68, 69; and detention for identification purposes, 43–44; edicts (misdemeanor regulations) of, 34–35; education levels of, 33, 52–53; expenditures, control and monitoring of, 39–40; external oversight of, 42–43; federal vs. municipal control of, 55, 57–59, 69–70; functions of, 39; history of, 29–31; human rights violations of, 43; inadequate remuneration of, 39; internal controls on, 41; investigative work of, 33; legislative and judicial control of, 43–45; military dictatorship's legacy and, 31–32; moonlighting of, 51–52; obligatory carrying of arms by, 46*n5;* officer class of, 32–33, 53; organization of,

227

About the Book

How Latin American governments will respond to popular outcry against unprecedented levels of both corruption and crime ranks among the principal political questions of this decade. *The State on the Streets* focuses on the tense interplay of police, democracy, state, and civil society in the region, using the cases of Argentina and Brazil as a lens.

Mercedes Hinton draws on her rare access to a wide spectrum of actors in the two countries—including top police officials and street patrolmen, military officers and legislators, clergy and prostitutes, business owners and shantytown residents—to present a vivid account of politics on the ground. Her in-depth comparative analysis reveals surprising parallels in the reform patterns adopted in Argentina and Brazil in the past decade, supporting conclusions that carry disturbing implications for the prospects for democratic consolidation in Latin America as a whole.

Mercedes S. Hinton is Nuffield Research Fellow at the London School of Economics and Political Science, where she works on issues of development and democracy.